THE TEXTS
IN ELEMENTARY
CLASSROOMS

D1715532

Center for Improvement of Early Reading Achievement
CIERA

Steven A. Stahl, University of Georgia
Susan B. Neuman, Temple University
P. David Pearson, University of California, Berkeley
Series Editors

Barbara M. Taylor and P. David Pearson
Teaching Reading: Effective Schools, Accomplished Teachers

Anne van Kleeck, Steven A. Stahl, and Eurydice B. Bauer
On Reading Books to Children: Parents and Teachers

THE TEXTS
IN ELEMENTARY
CLASSROOMS

Edited by

James V. Hoffman
Diane L. Schallert
University of Texas at Austin

LAWRENCE ERLBAUM ASSOCIATES, PUBLISHERS
2004   Mahwah, New Jersey   London

Lawrence Erlbaum Associates, Inc., Publishers
10 Industrial Avenue
Mahwah, New Jersey 07430

Cover design by Sean Trane Sciarrone

Library of Congress Cataloging-in-Publication Data

The texts in elementary classrooms / edited by James V. Hoffman and Diane L. Schallert.
      p. cm.
Includes bibliographical references and index.
ISBN 0-8058-4388-4 (cloth)
ISBN 0-8058-4389-2 (pbk)
    1. Reading (Primary) 2. Reading (Elementary) 3. Education, Primary—Curricula 4. Education, Elementary—Curricula 5. Children— Books and reading.   I. Hoffman, James V.   II. Schallert, Diane L.

LB1525.T45 2003
372.4—dc22

2003056140
CIP

Books published by Lawrence Erlbaum Associates are printed on acid-free paper, and their bindings are chosen for strength and durability.

Printed in the United States of America
10 9 8 7 6 5 4 3 2 1

Contents

       Beth Maloch, James V. Hoffman, and Elizabeth U. Patterson

9   Electronic Text in the Classroom   157
       Michael L. Kamil, Helen S. Kim, and Diane Lane

Part III: Some Issues Surrounding Text Selection

10 The Selection and Use of English Texts With Young English   177
       Language Learners
       Georgia Earnest García and Eurydice Bouchereau Bauer

11 Heavy (and Heavy-Handed) Issues Surrounding Book   195
       Selection
       Nancy Roser

Part IV: Assessing the Text Environment

12 Studying the Literacy Environment and Literacy Practices   213
       as the Basis for Critical Reflection and Change
       James V. Hoffman and Misty Sailors

       Author Index   241

       Subject Index   247

Preface

It is becoming increasingly clear in the minds of those who face the practical problems of improving instruction, that text books usually determine the success or failure of any educational method.

—Ernest Horn, 1922, p. 6

Perhaps Ernest Horn was accurate in his assessment of the role of textbooks in schools in the 1920s. However, times do change. Today we argue that it is the teacher, and not the method or materials, that is central to success. In this book, we assume a more contextualized and less controlling view of the texts in classrooms than that envisioned by Horn. Our stance is that the texts in classrooms offer students a range of opportunities to engage in literate activity. Our conception of texts reaches well beyond the "text books" as described by Horn to include a variety of texts that are imported into or created within the spaces of classroom teaching. We subscribe deeply to the Freirian notion that the reading of the word and the reading of the world are inextricably bound together. Our students deserve no less than a world of texts in their classrooms that engage them intellectually, socially, and emotionally.

We worked with our colleagues and CIERA (the Center for the Improvement of Early Reading Achievement) to develop this book on classroom texts. We asked each of the authors to draw on existing research in conceptualizing the issues, opportunities, and challenges related to the text environment in classrooms. The first section of the book focuses on basic processes of reading (comprehension, motivation, word recognition, and fluency) as they relate to features of texts. The second section focuses on the qualities of a various text types that are part of the classroom text environment. In Part III, the chapters deal with special issues related to texts in classrooms. Finally, Part IV, describes a process for teachers to use in assessing and reflecting on their own classroom text environment.

Our shared goal and vision is to assist classroom teachers as they work to improve instruction and learning.

—*James Hoffman*
—*Diane Schallert*

REFERENCE

Horn, E. (1922). Introduction. In R. H. Franzen & F. B. Knight (Eds.), *Textbook selection* (p. 6). Baltimore, MD: Warwick & York.

I

Basic Processes and Text Features

1

Texts in the Teaching and Learning of Reading

Victoria Purcell-Gates
Nell K. Duke
Michigan State University

"Look at this!" Michael pulled his mother's hand, directing her to the first-grade reader resting open on his desk to the most recent story he and his classmates had "mastered." Open House was in full swing, and parents and children milled about noisily in the brightly cluttered classroom.

"Listen!" Michael picked up the book and read:

You can not get it.

I will help.

I can, Mindy.

Mindy will get it for you.

"Isn't that funny? Isn't that WEIRD? It sounds so stupid! It doesn't even sound like a book!"

With that pronouncement, Michael, who had been quite well-read-to for all of his 6 years, passed judgment on the books he had encountered so far in first grade. It was not clear to his mother (one of the authors of this chapter) what connection he saw between the learning-to-read work he was struggling with in school and the rich literature he so enjoyed hearing at home.

Across town, another group of first-grade children sat in a circle listening to their teacher read to them from a wonderfully illustrated children's book. This group of inner-city, low-SES children were justly appreciative of the beautiful paintings (this was a magnet school with a focus on art) and enjoyed the rich use of language by the author. They were soon nonplussed, however, when their teacher stopped reading some pages before the end and handed the book, along with others by the same author, to the children and instructed them to finish it, or read and enjoy the other books, on their own. Alone, or in pairs, they proceeded to struggle over the complex text, identifying only a few words and soon losing interest and motivation, although they all exhibited great distress, begging teacher-aides (including one of the authors) to read it for them.

As Hiebert (1999) argued, "Text matters in learning to read." These children thought so, and so do we. Text is the *stuff* of reading: it is *what* is read. Thus, the nature of text is as critical to the beginning reader (or any reader, for that matter) as the nature of a mountain is to a mountain climber. For the beginning reader, text must be supportive of those initial steps that must be taken to gain mastery over a new symbol system: learning the system that codes meaning into language and speech into print, building automaticity in word and phrase recognition, learning strategies for comprehending written texts, understanding the social and personal uses that written texts can play, and so on. The texts that beginning readers encounter can serve to facilitate these learnings or to hinder them. Certainly, as educators, we wish to be knowledgeable and intentional about choosing texts that facilitate those beginning efforts and moves toward skilled reading.

IMPORTANT DIMENSIONS OF TEXTS FOR BEGINNING READERS

What are the important dimensions of texts for beginning readers? *What* matters in these texts that matter? There are, of course, many factors that matter and many ways to conceptualize them. We discuss these factors in terms of the units of text to which they apply. That is, we discuss important dimensions of *words* in texts for beginning readers, important dimensions of *sentences* in texts for beginning readers, important dimensions of *discourse* (text beyond the sentence level) for beginning readers, and important dimensions of *illustrations* in texts for beginning readers. Consider the following example:

(a) a (× 2), bukonin, ghifilten, lived, on, there, was

(b) On a bukonin, there lived a ghifilten..

(c) Once upon a time, on a bukonin, there lived a ghifiltin....

(d) [Imagine a picture of a ghifilten (perhaps a troll-like creature) living in a bukonin (perhaps a crevice in a mountain or under the overhang of a riverbank or something)] Once upon a time, there was a ghifilten who lived in a bukonin ...

In (a), we have a list of words in the opening line of a text. Some of these words are likely to be in the child's existing vocabulary (a, lived, on, there, was); some are not (bukonin, ghifilten). Some are clearly high frequency or common words in print (a, on, there, was); others perhaps not (e.g., lived), and others certainly not (bukonin, ghifilten). Some are easily decoded by very common sound–letter relationships or phonograms (e.g., on, a); others are not (e.g., was, ghifilten). Some are likely to carry considerable meaning in the text (bukonin, ghifilten); others are not (e.g., there, a). These different words pose different challenges to, and require different strategies of, the beginning readers. *Dimensions at the level of the word matter.*

In (b), the words are put together to make a sentence. Viewed from this perspective, not only are dimensions of the individual words of importance, but also dimensions of the way in which the words are put together in a sentence. The syntactic complexity of the sentence is relatively high, as it contains a subordinate clause and embedded prepositional phrase with a transformed order of units, putting the adverbial prepositional phrase before the subject and verb. The resulting "written-ness" of the sentence is high—it is relatively unlikely that a string of words with this structure would be spoken in everyday conversation, yet it is relatively common in written texts. For the beginning reader, the degree of familiarity with this kind of complex syntax and this very written-like language (language register) would likely impact the difficulty of both decoding and comprehending the sentence. *Dimensions at the level of the sentence matter.*

In (c), the phrase "Once upon a time" is added to the sentence. The simple addition of this convention of Western fairy tales signals the genre of the entire text, and with it particular kinds of vocabulary (e.g., princess, castle), syntax (e.g. "Of course," said she.), meanings (e.g., good vs. evil, particular moral codes), and purposes and settings (e.g., bedtime, pleasure reading) associated with that type of text. The experience of reading a text beginning with those words will likely be very different for children familiar with this convention and genre of text as compared to that of children who are unfamiliar with it. Children's own reading preferences (e.g., whether or not they tend to like fairy tales, what associations they have with fairy tales) will also likely affect their reading. *Dimensions at the level of discourse matter.*

Finally, in (d) an illustration depicts what is (for those who know to make links between picture and text) presumably a ghifilten living on a bukonin. The illustration adds considerable meaning to the text—among other things provid-

ing some information as to what a bukonin and ghifilten are, further signaling or
at least reinforcing the kind of genre this is (that it is fiction with magical or mys-
tical elements), and perhaps triggering predictions about what is to come in the
narrative. The extent to which children are able to glean this kind of information from the illustration, and the kinds of interpretations that they do and do
not make on the basis of it, will also impact their reading experience. Their basic
understanding of the text, the level of activity of their text processing (e.g.,
whether they are making predictions, whether they are making associations
with other texts they have read), and their degree of interest in the text, are all
likely affected by the presence and nature of the illustration. *Dimensions at the
level of illustration matter.*

In the sections that follow, we discuss specific text characteristics at the level
of word, sentence, whole text, and illustration that appear to be salient for
young readers. For each characteristic, the first paragraph describes the characteristic and its relevance to beginning reading. The second paragraph discusses
how texts for beginning readers vary in terms of that characteristic.[1]

Dimensions at the Level of the Word

Frequency. Research indicates that some words appear more frequently in
text than others. Moreover, because some words appear so often, a relatively
small set of words actually comprises a very large proportion of all words encountered in text. The presence of so many high-frequency words in text means
that children's ability to read high-frequency words will be related to their ability to read the text. The beginning reader who recognizes a substantial number
of high-frequency words is likely to read better than one who does not.

The number and proportion of high-frequency words in a text does vary naturally from text to text. In addition, some texts for beginning readers are written
specifically to have a high number and proportion of high-frequency words, either to serve as a support to the young reader and/or to build his or her knowledge of those words. For example, the book *Big* (Blevins, 2000) from
Scholastic's *Literacy Place High Frequency Readers* contains five words they identify as high frequency: *I, it, looks, see,* and *the,* and focuses on a sixth word, *big.*
The text reads:

I see the elephant.

---

[1]For the purposes of this chapter, examples come from individual books for beginning readers, as opposed to from bound collections of texts for beginning readers commonly known as primers, basal readers, or anthologies. However, many of the points made could also apply to these more traditional forms.

It looks big.

I see the camel.

It looks big.

I see the lion.

It looks big.

I see the cow.

It looks big.

I see the horse.

It looks big.

I see the turtle.

It looks big.

I see the puppy.

It looks little!

The extent to which texts like this are helpful for beginning readers, and for *which* beginning readers, is an important area for consideration, as are relationships among the proportion of high-frequency words in texts in general and beginning readers' success in reading and learning to read.

Meaning/Content. Perhaps inversely related to how frequently a word appears in text is how much content or meaning that word carries. The word *dinosaur*, for example, is certainly low frequency in the corpus of words in English texts, but it is high meaning/content for many young learners. The literature on beginning reading contains several testimonies to the power of high-meaning words for children. Perhaps most famous is the work of Sylvia Ashton-Warner (1963), who used words of great meaning to individual children (what she called *key vocabulary*) as their entrée into literacy. These words comprised in large part the first texts that these children came to write and to read. By Ashton-Warner's account, the words helped spur children's success as both readers and writers.

As with high-frequency words, there is natural variability among texts in the number and proportion of high-meaning/content words they contain. However, unlike with high-frequency words, we are not aware of texts written specifically for the purpose of containing a great density of such words. Rather, texts written primarily for the purpose of conveying a compelling story, a vivid description, significant information, rather than the purpose of reading instruction, are more likely to contain many high-content/density words. How variations among texts in this regard impact children's reading performance and development is an important area for consideration in texts for beginning readers.[2]

Decodability. Research on the nature of sound–letter relationships in English reveals that whereas some relationships or patterns are quite common (e.g., *ch* representing the sound heard at the beginning of *cheese*), others are far less so (e.g., *ch* representing the sound heard at the beginning of *chalet*) (Venezky, 1999). The term *decodability* is commonly used to refer to the extent to which readers can decode a text based on their knowledge of sound–letter relationships. All other things being equal, if a text contains words with many sound–letter relationships familiar to the reader, it is likely to be read more successfully by that reader than a text that contains words with fewer known sound–letter patterns. Moreover, the decodability of words in texts used with beginning readers may impact the kinds of word identification strategies those readers use in that and future reading (Juel & Roper/Schneider, 1985).

The decodability of words in a text varies from text to text, but also from reader to reader (because which sound–letter relationships are and are not known varies from reader to reader). At many points in the history of American reading instruction, texts for beginning readers have been written specifically to be highly decodable by a small set of sound–letter patterns, and then to increase the number of patterns as the reader increases in pattern knowledge. For example, book one, *Mat* (Maslen, 1976a), of the *Bob Books* series reads:

> Mat.
>
> Mat sat.
>
> Sam.
>
> Sam sat.
>
> Mat sat. Sam sat.
>
> Mat sat on Sam.
>
> Sam sat on Mat.
>
> Mat sat. Sam sat.
>
> The End

Book four, *Mac* (Maslen, 1976b) reads:

> Mac had a bag.

---

[2]The interest or engagingness of text may be related to the presence or absence of high meaning/content words, as well as to whole text level factors. This is discussed in greater depth in chapter 4 of this volume.

The bag had a dog.

Mac had a bag and a dog.

Mac had a rag.

Mac can tag Mag.

Mac got the rag.

Mac sat on the rag.

Mag sat on the bag.

The End

As discussed at greater depth in chapter 2 of this volume, some research has examined the impact of books like these on children's reading development. Research on the impact of texts varying naturally along this dimension is less common but also important.

Dimensions at the Level of the Sentence

Predictability. An aspect of text at the sentence level (as well as at the letter and word levels) thought to be important is its degree of predictability. In general, *prediction* is defined as the elimination of unlikely occurrences. It is a naturally occurring process done by the brain at the level of information processing (Smith, 1978). Predictability at the sentence level (see later discussion regarding predictability at the whole text level) refers to the extent to which what comes later in a sentence can be predicted, or is at least constrained, by what has come before. Good readers attend simultaneously to meaning (semantics) and order (syntax) of words, as well as their sound–letter (graphophonic) composition (e.g., Goodman, 1973); how these factors have played out earlier in a sentence, or in prior sentences, can inform the process of decoding or recognizing words later in the sentence (Adams, 1990). Consider the following sentences, for example:

The teacher wrote the following on the board and asked students to identify the number: 13. All of the students "saw" the number 13.

The teacher wrote the following on the board and asked the students to identify the letter: 13. All of the students "saw" the letter B.

The perception of letters and words is informed by the meaning and word order of letters and words before them.

Of course, sentences vary in the degree to which they provide rich meaning and word order cues for the reader. In some cases, meaning and word order may even mislead the reader about subsequent words, as in so-called "garden path" sentences such as:

The old train the young. (Just & Carpenter, 1987; cited in Adams, 1990)

The degree to which texts for beginning readers provide rich meaning and word-order cues is yet another important consideration in texts for beginning readers.

Written-ness.   It is now well documented that written language differs in significant ways from oral language (Chafe, 1982; Purcell-Gates, 1988). For example, attributive adjectives (*the brown dog, the brave knight*) are often found in written narrative language but less often found in oral narrative language (where phrasings such as *the dog is brown* and *the knight was brave* would be more common). Research indicates that young children vary in the extent to which they have knowledge of written language registers (Purcell-Gates, McIntyre, & Freppon, 1995), and that these variations relate to other differences in achievement (Purcell-Gates, 1998, 2000). Because of their greater familiarity with the meanings and word orders associated with written language, children with greater knowledge of written language registers are in a better position to do the kind of predicting and expecting just described.

As with all of the aspects of text thus far discussed, texts vary in the degree of written-ness of the language within them. Some texts for young readers are written to be much more like oral language, as in Mayer's *Little Critters Books* (e.g., *Just Me and My Puppy,* [1985] and *I Was So Mad* [1983]). Others are written such that they are particularly unlike language that is spoken, as in many written fairy tales, for example. Given the variation among children in their knowledge of written registers, documented earlier, as well as the importance of acquiring such registers, the written-ness of texts clearly constitutes an important consideration in their use with beginning readers.

Dimensions at the Level of Text

Familiarity of Topic/Content.   Perhaps more so than some other factors, familiarity with the topic or content of a given text substantially impacts all readers. Even the strongest adult reader may struggle greatly with a text in an area that is unfamiliar—*Identification of Cell Wall-Deficient Mycobacteria with Polyacrylamide Gel Electrophoresis* (Steffen & Mattman, 1986), for example, or *A Case for the Predominance of Melody over Text in Troubadour Lyric: Bernart de Ventadorn's "Can Vei La Lauzeta Mover"* (Steel, 1982). Lack of relevant background knowledge, failure to understand key assumptions of the area, lack of familiarity with the vocabulary and concepts employed, and other factors make it very difficult for us to comprehend and in some cases even decode the text. For young readers, too, texts with familiar topics, characters, language, and so on are likely to be read more easily than those that are less familiar, perhaps explaining, among other things, children's interest in series books, which are typically predictable in many respects, including setting, characters, plot line, and so on.

Texts vary in the extent to which they are familiar to readers, and of course readers themselves vary in the extent to which particular content or experiences are familiar. The most direct means of matching text to reader along dimensions of familiarity are found in language experience approaches (Lee & Van Allen, 1963). In these approaches, children dictate their own texts, which then become the children's reading material; this ensures that the text, including its language, structure, content, and so on will be highly familiar to the child.[3] Use of texts that children have memorized or read repeatedly also increases the likelihood of familiarity. As discussed in chapter 3 of this volume, this may in turn help develop reading fluency.

Predictability.   One type of text often written to generate familiarity in children is predictable text. At the whole-text level, predictability refers to the extent to which what is written in the text can be predicted based on previous pages in the text, illustrations, content, or other factors. In "patterned-predictable" texts, for example, the first few pages of a book establish a pattern that is found throughout the remainder of the book. A classic example of this is *Brown Bear, Brown Bear, What Do You See?* (Martin, 1967). It begins:

Brown Bear, Brown Bear, What do you see?

I see a red bird looking at me.

Red Bird, Red Bird, What do you see?

I see a yellow duck looking at me.

The book continues through this pattern, with illustrations to match in each case, for a blue horse, green frog, purple cat, white dog, black sheep, goldfish, teacher, and children. In our experience, even on first hearing, many children can predict the language of each page of the text beyond the first two. The theory behind use of predictable texts is that the predictability of the text supports the beginning reader's ability to actually read it, thus allowing the experience of fluent reading and freeing up some attention (from the process of decoding each word based solely or largely on graphophonic cues) for learning of other kinds (LaBerge & Samuels, 1974; Smith, 1973). For example, reading predictable

---

[3]See chapter 8 in this volume for further discussion of texts authored or co-authored by children and teachers.

texts could develop or reinforce recognition of high-frequency words appearing in the text (e.g., *what, see* in the earlier text), phonological awareness (many predictable texts include considerable rhyme and phoneme manipulation), print directionality, and awareness of language patterns.

Only some texts for beginning readers are predictable along the lines just described, and of course texts vary in their degrees of predictability. Following the thinking described earlier, the key issue is the extent to which the text is sufficiently predictable to allow for fluent reading and to free up attention for learning in particular areas. Like the other factors discussed, this too depends not only on the text but also on the reader (what she or he finds predictable; how much attention she or he has for other foci) and the task (whether the text has been read before, what kinds of external supports are provided during the text reading, and so forth). Predictability is yet another aspect of text for beginning readers important to consider. Chapter 6 explores how predictability, along with other text dimensions, informs decisions about text leveling for young readers.

Genre.   Whether using more modern definitions of genre as rhetorical function and situation, or more traditional definitions of genre as a particular set of features or conventions, it is clear that texts for children come in multiple genres. The rhetorical function, as well as the linguistic features, of a fairy tale differ in substantial ways from the rhetorical function and linguistic features of an alphabet book, which in turn differ from a book on how to make paper airplanes, a collection of Bible stories for children, or a book all about firefighters. There is considerable research that genre differences are salient even to young children (see Duke & Purcell-Gates, 2003, for a review). Children are able to produce texts clearly reflective of one genre or another (e.g., Harste, Woodward, & Burke, 1984), they show differential competence with different genres (e.g., Kamberelis, 1999), and different preferences for different genres (Kletzien, 1999). Sustained exposure to particular genres appears to impact children's emergent readings and writings of that genre (Duke & Kays, 1998; Kamberelis, 1998).

Although books written for young children represent a whole range of genres (e.g., Huck, Hepler, Hickman, 1993), research indicates that children typically receive a more limited diet of genres in school (e.g., Duke, 2000). Many scholars have challenged this pattern, however, and the trend seems to be toward calling for a greater range of genres in texts for beginning readers (see Duke & Bennett-Armistead, 2003, for a review). Yet to be documented, however, is the long-term impact on children's overall and genre-specific reading and writing development of experiencing a greater diversity of genres in early schooling. Also yet to be fully understood is the extent to which different genres are more or less appropriate for different learners and in different curricular situations (see chaps. 5, 7, and 9 in this volume for further discussion of particular genres in texts for beginning readers).

Dimensions of Illustrations

There is substantial evidence that illustrations in text affect both reading accuracy and reading comprehension (Filippatou & Pumfrey, 1996). Just how illustrations affect reading accuracy and comprehension, however, is a complex and not yet fully resolved matter. It appears that all three points of the classic triangle of reader, text, and task (Anderson, Hiebert, Scott, & Wilkinson, 1985) are influential. With regard to the reader, level of reading skill is one important factor. Learning disabled and poor readers are more likely to have their reading performance diminished by the presence of illustrations than higher skilled readers, for whom illustrations seem to be comprehension facilitative in most cases; and across readers, illustrations are more likely to be facilitative when the texts are easier for the reader than when they are quite difficult for that reader (Filippatou & Pumfrey, 1996).

Characteristics of the text and illustrations themselves are also important. For example, illustrations are more likely to be facilitative when they correspond to the particular challenges of or focus of the text, for instance if the text requires substantial attention to detail and the illustrations include a great deal of detail or if the text has explanatory purposes and the illustrations are also explanatory (Filippatou & Pumfrey, 1996). Characteristics of the task also seem to be influential in determining the effect of illustrations on the reader. For example, one study suggested that combining mental imagery with attention to text illustrations results in greater comprehension than attention to text illustrations alone (Gambrell & Jawitz, 1993).

Exacerbating the complexity of the relationship between illustrations and reading performance is the tremendous range of illustrations in texts for young readers. Some texts have no illustrations at all, some only a few, some have one for nearly every word or sentence. Some illustrations are almost entirely redundant with the content of the written text, such as a text that reads "A blue ball" and depicts a blue ball. Others carry a great deal of meaning beyond what is entailed in the written text. For example, in the book *Rosie's Walk* (Hutchins, 1968), the entire written text reads:

> Rosie the hen went for a walk across the yard around the pond over the haystack past the mill through the fence under the beehives and got back in time for dinner.

It is only through the illustrations that one sees that the book is about a fox chasing Rosie, unbeknownst to her, and foiled in one way or another at each turn. Perhaps even more extreme are wordless books for young readers, in which the illustrations convey the entire meaning of the text (e.g., Goodall, 1975: Mayer, 1969). There is considerable instructional research yet to be done on how what types and range of illustrations and text–illustration relationships best serve young readers, which readers, in which tasks, and at what points in development.

THE RECURSIVE NATURE
OF TEXT DIMENSIONS THAT MATTER

It is important to keep in mind that the text dimensions just identified and described do not exist as separate dimensions for the reader during the act of reading. Rather they occur and matter to beginning readers in a synergistic fashion, each dimension informing and helping to shape the others, recursively. Individual words become familiar as they are encountered either through being read to or reading in textual contents—contents that reflect specific genre purposes, conventions, and textual features. Words become more or less predictable as they occur in more or less predictable sentences, more or less familiar contents or discourse styles. Furthermore, decodable words can make sentences more predictable than words that the reader cannot decode (thus missing the meaning). Sentences become more or less predictable as they occur in more or less predictable texts. Texts become more or less predictable, and decodable, as their meanings are more or less supported by illustrations, and so forth. Furthermore, each of these effects and countereffects differ as the readers of texts, with their different backgrounds, experiences, strengths, and purposes for reading, differ.

It would be a mistake to read our discussion of textual dimensions as an argument for teaching these dimensions as isolated units in a building-block fashion: first words, then sentences, then whole texts. No, *texts*, by definition, are whole units of language, and they are made up of words and sentences, language features, macrostructures, and illustrations. When considering the facilitative nature of texts for beginning readers, as we are doing here, it is critical to remember this whole–part–whole relationship.

There is another caution we wish to put forward. It would be unfortunate to interpret the discussion we present here, and the way in which we have structured it, as indicating that a given text is *either* decodable *or* predictable, and so on. Rather it is critical to recognize that although there are texts that are extreme prototypes of one or another of the textual aspects discussed, most texts have a mixture of them. Garcia and Bauer in chapter 10 make a compelling argument for selecting texts, for example, for bilingual learners along a number of dimensions important for their oral and written language development.

A final note for those collecting texts for their classrooms: Be sure to consider texts other than books. Remember that texts come in all types of forms and packagings. Flyers are texts; pamphlets are texts; web sites are texts; advertisements are texts; magazines and journals are texts; and student-written and published texts may be in nonbook form, as may be many texts written by teachers. Consider the total print environment as the texts available to young readers and writers (see chaps. 8 and 12 for further elaboration of this point).

TEXT IS FOR COMPREHENDING ⚹

Within our understanding of the different features of text and their relationships to reading development is the basic assumption underlying our current model of reading—that reading equals comprehending. To simply "say" a word in response to seeing it in print is not *reading* unless one understands what that word means—and ultimately what the textual content, in which that word appears, means. Simply saying a word without comprehension is decoding, but it is not reading. This is not to say that decoding is not important, or absolutely critical, to reading (comprehending) but that it is not the same. It is a necessary but not sufficient component of reading.

The point of this point is that when we argue that *text matters*, we are arguing that text matters as it relates to beginning *reading*, to beginning *comprehending*. It is as important that teachers keep their eyes on this goal of comprehending as it is that novice bicycle riders keep their eyes on where they are going rather than the components of how they are going there (i.e., on the handlebars, the front tire, the pedals, and so on). The comprehensibility of a text will impact young readers, as will the comprehension strategies, and relevant background knowledge they bring to the text.

Similarly, beginning reading involves more than alphabetic knowledge. Alphabetic knowledge is critical to decoding print. Decoding print is critical to developing automaticity of word recognition. Automaticity is critical to comprehending texts. Decoding is facilitated by many of the dimensions of text introduced in this chapter. Thus, automaticity is facilitated by these dimensions, and comprehension is facilitated by these dimensions (Pressley, 2000). Finally, the goal of comprehension, the drive on the part of the reader (beginning and skilled), fuels the application of skills and strategies that enable decoding and word recognition. And all of those dimensions of texts that facilitate decoding and word recognition also facilitate, and are facilitated by, comprehension.

METHODS OF BEGINNING READING INSTRUCTION
AND TEXT DIMENSIONS

We conclude this chapter with some thoughts about beginning reading instruction and text dimensions. This, after all, is the ultimate point of learning about the aspects of text that matter to beginning readers: What can we, as teachers, do with different texts to help our young students develop into fluent and effective comprehenders of print? We approach this in two ways: matching the texts used to the type of instruction; and matching the texts used to the stages of reading development of your students.

Types of Beginning Reading Instruction

Districts and teachers differ in the approaches they take to beginning reading instruction. Some take a very skills-based, building-block approach with a carefully sequenced program of decoding instruction (including sight words), followed by increased focus on comprehension, accompanied by increasingly complex texts. Others take a more holistic approach, with more natural, complex texts introduced early while word-level skills are more slowly taught within the context of a comprehension focus. Other programs, and/or teachers, mix these two in individual ways. The point we wish to make is the need for teachers with any approach to attend very carefully to the texts they use for their instruction and to match the types of texts (re their different dimensions) to the focus of their instruction.

Hiebert (1999) reminded us that it is potentially confusing to developing readers, and thus counterproductive as a teaching tool, to try to practice the skills or strategies being presented to them with texts that do not allow them to do this and get meaning. Juel and Roper/Schneider's (1985) work illustrated this with their documentation of the relative difficulty children face in learning and practicing decoding skills in the context of books that do not contain many regularly decodable words.

Similarly, teachers focusing on teaching students about the ways that texts "sound" and "mean" and ways that readers can use their predictive and meaning-making strategies to glean the meaning of authentic texts, will not want to demonstrate this with texts written primarily to reinforce decoding principles. MAT SAT ON THE HAT; THE CAT SAT ON THE HAT do not allow children to practice their language prediction abilities, and if this is what the teacher wishes to teach, the MAT text is the wrong one to use.

Stages of Reading Development

One can also look at this issue not through the lens of instructional program focus, but through the lens of stages of development toward reading competence. The same principle holds: The teacher needs to carefully consider the dimensions of the texts she uses to ensure that it supports that aspect of the reading process she is currently focusing on with groups of children or with individual children within the group. The following examples illustrate this point.

Teaching Focus: Semiotic Nature of Print.   Let us say that several, if not most, of the children enter kindergarten or first grade with very little experience with people reading and writing. Clearly, they will be starting the learning-to-read process at a very different place than will those children who come from high print-use homes (Purcell-Gates, 1995, 1998). It is necessary to provide experiences with print in use for such children to learn the very basic concept of the semiotic nature of print (that print "says" something, that is, it is more than just decorative marks but is a linguistic symbol system; Harste, Burke, & Woodward, 1984). Many examples of environmental print (together with logos or illustrations) are called for; different text types like stories, information, regulatory signs, menus, and so on are also called for. This is not the time to limit the exposure of text to that which is created to teach word-level skills such as sight word lists and highly decodable text.

Teaching Focus: Concept of Word.   The scenario here would consist of children who understand the semiotic nature of print but have not attended to people actually reading the words enough to understand the concept of a "word" (Clay, 1991). An excellent type of text to use to help children master this concept is text that is memorized, or almost memorized. This could consist of familiar rhymes, jump rope chants, commercial jingles, songs, and so on. Written out, this text can be "read" by the children from their knowledge of the words while the teacher can explicitly show them and help them to practice matching the known words to the printed words. Part of this explanation of "word" would of course involve an explanation of the white spaces between the words.

Teaching Focus: Short Vowels.   For this scenario, the children are learning the alphabetic principle underlying written English (and many other languages): the match between graphic symbols and aural phonemes (isolable "sounds" of the language). A few consonant sound–symbol matches have been taught and the teacher is now moving to what many call *short vowels* such as /ae/ in "cat." After focusing the children on this first short vowel, /ae/, with some word family lists, the teacher wants to let the children apply their new phonic knowledge to written text. She needs to locate texts that have many CVC (consonant–vowel–consonant) words in them that include this sound–letter relationship.

As the children move through the short vowels, texts can be located that contain a high percentage (70%–80%) of regular application of the short-vowel sound–symbol matches that they have learned. This would not be the time to ask the children to read from complex text within which they will encounter only a few words that illustrate the vowel sounds they are in the process of learning.

Teaching Focus: Difference Between Story and Information Text. In this scenario, the teacher wants to explicitly point out to the children some of the basic differences between story text and information text (genre). She knows that they will need to know these differences in order to comprehend fully and accurately the two different types of text. She begins with the simple difference of timed versus timeless verbs and the specific versus generic subjects they imply. She points out to them that stories are usually about some specific person or animal or thing (e.g. Jonah, the whale, or Ollie, the owl). These characters do something and the words that talk about that usually show that they do these things either in the past (swam), in the present (swims, is swimming), or in the future (will swim). Information texts, though, are usually about generic subjects like whales, or birds, or machines and the words about what they do are usually timeless—for example, whales swim in the ocean; owls hunt at night; elevators carry people. To help make this point, the teacher needs to locate both story texts and information texts for the children to examine and read as they focus on differences between the two. Simply presenting sample sentences on the board to illustrate generic and specific nouns and timed and timeless verbs, while continuing a diet of 100% storybooks for reading, does not accomplish the desired teaching task.

TEXTS MATTER

We hope we have presented a convincing case that texts do matter to beginning readers and to teachers of beginning readers. Moreover, we hope we have demonstrated that different dimensions of text matter, at different times, and for different reasons. It is this simple, and it is this complex. We hope that as you read other chapters in this volume, which treat many of the issues we raise in greater depth, you bear both this simplicity and complexity in mind. The simple fact is that considering text is absolutely critical to teaching beginning readers; the complex fact is the myriad of dimensions and factors to consider when a begin‐ ning reader interacts with a text.

REFERENCES

Adams, M. J. (1990). *Beginning to read: Thinking and learning about print.* Cambridge, MA: The MIT Press.

Anderson, R. C., Hiebert, E. H., Scott, J. A., & Wilkinson, I. G. (1985). *Becoming a nation of readers: The report of the Commission on Reading.* Washington, DC: The National Institute of Education..

Ashton-Warner, S. (1963). *Teacher.* New York: Simon & Schuster

Chafe, W. (1982). Integration and involvement in speaking, writing and oral literature. In D. Tannen (Ed.), *Spoken and written language: Exploring orality and literacy. Vol. IX. Advances in discourse processes* (pp. 35–53). Norwood, NJ: Ablex.

Clay, M. M. (1991). *Becoming literate: The construction of inner control.* Auckland, NZ: Heinemann Education.

Duke, N. K. (2000). 3.6 minutes per day: The scarcity of informational texts in first grade. *Reading Research Quarterly, 35,* 202–224.

Duke, N. K., & Bennett-Armistead, V. S., with Huxley, A., Johnson, M., McLurkin, D., Rob‐ erts, E., Rosen, C., & Vogel, E. (2003). *Reading and writing informational text in the primary grades: Research-based practices.* New York: Scholastic.

Duke, N. K., & Kays, J. (1998). "Can I say 'once upon a time'?": Kindergarten children devel‐ oping knowledge of information book language. *Early Childhood Research Quarterly, 13*(2), 295–318.

Duke, N. K., & Purcell-Gates, V. (2003). Genres at home and school: Bridging the new to the known. *The Reading Teacher, 57,* 30–37.

Filippatou, D., & Pumfrey, P. D. (1996). Pictures, titles, reading accuracy and reading com‐ prehension: A research review. *Educational Research, 38,* 259–291.

Gambrell, L. B., & Jawitz, P. B. (1993). Mental imagery, text illustrations and children's story comprehension and recall. *Reading Research Quarterly, 28,* 265–276.

Goodman, K. S. (1973). Psycholinguistic universals in the reading process. In F. Smith (Ed.), *Psycholinguistics and reading* (pp. 21–27). New York: Holt, Rinehart and Winston.

Harste, J. C., Woodward, V. A., & Burke, C. (1984). *Language stories and literacy lessons.* Portsmouth, NH: Heinemann.

Hiebert, E. H. (1999). Text matters in learning to read. *The Reading Teacher, 52,* 552–566.

Huck, C. S., Hepler, S., & Hickman, J. (1993). *Children's literature in the elementary school.* Fort Worth : Harcourt Brace Jovanovich.

Juel, C., & Roper/Schneider, D. (1985). The influence of basal readers on first grade reading. *Reading Research Quarterly, 20,* 134–152.

Just, M. A., & Carpenter, P. A. (1987). *The psychology of reading and language comprehension.* Boston: Allyn & Bacon.

Kamberelis, G. (1998). Relations between children's literacy diets and genre development: You write what you read. *Literacy Teaching and Learning, 3,* 7–53.

Kamberelis, G. (1999). Genre development and learning: Children writing stories, science reports, and poems. *Research in the Teaching of English, 33,* 403–460.

Kletzien, S. B. (1999). *Children's reading preferences and information books.* Paper presented at the National Reading Conference, Orlando, FL.

LaBerge, D., & Samuels, S. (1974). Toward a theory of automatic information processing in reading. *Cognitive Psychology, 6,* 293–323.

Lee, D., & Van Allen, R. (1963). *Learning to read through experience.* New York: Appleton Century Crofts.

Nash-Webber, B. (1975). The role of semantics in automatic speech understanding. In D. G. Bobrow & A. Collins (Eds.), *Representation and understanding* (pp. 351–382). New York: Academic Press.

Pressley, M. (2000). What should comprehension instruction be the instruction of? In M. Kamil, P. Mosenthal, P. D. Pearson, & R. Barr (Eds.), *Handbook of reading research* (Vol 3, pp. 545–561). Hillsdale, NJ: Lawrence Erlbaum Associates.

Purcell-Gates, V. (1988). Lexical and syntactic knowledge of written narrative held by well-read-to kindergartners and second graders. *Research in the Teaching of English, 22*(2), 128–160.

Purcell-Gates, V. (1995). *Other people's words: The cycle of low literacy.* Cambridge, MA: Harvard University Press.

Purcell-Gates, V. (1998). Growing successful readers: Homes, communities, and schools. In F. Lehr & J. Osborn (Eds.), *Literacy for all: Issues for teaching and learning* (pp. 51–72). New York, NY: Guilford.

Purcell-Gates, V. (2000). Family literacy: A research review. *Handbook of Reading Research.* (Vol. 3, 853–870). New York: NY: Lawrence Erlbaum Associates.

Purcell-Gates, V., McIntyre, E., & Freppon, P. A. (1995). Learning written storybook language in school: A comparison of low-SES children in skills-based and whole language classrooms. *American Educational Research Journal, 32,* 659–685.

Smith, F. (1973). Psycholinguistics and reading. In F. Smith (Ed.), *Psycholinguistics and reading* (pp. 1–9). New York: Holt, Rinehart and Winston.

Smith, F. (1978). *Understanding reading: A psycholinguistic analysis of reading and learning to read, 2nd edition.* New York: Holt, Rinehart and Winston.

Steel, M. C. (1982). A case for the predominance of melody over text in troubadour lyric: Bernart de Ventadorn's "Can Vei La Lauzeta Mover." *Michigan Academician, 14,* 259–271.

Steffen, C. M., & Mattman, L. H. (1986). Identification of cell wall-deficient mycobacteria with polyacrylamide gel electrophoresis. *Michigan Academician, 18,* 303–313.

Venezky, R. L. (1999). *The American way of spelling: The structure and origins of American English orthography.* New York: Guilford.

CHILDREN'S BOOKS CITED

Blevins, W. (2000). *Big.* New York: Scholastic.

Goodall, J. S. (1975). *Creepy castle.* New York: Simon & Schuster.

Hutchins, P. (1968). *Rosie's Walk.* New York: Aladdin.

Martin, B. M., Jr. (1967). *Brown bear, brown bear, what do you see?* New York: Henry Holt and Company.

Maslen, B. L. (1976a). *Mat.* New York: Scholastic.

Maslen, B. L. (1976b). *Mac.* New York: Scholastic.

Mayer, M. (1969). *Frog, where are you?* New York: Dial Press.

Mayer, M. (1983). *I was so mad.* New York: Golden Press.

Mayer, M. (1985). *Just me and my puppy.* New York: Golden Press.

2

Word Identification
and Text Characteristics

James W. Cunningham
University of North Carolina at Chapel Hill

David A. Koppenhaver
Gustavus Adolphus College

Karen A. Erickson
University of North Carolina at Chapel Hill

Stephanie A. Spadorcia
Lesley University

Trends in reading instruction can be traced back decades to reveal a cyclical discussion of the importance of word-level instruction and of modified or engineered texts to literacy learning success (J. Cunningham, 1999). Not long ago, authentic literature was widely considered essential for young readers. Currently, at least two states and many school districts in the United States have mandated the use of highly decodable texts in primary-grade classrooms. This return to engineered texts for reading instruction has fueled a new round of debate. This chapter discusses the relationship between word identification instruction and the characteristics of texts that are most likely to support successful word identification learning.

WORD IDENTIFICATION

There is no single set of clearly defined and commonly used expressions to talk about the part of reading that we, the authors of this chapter, call *word identification*. Our work fits into the tradition that uses the term word identification as the umbrella term for the component of the reading process that translates both familiar and unfamiliar printed words into sound (J. Cunningham, 1993; P. Cunningham, 1975–1976; Smith, 1971). Good readers turn printed words into pronounced words vocally (during oral reading), subvocally (during silent reading), and neurologically (during silent reading without subvocalization). They can simultaneously or subsequently access word meanings as they identify words, but good readers can also identify words that have no meaning (nonwords) or for which they do not yet know any meaning. In short, we agree with the body of theory and research supporting that good readers, from the beginning, have a component within their reading process that has a single, but essential role: to turn printed words into pronounced words, whether aloud, in inner speech, or represented only in the mind. We also hold that a different, but equally essential, component of the reading process functions simultaneously to comprehend the language represented by printed words plus other signals. For us, knowing word meanings is a part of the language comprehension component of reading rather than the word identification component.

Because word identification is our term for the entire component of reading that translates printed words into pronounced words, we need different terms for the subcomponents of word identification. There are two main ways that good readers identify words, whether orally, silently, or neurologically. The terms we use for these two subcomponents, or ways of turning printed words into pronounced words, are *decoding* and *word recognition*. During decoding, as we define it, children use their knowledge of letter–sound relationships to construct a pronunciation for an unfamiliar printed word. Other names for this same subcomponent are *mediated word identification* and *phonological recoding*. For us, decoding is always an act of problem solving requiring that the reader attend to different letters or letter clusters within the printed word. Decoding requires *phonics*, which we define as general knowledge about how printed words encode sounds. When decoding happens quickly, with little effort, it is said to be efficient decoding. For example, good readers past first grade are usually able to decode the low-frequency word *snide* efficiently.

In contrast, during word recognition, as we define it, children use their familiarity with a word's full print array to match it with a representation of that word stored in memory. Other names for this same subcomponent are *immediate word identification* and *sight word reading*. For us, word recognition is always an act of accessing a pronunciation that is attached in memory to the entire printed word. Word recognition can be increased by *word study*, which we define as working with specific printed words to learn the particular pattern of letters that comprise each one. When word recognition happens very quickly, with no effort, it is said to be automatic word recognition. For example, good readers in late first grade are usually able to recognize the high frequency word *how* automatically.

The two subcomponents of word identification, word recognition and decoding, are two different ways to turn printed words into pronounced words, but they are related. The better and more efficiently a child can decode unfamiliar printed words, the easier it is for him or her to learn to recognize more and more words automatically (Ehri, 1992). Words are recognized as patterns or arrays of letters. The more a reader knows about letters and how they represent sounds individually and in clusters, the better she or he will be at learning to recognize specific words.

Likewise, the more words a child can recognize, the more other words that child can decode by analogy with one or more known words (P. Cunningham, 2000). For example, it is often easier for a child to decode the word *blind* if that child recognizes *black* and *blue*. It is often easier for a child to decode the word *mall* if that child recognizes *ball* and *fall*.

WORD IDENTIFICATION INSTRUCTION
AND TEXTS THAT SUPPORT IT

Although there is much theory, research, and common sense to support the existence of a separate component of the reading process given to translating printed words into pronounced words, there is certainly no consensus among teachers or reading researchers on how best to teach the word identification component or what kinds of texts best support whatever instruction is provided.

In the remainder of this chapter, we first make the case that children learn word identification better when they can apply their developing word recognition and decoding abilities to reading interesting and meaningful texts from the beginning. Then, we make the case that children also learn word identification better when they receive systematic phonics and word study instruction from the beginning. After these two sections, we discuss implications of our view for improving children's word identification.

WHY ARE INTERESTING AND MEANINGFUL TEXTS NECESSARY FOR WORD IDENTIFICATION DEVELOPMENT?

We, the authors, have systematically examined the highly decodable text recently adopted in at least two states and numerous school districts around the country. These materials are based on a definition of decodability that does not count either word recognition or contextual support. Rather, for a word to be considered *decodable* in these programs, its pronunciation must be achievable by the sole application of the phonics instructional elements taught to date in the program. Some who argue that primary-grade texts can be decodable as well as interesting and meaningful usually have a wider definition of what decodable means or advocate a lower percentage of decodability than is generally applied today by those who insist on highly decodable texts for early reading instruction. As is apparent later, we too feel that some decodability is compatible with good texts for comprehension and enjoyment. However, we find the very few texts available today that are interesting and meaningful as well as highly phonetically decodable to be the exceptions that prove the rule.

We believe a persuasive case can and must be made that decoding and word recognition develop better, in the long run, if from the beginning, children read good texts that support their developing word identification abilities. As of now, we do not believe the case has been adequately made, and the purpose of this section is to make it.

There are at least five reasons why word identification cannot be successfully taught to most children without meaningful and interesting texts that support the development of automatic word recognition and efficient decoding. This section discusses these five reasons as five needs children have during their word identification development.

The Need for Metacognition of Word Identification

All good readers use context to monitor their word identification during reading. Once good readers have identified a word by recognizing or decoding it, they attend to whether the pronunciation sounds like a word that they have heard before, that fits grammatically with the language context, and that makes sense within the meaning context. When a pronunciation fails to sound familiar, grammatical, or meaningful to them, good readers often look back at that word again to see if it might be a different one than they thought when they first recognized or decoded it.

Metacognition involves the thinking that readers do about their own thinking while performing a task, in this case the thinking that readers do about their word recognition or decoding. Good readers constantly think about their word identification to ensure that it is going well and does not need to be redone. This monitoring of word identification takes place in an internal dialogue as readers listen to themselves during oral or silent reading. The metacognitive process constantly raises and answers questions about whether the words being identified by the reader fit with what the reader knows about words, language, the world, and the meaning of the text so far.

Moreover, while independently reading a text, a successfully developing reader is constantly testing out her or his current knowledge of word identification. In other words, a growing reader is not only concerned with reading this particular text well, but also in learning how to read better while reading this particular text. Children who are becoming good readers metacognitively test their current knowledge of word identification against the word-level demands of the texts they read.

Texts that best support the development of word identification provide the young reader with the opportunity to practice his or her developing decoding and word recognition abilities (Juel & Roper/Schneider, 1985), as well as the opportunity to learn to monitor and control decoding and word recognition during reading (Clay, 1991). To do so, the texts must contain higher frequency words that the children have been studying and lower frequency words that can be decoded using the phonics they have been taught. In addition, these texts must be very meaningful to the children in order to promote the development of their metacognition of word identification.

The Need for Transfer of Word Identification to Oral and Silent Reading

The second reason why it is necessary to use interesting and meaningful texts with most students to teach them word recognition and decoding is that it is not enough for readers to be able to identify words; they must be able to identify words during oral and silent reading. The challenge of transferring what is learned during systematic phonics and word study instruction to oral and silent reading is primarily caused by the need to learn to integrate or juggle the word identification component of reading with the component that may be called *print processing beyond word identification* (J. Cunningham, 1993).

Print processing beyond word identification is the third major component of the reading process, separate from the word identification and language comprehension components, but equally essential. Print processing beyond word identification involves at least five basic subcomponents: eye movements beyond the word, projecting prosody, reading in inner speech, making print-to-meaning links, and integration. Helping children develop these subcomponents requires much practice reading texts that are largely comprised of words a reader can successfully identify through a combination of automatic word recognition and efficient decoding, with context that is rich enough to enable ongoing metacognition of word identification. When the reader cannot recognize or decode the words in a text, or is reading a text with too little context to monitor whether a word has been successfully identified, the task is akin to reading words in isolation because the reader's attention is overly focused on word identification of one word at a time. The reader has little attention left over to concentrate on a different component of the reading process, in this case print processing beyond word identification.

Eye Movements Beyond the Word.   Good readers look at almost every word and most letters on the page when they are reading even the most familiar words (Rayner, 1985). Their eyes move in predictable patterns that vary, depending on a variety of text-based factors including the relative difficulty of the words in the text (Starr & Rayner, 2001; Wiley & Rayner, 2000). Good readers move their eyes effortlessly through the text and, therefore, can allocate more attention to reading and understanding the words in it (Stanovich, 1992). Their eye movements are strategic rather than mechanical or habitual. Struggling readers, on the other hand, often have difficulty with eye movements, yet research suggests that a behavioral approach of training those readers to make more accurate and efficient eye movements does not improve their reading (Rayner, 1985) and is widely viewed as one way to make learning to read very difficult (Flippo, 1998). To develop, good strategic eye movements appear to require a substantial quantity of successful experience reading connected and meaningful texts until the reader gains knowledge of how print is processed during successful reading. To learn to move their eyes properly while identifying words during oral or silent reading, children need to identify those words while reading meaningful and interesting texts that foster good eye movements beyond the word.

Projecting Prosody.   Prosody is the rhythm (pitch, juncture, and stress) oral language has that helps to make it understandable. Prosody helps the listener to parse the syntax within each utterance, follow the cohesive links between utterances, and assign emphasis to the most important words and phrases. Printed language provides only a few meager clues (e.g., punctuation, underlining, italics) to its rhythm and phrasing. Children must learn to project prosody onto printed language to help them assign proper syntax, cohesion, and emphasis during oral and silent reading.

Projecting prosody onto print requires readers to take information received visually and hold it in an auditory channel while processing connected text (Wilkenfeld, 1980). The reader must learn to interpret morphological and syntactic cues within a text in addition to identifying the words in the text in order to project the prosody accurately (Schreiber, 1980). Like eye movements, teaching children prosodic structure on its own does not produce improvements in reading unless that teaching includes reading intact texts with words the child can read effectively (Young, Bowers, & MacKinnon, 1996). Learning to read texts orally with expression (Erekson, 2001) and silently with comprehension are the principal means by which readers acquire the ability to project prosody. Both kinds of learning require that students read meaningful texts with natural language patterns.

Reading in Inner Speech.   Subvocalization is another essential subcomponent of the reading process that children cannot acquire through systematic word identification instruction or listening to another person read aloud. The importance of inner speech in reading is that it allows the reader to hold and integrate ideas (Daneman & Newson, 1992). When inner speech is suppressed during reading, the reader can remember the words themselves, but has difficulty integrating ideas across the entire text because inner speech is believed to enable prosodic restructuring of the text during silent reading (Daneman & Newson, 1992; Slowiaczek & Clifton, 1980). Obviously, reading in inner speech also makes it possible for the reader to read silently so as not to disturb others nearby, an indispensable reading ability for all to acquire.

Making Print-to-Meaning Links.   When a reader is able to recognize a word automatically and also knows one or more meanings for that word, it becomes possible for the reader to go directly from print to meaning when encountering that word. If so, the reader has learned to link meaning directly to the word's print array without having to first translate the print into sound before accessing the word's meaning. This degree of knowledge of a word (direct lexical access) only occurs through repeated encounters with a word in meaningful context. A good reader uses this ability along with the ability to read in inner speech in order to monitor both word identification and silent reading comprehension. To understand how this special kind of metacognition works, read the following sentence silently:

Eye red the sine be sighed the rode.

If you simultaneously performed two subcomponents of print processing, reading in inner speech and making print-to-meaning links, you had a schizophrenic experience. Your reading in inner speech yielded a perfectly sensible piece of language, "I read the sign beside the road." No problem there. But, the print-to-meaning links you made yielded a garbled mass of incoherent meanings—the organ of vision/a color of a fire engine/a trig function/etc. A serious problem there. By engaging in these two subcomponents of reading at the same time, a reader has another way of checking to see if reading (or the text) is making sense. As long as both make sense and agree with each other, reading can continue without a concern.

Integration. To achieve the complexity and fluidity of understanding that characterize good reading, children require much successful experience integrating the many components and subcomponents of the reading process. Juggling all the other subcomponents while applying newly acquired word identification abilities is a challenging task that requires readers to apply the words and decoding skills they are learning to the reading of interesting and meaningful texts. Some advocates have suggested that teacher read-aloud is adequate to build the comprehension and affective aspects of reading, but we teachers cannot read texts aloud to children and expect the experience to be an adequate complement to our word identification instruction. Why not? Because teacher read-aloud cannot help children acquire either print processing beyond word identification or the ability to integrate it with decoding and word recognition. Teacher read-aloud has value, but it cannot replace the need for students to learn to comprehend the language of texts while simultaneously identifying the words and processing the print beyond what word identification requires.

Print Processing Beyond Word Identification. Even if children learn to decode and recognize words well in isolation, they will not be good readers unless they also learn to transfer their word identification abilities to oral and silent reading. Transfer requires that they learn to identify words while moving their eyes strategically through the text, reading in inner speech, projecting prosody, making print-to-meaning links, and integrating the many parts of the reading process together. Only by reading meaningful texts that require decoding and word recognition as well as print processing beyond word identification will a child develop word identification ability he or she can use.

The Need for Cognitive Clarity About the Role of Word Identification in Reading

The third reason that most young children must read interesting and meaningful texts that support their word recognition and decoding instruction is their need for cognitive clarity about the role of word identification in reading. Cognitive clarity, a lucid understanding that can lead to learning, results when children perceive instructional activities as significant and worthwhile (Downing, 1979; Good & Brophy, 2000). When children do not understand the purpose of an activity, do not find it particularly interesting, or do not understand how an activity relates to improving their lives or learning, they lack cognitive clarity about that activity.

Cognitive clarity is necessary to help children decide what information or processes to attend to, how to relate what is being experienced to previous knowledge, what learning strategies to apply, and how to self-monitor strategy application in relation to learning. Children often lack the experience and understanding of the big picture to achieve cognitive clarity in relation to given instructional activities unless the teacher or the situation provide it.

When children have cognitive clarity about learning to identify words, they are more likely to persist in their efforts because they anticipate being able to recognize many words when they read and being able to decode most of the rest. They can use this understanding of the purpose of their word identification instruction to self-monitor their learning, even when words are presented out of context. They are better able to cooperate with the word identification instruction they receive because they know what their teacher is trying to help them learn to do.

The best way to build children's cognitive clarity for word identification is to provide them with meaningful and interesting texts that contain many words they have learned to recognize or decode. Another good way is to point out frequently and concretely to them how they are using what they have learned as they read these texts.

The Need for Motivation to Learn Word Identification

Proficient word identification must be learned by anyone who will become a good reader, but that fact may not be at all obvious to primary-grade children. They must perceive in real terms (i.e., observe and experience) that word identification helps them read and/or write something that matters to them personally, or many will pay less attention during word identification instructional activities, or during reading and writing. As teachers, we can support children's development of motivation to learn and apply word identification.

Student motivation is dependent on two factors: the degree of success that students anticipate when engaging in a particular task, and the value they place on the rewards associated with successful task performance (Feather, 1982). Before children will invest significant effort in a task, such as learning to identify words or trying to identify words in a text, they must first believe they will be able to succeed if they try. Yet self-confidence, though necessary, is not sufficient for student motivation. Everyone knows skills or activities they can do successfully but still do not or will not do. In addition to self-confidence, if children are to engage with word identification instruction and identifying words in order to read a text, they must value the learning and reading they can do. The value may be intrinsic (e.g., enjoying learning or the content of the text) or extrinsic to the activity (e.g., being the first member of the class to read a particular text successfully). If students are motivated solely by extrinsic rewards, they tend to focus on the short-term acquisition of those rewards rather than the longer term acquisition of strategies, skills, or understanding (Good & Brophy, 2000). Usually, intrinsic motivation has greater value for long-term reading development.

Thus, motivating children to learn word identification employs two tactics: (a) making the instruction itself successful, interesting, and applicable to reading; and (b) providing children with interesting and meaningful texts that provide a number of opportunities for the children to apply the decoding and word recognition they are learning. Both tactics help students value learning and using word identification.

The Need for Self-Teaching of Word Recognition

The fifth reason why meaningful and interesting texts play an essential role in the development of children's word identification ability is that good decoders teach themselves to recognize many words as they read for enjoyment. Jorm and Share (1983; Share, 1995) have written about the self-teaching of word recognition that can occur while a reader is decoding words during independent reading. This self-teaching of word recognition depends on the frequency of the words that are encountered within texts (Share, 1999). Texts expose readers to a variety of words, many of which occur frequently enough across texts to be learned through repeated decoding of them.

If children work on the highest frequency words in word study instruction, they do not need to learn them through self-teaching. On the other hand, learning to recognize words of moderate or lower frequency in texts generally requires self-teaching by decoding while reading because the words are not likely to be studied in reading or spelling instruction. The need for self-teaching explains why exposure to print (text) is a key factor in students' growth in automatic word recognition (Stanovich & West, 1989).

Summary: The Necessity of Meaningful and Interesting Texts for Word Identification Development

Regardless of how well or how long phonics and word study are taught, many children only develop word identification ability they use during reading if they also develop metacognition of word identification, transfer of word identification to oral and silent reading, cognitive clarity about the role of word identification in reading, motivation to learn word identification, and self-teaching of word recognition. Helping the children we teach meet these five needs is vital for the word identification component to function properly during the reading process. These five needs will only be met well enough and early enough for most children if they read enough meaningful and interesting texts that provide adequate opportunities for them to apply their developing decoding and word recognition.

WHY IS SYSTEMATIC WORD RECOGNITION AND DECODING INSTRUCTION NECESSARY FOR WORD IDENTIFICATION DEVELOPMENT?

If texts with rich language and meaning that provide a number of opportunities to recognize and decode words are so valuable for children's word identification development, why is systematic instruction also necessary? Why not have children read orally and silently in good texts of appropriate difficulty that support word recognition and decoding and have their word identification develop by reading?

Systematic instruction has a scope or curriculum to transmit and is regular, planned, and teacher-directed. There are at least two reasons why many children will not successfully develop facility with word identification unless they receive systematic instruction in decoding and word recognition from the beginning. This section discusses these two reasons as two more needs that children have during their word identification development.

The Need to Focus Extensively on the Sounds of Letters, Letter Clusters, and Words

Interesting and meaningful texts that allow young children to apply the decoding and word recognition they are learning are crucial if children are to learn to read well in every sense of that term. Unfortunately, the very aspects of these texts that make them so valuable also make them inadequate as stand-alone means for helping most children learn the letter–sound relationships and words that comprise adept word identification ability. The interestingness and meaningfulness of texts tend to distract readers from concentrating on the phonology and orthography of the words in those texts. Such distractions are not problematic for the application of word identification to reading; indeed, learning to use word identification while being distracted by interesting and meaningful language and content is exactly what developing word identifiers must do! However, such distractions are problematic for the learning of decoding and word recognition in the first place. Only by attending carefully and repeatedly to letters, groups of letters, and the full visual array of each specific word, as well as the sounds those letters and words represent, can the child master the word identification component of reading. Most young children must receive systematic phonics and word study instruction of some kind outside of reading to provide the extensive focus required.

The Need for Sufficient Repetition in the Beginning on the Words and Decoding Skills Essential for Reading

The more interesting and meaningful texts for early readers are, the less likely the texts are to supply enough repetition with the most important words and letter–sound relationships. Unfortunately, when texts for early readers are engineered to provide high percentages of high-frequency words (as in the "Sally, Dick, and Jane" era) or high percentages of decodable words (as currently mandated in Texas, California, and elsewhere), they almost always lack the rich language and content necessary to foster the development of the other components and abilities of reading. Systematic phonics and word study instruction are often more effective than such "untexts" in providing the needed repetition on the words and decoding skills that young readers must learn.

Summary: The Necessity of Systematic Instruction for Word Identification Development

Most children only develop proficient word identification ability if they focus extensively on the sounds of letters, clusters of letters, and words, and receive sufficient repetition in the beginning on the words and decoding skills essential for reading. Regardless of how meaningful, interesting, and supportive of the development of decoding and word recognition that the texts they read are, most children also need systematic phonics and word study instruction outside of connected reading.

IMPLICATIONS OF THE CASE FOR INTERESTING AND MEANINGFUL TEXTS THAT SUPPORT WORD IDENTIFICATION DEVELOPMENT FROM THE BEGINNING

In this chapter, we have made a strong case for having young children read good texts with adequate opportunities to recognize and decode words. There are three main implications of this case for practice.

Most of the Texts Young Children Are Asked to Read Should Be Interesting and Meaningful to Them

What is an interesting and meaningful text? It is a text that a teacher can read aloud to the class and have the children engaged in what they are hearing. To find out whether available texts are good for young children to read, teachers without much experience, or early in the school year, may need to read a sample of the books aloud to the class. Teachers with experience, or later in the school year, are able to anticipate which books would make successful read-alouds without actually having to read any of them to the class. Books for guided and self-selected reading do not need to be *excellent* read-alouds. However, unless children would remain engaged if they listened to them, they are not meaningful and interesting enough for children to read in order to foster the development of word identification ability they use over the long run.

Many of the Texts Young Children Are Asked to Read Should Support Their Developing Word Identification Abilities

Books that support word identification development have two essential features. First, they work together as a collection of books that provide adequate repetition of high-frequency words and words that can be decoded with a certain level of phonics knowledge. Second, this collection of books gradually decreases in the repetition it provides on any particular subset of high-frequency words and any particular level of decoding skill. That is, the word identification demands of the texts gradually increase. If there is no critical mass of books with both features available for young children to read during guided and self-selected reading, the books may be interesting and meaningful to children, but they cannot be aligned with systematic word identification instruction.

At present, there are many good books available to teachers that support in-struction in the use of the three cuing systems in figuring out unfamiliar words. Unfortunately, in our examination of these books we did not find that they gen-erally have the two features needed to support either word recognition or de-coding development.

Although the highly decodable texts we also examined possess both features needed to support the development of decoding, they do not generally support the development of word recognition. Moreover, very few of these texts could be read aloud to young children and maintain their engagement. Therefore, they cannot be expected to foster metacognition of word identification, transfer of word identification to oral and silent reading, cognitive clarity about the role of word identification in reading, motivation to learn word identification, or self-teaching of word recognition.

Reading Educators Should Select Subsets of Interesting and Meaningful Texts That Support the Development of Both Word Recognition and Decoding

There are so many good books available for young children to read that there is much reason for optimism about the possibility of finding subsets of these books that have the essential features needed for them to foster the development of both word recognition and decoding. Books that collectively have these characteristics would qualify as "multiple-criteria" texts (Hiebert, 1999). Of course, there may be readers with disabilities who need "single-criterion" texts (Hiebert, 1999) for a pe-riod of time, but prescribing those texts for readers without disabilities would violate the research, as we read it, and the logic we present in this chapter.

Finding these subsets of texts requires the will, as well as the time and exper-tise, on the part of teachers and other reading educators to analyze a great many good books. Happily, these analyses can lead to sequenced or leveled lists of in-teresting and meaningful books that help teachers of early literacy teach their students word identification they use in real reading.

IMPLICATIONS OF THE CASE FOR SYSTEMATIC WORD IDENTIFICATION INSTRUCTION FROM THE BEGINNING

We have also made a strong case that systematic teaching of word recognition and decoding are necessary for most children from the beginning. There are three additional implications of this case for practice.

Most of the Word Recognition and Decoding Instruction Children Receive Should Be Directly Provided by the Teacher

To date, there is little evidence that worksheets, workbooks, computers, or learning centers can teach children word recognition or decoding. Rather, direct instruction by teachers is usually required (Stahl, Duffy-Hester, Stahl, 1998). We are advocates of a particular approach to word study instruction (Word Wall with daily On-the-Back Activities) and phonics instruction (Tongue Twisters, Making Words, Rounding Up the Rhymes, Reading/Writing Rhymes, etc.; P. Cunningham, 2000). No doubt, other approaches to teaching word identification can also be effective if they are sound and include an adequate amount of direct teacher instruction.

Most of the Word Recognition and Decoding Instruction Children Receive Should Have a Curriculum to Transmit and Be Regular and Planned

A long tradition in reading education supports the value of a strand in the reading curriculum dedicated to teaching children the high-utility letter–sound associations for letters and clusters of letters. Children need to learn the common sounds spelled by single onsets (initial consonant sounds), digraph onsets, and blend onsets. At the very least, they need to learn the common sounds of high-utility phonograms (orthographic rimes). They must either induce the vowel and final consonant letter–sound relationships or be taught those as well. Similarly, a long tradition in reading education supports the need to teach children the most common words in printed language, especially the words that are not phonetically regular. We advocate teaching children to recognize the first few hundred most common words, whether or not they are phonetically regular.

Too many children will fail to learn these words and letter–sound relationships if we rely on hit-or-miss instruction that waits for children to make an error in oral reading or spelling. We know what words, letters, and letter clusters children most need to know; it is only common sense to teach them this knowledge in a clear and logical sequence, with adequate repetition and good examples.

The Word Identification Instruction Children Receive Should Be Aligned With the Word Recognition and Decoding Demands of Many of the Texts They Read During Guided and Self-Selected Reading

If children are to apply their developing word recognition and decoding abilities when reading, most of them need instruction and practice in doing so. A logical sequence of word identification instruction should inform any attempt to select and align a subset of good texts with that instruction. On the other hand, the high-frequency and phonetically regular words in a collection of good texts should also shape the scope and sequence of word study and phonics instruction aligned with those texts.

THE RECIPROCAL RELATIONSHIP BETWEEN WORD IDENTIFICATION INSTRUCTION AND GOOD TEXTS THAT ARE INSTRUCTIONALLY SUPPORTIVE

Our goal in this chapter was to demonstrate the reciprocal relationship that can and should exist between the phonics and word-study lessons teachers provide young children and the texts they offer them during guided and self-selected reading. When the lessons are systematic, the texts are meaningful and interesting, and the lessons and texts are aligned so the children have adequate opportunities to apply the word recognition and decoding they have been taught, word identification develops in a way that is complementary and not competitive with the other purposes of reading instruction.

REFERENCES

Clay, M. M. (1991). *Becoming literate: The construction of inner control.* Portsmouth, NH: Heinemann.
Cunningham, J. W. (1993). Whole-to-part reading diagnosis. *Reading and Writing Quarterly: Overcoming Learning Difficulties, 9,* 31–49.
Cunningham, J. W. (1999). How we can achieve best practices in literacy instruction. In L. B. Gambrell, L. M. Morrow, S. B. Neuman, & M. Pressley (Eds.), *Best practices in literacy instruction* (pp. 34–45). New York: Guilford.
Cunningham, P. M. (1975–1976). Investigating a synthesized theory of mediated word identification. *Reading Research Quarterly, 11,* 127–143.
Cunningham, P. M. (2000). *Phonics they use: Words for reading and writing* (3rd ed.). New York: Longman.
Daneman, M., & Newson, M. (1992). Assessing the importance of subvocalization during normal silent reading. *Reading & Writing, 4*(1), 55–77.
Downing, J. (1979). *Reading and reasoning.* New York: Springer-Verlag.
Ehri, L. C. (1992). Reconceptualizing the development of sight word reading and its relationship to recoding. In P. B. Gough, L. C. Ehri, & R. Treiman (Eds.), *Reading acquisition* (pp. 107–143). Hillsdale, NJ: Lawrence Erlbaum Associates..
Erekson, J. A. (2001). Prosody and performance: Children talking the text in elementary school (Doctoral dissertation, Michigan State University, 2001). *Dissertation Abstracts International, 62,* A947.
Feather, N. (Ed.). (1982). *Expectations and actions.* Hillsdale, NJ: Lawrence Erlbaum Associates.
Flippo, R. F. (1998). Points of agreement: A display of professional unity in our field. *The Reading Teacher, 52,* 30–40.

Good, T. L., & Brophy, J. E. (2000). *Looking in classrooms* (8th ed.). New York: Longman.

Hiebert, E. H. (1999). Text matters in learning to read. *The Reading Teacher, 52*, 552–566.

Jorm, A. F., & Share, D. L. (1983). Phonological recoding and reading acquisition. *Applied Psycholinguistics, 4*, 103–147.

Juel, C., & Roper/Schneider, D. (1985). The influence of basal readers on first grade reading. *Reading Research Quarterly, 20*, 134–152.

Rayner, K. (1985). The role of eye movements in learning to read and reading disability. *Remedial and Special Education, 6*(6), 53–60.

Schreiber, P. A. (1980). On the acquisition of reading fluency. *Journal of Reading Behavior, 12*, 177–186.

Share, D. L. (1995). Phonological recoding and self-teaching: *Sine qua non* of reading acquisition. *Cognition, 55*, 151–218.

Share, D. L. (1999). Phonological recoding and orthographic learning: A direct test of the self-teaching hypothesis. *Journal of Experimental Child Psychology, 72*, 95–129.

Slowiaczek, M. L., & Clifton, C. (1980). Subvocalization and reading for meaning. *Journal of Verbal Learning and Verbal Behavior, 19*, 573–582.

Smith, F. (1971). *Understanding reading: A psycholinguistic analysis of reading and learning to read.* New York: Holt, Rinehart & Winston.

Stahl, S. A., Duffy-Hester, A. M., Stahl, K. A. D. (1998). Everything you wanted to know about phonics (but were afraid to ask). *Reading Research Quarterly, 33*, 338–355.

Stanovich, K. E. (1992). Speculations on the causes and consequences of individual differences in early reading acquisition. In P. B. Gough, L. C. Ehri, & R. Treiman (Eds.), *Reading acquisition* (pp. 307–342). Hillsdale, NJ: Lawrence Erlbaum Associates.

Stanovich, K. E., & West, R. F. (1989). Exposure to print and orthographic processing. *Reading Research Quarterly, 24*, 402–433.

Starr, M. S., & Rayner, K. (2001). Eye movements during reading: Some current controversies. *Trends in Cognitive Sciences, 5*(4), 156–163.

Wiley, J., & Rayner, K. (2000). Effects of titles on the processing of text and lexically ambiguous words: Evidence from eye movements. *Memory & Cognition, 28*, 1011–1021.

Wilkenfeld, D. (1980). Prosodic encoding in silent reading. *CUNY Forum (no. 7–8)*, 230–236.

Young, A. R., Bowers, P. G., & MacKinnon, G. E. (1996). Effects of prosodic modeling and repeated reading on poor readers' fluency and comprehension. *Applied Psycholinguistics, 17*, 59–84.

3

From *Brown Bear* to *Paddington Bear*: The Role of Text in the Development of Fluency

Steven A. Stahl
Center for the Improvement of Early Reading Achievement
University of Illinois, Urbana-Champaign

Katherine A. Dougherty Stahl
University of Illinois, Urbana-Champaign

What is fluency? To some degree, we know it when we see it, but we do not know, yet, how precisely to define it. We know that a first grader stumbling over words in a preprimer is not fluent. Nor is the struggling reader in third grade whose reading is full of self-corrections and hesitations. We know that the child whose reading is smooth and prosodic is fluent, but what of adults, like an old high school history teacher we know, whose reading is still a monotone?

This chapter looks at how text informs the development of fluency. For the purposes of the chapter, we foreground text, as might be expected in a book on text, relegating instruction to a lesser focus. This does not mean that instruction is unimportant—it most assuredly is—but that here we choose to talk about text.

Fluency must be defined in terms of both automatic word recognition and prosodic or expressive reading (Kuhn & Stahl, 2003). In this chapter, however, we devote more of our discussion to the development of automatic word recognition, simply because we know more about how word recognition develops than about how children's reading becomes prosodic. Prosody may develop as a result of a child's ability to read words quickly and automatically, or it may have a separate developmental trajectory, so that the focus for now on the automaticity aspect of fluency seems warranted.

FLUENT READING AS AUTOMATIC WORD RECOGNITION

Proficient readers can read words automatically, without conscious attention to the word forms, unless there is a problem with the print that calls attention to the print itself, such as writing in a different FoNt or including an anomalous succotash in a sentence. Before turning to a discussion of how automatic word recognition develops, we address two models that researchers have suggested for the development of automaticity, one based on learning through repetition of words, the other based on repetition of spelling patterns. These models have different implications for children's learning to develop automaticity from exposure to words in text.

Two Models of the Development of Automaticity

"Practice Makes Perfect."   One model suggests that children need repeated exposure to the same word in order to recognize it automatically. Logan's instance theory suggested that words are recognized as wholes (e.g., Logan, 1990; Logan, Taylor, & Etherton, 1999). He proposed that automaticity develops from repeated exposure to the same stimulus. Once a word is automatized, its processing is obligatory, that is a person cannot *not* process the word. Earlier versions of Logan's theory suggested that mere repetition may be enough to lead to automaticity. Later formulations (e.g., Logan et al., 1999) suggested that mere exposure is not enough. The learner must attend to the word and actively encode it in short-term memory until it is established in long-term memory and thus, automatized. It is the attention that enables the learner to form that stable memory trace that leads to automaticity. Thus, highly predictable texts, which do not require the child to analyze the word but instead allow the child to use context to predict the print, may work against the development of automaticity.

Orthographic Models.   Mere repetition, however, cannot explain why proficient readers can read words such as *quotidian*, *perspicacious*, and *approbation*, words we encounter rarely. In LaBerge and Samuels' (1974) model, words can be recognized by a number of routes, including as whole words, through spelling patterns, and through an automatized synthesis of individual letters. There is an assumption, however, that a written word unit must be securely represented in long-term memory for it to be recognized automatically. Adams' (1990) model suggest that words

are stored in long-term memory as networks of letters (which, in turn, are represented by networks of features). With repeated exposures, links between the letters
on the network are strengthened. As a word is read, activation spreads first between
the letters on the network whose links are strongest, only later spreading to weaker
links. Adams suggested that phonograms that are encountered more frequently
than specific words are a basic unit of word recognition, and that proficient readers
use phonograms (or rimes) to recognize words. For example, a child may use knowledge of *train, main,* and *rain,* to decode *chain* and *drain* automatically, even if these
new words have up until then been seen less frequently or not at all. There is some
evidence that letter clusters in the form of rimes or trigrams that occur more frequently are recognized more quickly than those which are less frequent. This is especially true for children reading past the second grade level who encounter
common rimes and come to read them automatically (Leslie & Calhoon, 1995).

Adams also stressed the importance of the child attending to individual letters in word learning. Similar to Share (1995; Share & Stanovich, 1995), she
suggested that children need to analyze words fully, through "sounding out" or
some other mechanism, in order to develop the representations necessary for
the development of automaticity. Thus, whether the representation is word by
word or through links of letters into phonograms or spelling patterns, children
need to examine the internal structures of words in order to develop the lasting
long-term memory traces that underlie automaticity.

We learn words by making connections of their particular spelling (as in irregular words), their spelling patterns, or parts of their spelling patterns (such as using
a first letter as a cue). As the words are encountered more frequently, information
about the word is tied to a number of different contexts, and we forget about the
specific contexts and learn to recognize the word automatically. Thus, we may remember where we first encountered words like *minatory, calliope,* and
broustophedon, but not more common words, such as *the, tree,* or even *exterminate.*

Because we recognize words not only by their particular spelling, but also as
collections of spelling patterns within the words (Adams, 1990), we need to internalize patterns as well as individual words. If a word is predictable, by virtue
of the language pattern of the book or the repetition of a spelling pattern in the
book, it is not learned as well as if the reader had to analyze it and connect it
with already known words. In order to learn a word, the child must devote attention to it. Because predictable words do not require much focused attention,
they might not be learned as well as nonpredictable words that may elicit more
attention (Johnston, 2000).

In early reading, the relative difficulty of the text depends on the amount of
knowledge that the child has about words. When there are too many words
needing to be analyzed, the child must spend an inordinate amount of attention

on the analysis, allowing less attention to be available for making connections. When there are too few words to be analyzed, the child will learn fewer new words simply because there are fewer to be learned. These principles are at the heart of the recommendation that the child should read text at a moderate level of difficulty. The text cannot contain all new words or all known words, but must provide enough support for the child to develop rich connections for a moderate number of new words. Thus, each text must contain known words, some in the process of being learned to automaticity, and some new words. In the beginning stages of reading, the known words may be "known" because they are cued by a language pattern or by pictures. The point is that these words should not require the child to process them, so that attention can be focused on new words or even parts of words.

Instruction that promotes automaticity requires the child to analyze words in order to make connections between the words and information already in long-term memory. With repetition, more connections are made between newly encoded words and spelling patterns and other information already known. The greater number of connections and the greater number of contexts in which a word is learned, the more automatic the recognition becomes. This continues until the word is learned well enough that all information about the contexts in which it first appeared are forgotten.

The Development of Automatic Word Recognition

Ehri suggested that there are a series of phases through which children pass as they learn to recognize words (Ehri, 1995, 1998). As children learn to recognize words, they first recognize them holistically, as a single logograph. Ehri called this phase *visual cue reading* or *pre-alphabetic* reading. Children at this phase may recognize words like *look* through the two "eyes" in the middle or the word *monkey* by its "tail." This is a *pre-alphabetic phase* (Ehri, 1995) because children are not using letters and sounds, but are instead using the look of each word to recognize it. As children develop phonological awareness, they may begin to use partial sound information in the word, such as an initial or final sound (see Stahl & Murray, 1998). Ehri called this phase the *partial alphabetic phase*. In this phase, a child might substitute a word that begins with the same letter, such as *bird* for *bear*, when reading words in text or in lists. As children learn more words, phonetic cue reading becomes less efficient and children analyze the word more deeply. In the *full alphabetic phase* (Ehri, 1995), children use all the letters and sounds. At this phase, children's reading can still be labored, relying on sounding out the word or other, less efficient strategies. At this point, they are either sounding the word out or using analogies to identify the whole word.

Following this phase, children move to *automatic word recognition*, a stage when they are able to identify the word seemingly as a whole or through rapid recognition of chunks within the word. At this point, children are free to put all of their attention toward comprehension, for word recognition has become fluent and transparent. With greater practice, children will develop automatic word recognition so that they do not have to think about the words in a text and can concentrate fully on the meaning of the text (Chall, 1996; Ehri, 1995). Ehri called this last phase *consolidated word recognition* because readers have consolidated all their information about words into a single representation. At the consolidated phase, a word is recognized automatically, so that the reader goes from text to meaning transparently.

In Ehri's model, children in this last phase have automatic word recognition. Perfetti (1992) suggested that this phase model does not as much describe readers' development but instead, the development of knowledge each reader undergoes for each individual word. That is, a reader may have a consolidated representation of some words, partial alphabetic knowledge of other words, and need to sound out other words. Even proficient readers may use visual cues to recognize words, as in the names in a Russian novel.

A synthesis of these two positions suggests that the first three phases of Ehri's (1995, 1998) model represent three successive awarenesses that children need to acquire. Thus, visual cue reading represents the child's understanding that print carries meaning and that one reads the written words, not the pictures (Clay, 1991). Partial alphabetic cueing represents the initial stages of awareness that letters in words represent sounds, the alphabetic principle. This is tied to the initial stages of phonological awareness (see Stahl & Murray, 1998; Stahl, McKenna, & Kovach, in press), essentially an awareness of consonants and how letters represents them. The next phase, full alphabetic cueing, represents an awareness of vowels. Vowels are difficult to isolate because in spoken syllables, consonants are folded into the vowel (Shankweiler & Liberman, 1972). There is an awareness that words are constructed from each letter in a sequential order. However, at this stage the children do not have enough experience with the variations in vowels to know quite what to do with them. Children also begin to notice patterns in longer words during the full alphabetic phase. These three phases are primarily awarenesses, concepts that are attained in relatively all-or-none fashion.

In contrast, the movement from the full alphabetic cueing phase, in which the child has the capacity to sound out words but still sees them as collections of letters, to the consolidated phase, in which the reader recognizes new or rarely seen words through the use of spelling patterns, happens through a gradual accretion of learned patterns. That is, once a child "gets" the idea that words can be sounded out through looking at all of the letters, progress occurs pattern by pattern, until the child has a well-articulated network of letters (Adams, 1990) or a large number of well-learned words in memory (Logan, 1990).

Thus, a word will go through two phases in order to be automatic. First, the word must be encoded into long-term memory, through a process of analysis. Then the word must be seen in a number of different contexts until its recall is automatic. The same process occurs with spelling patterns within words. First, they are learned, as parts of words. With exposure to the same spelling pattern in different words, the pattern becomes automatically activated. Thus, more common rimes become recognized automatically prior to less common rimes (Leslie & Calhoon, 1995).

Text will have two different roles in the development of automatic word recognition. In the early phases, text will support these ongoing insights. In the transition from full alphabetic coding to consolidated word reading, text will provide structured practice, supporting the acquisition of new word patterns.

Reading Words in Context.   Ehri's (1995, 1998) model refers only to the recognition of words in isolation. There is some evidence that words are recognized differently in context. In an early study, Goodman (1965) found that children recognized words in context that they could not recognize in isolation. Nicholson (1991) suggested that these results were an artifact of the experimental process that Goodman used, and that, if there is a context facilitation effect, it is smaller than Goodman claimed. However, there is some evidence that text provides at least some support for word recognition. Adams and Huggins (1985) found that second- through fifth-grade students could read irregular words such as *island* or *anchor* in sentence contexts significantly better than they could read them in isolation.

Adams (1990) proposed that contextual facilitation may not be enough to recognize a word by itself, but context may provide enough information to boost a weak or partial representation of a word so that the word is recognized. Thus, the words in Adams and Huggins' (1985) study may have been partially known, or not known well enough to be recognized by themselves, but have been recognized with the facilitation given from context.

Contextual facilitation may be a two-edged sword, however. Context may help a person recognize partially known words, but also may inhibit the learning of other words, when the salience of the context overpowers the need to examine the word. This can happen in the early phases of reading, with predictable texts. We turn next to a discussion of text characteristics such as predictability that may or may not contribute to fluency development.

PREDICTABILITY AND OTHER TEXT FACTORS IN THE DEVELOPMENT OF FLUENCY

Children's early texts can be described in a number of ways. Here, we focus on the texts' predictability and on how predictability relates to their decodability and their vocabulary load. Each of these characteristics makes different contributions to the development of automatic word recognition. Although we talk about "predictable books" and "decodable text," neither of these characteristics are absolute. Instead, books vary in terms of the predictability of the text from language patterns and pictures, and vary in terms of the number of words that can be decoded, given the content covered in the child's phonics lessons.

Predictable books use a repeated language pattern in order to scaffold children's acquisition of the text. Early predictable books, such as *Brown Bear, Brown Bear, What Do You See?* (Martin, 1967), have a single pattern repeated until the end, when there is a variation in the pattern, for interest. Later predictable books, such as *Ms. Wishy-Washy* (Cowley, 1980) or *The Red Rose* (Cowley, 1991), have two patterns. In *Ms. Wishy-Washy*, a series of animals see a mud puddle and say, "What lovely mud," and jump in. In the second pattern, Ms. Wishy-Washy scrubs each animal in turn. The end is when the animals, newly clean, see the mud again and exclaim, "What lovely mud." The double pattern adds some complexity and interest.

Another source of predictability is the degree to which the pictures reflect the text. In very early predictable books, the text merely labels the picture ("A blue box," "A red ball," etc.). As texts become less predictable, the pictures provide fewer and fewer cues.

The movement away from predictability is characteristic of texts leveled for the Reading Recovery system (Clay, 1991; Fountas & Pinnell, 1996; Peterson, 1991). Indeed, the lessons in Reading Recovery gradually introduce children to greater analysis of the visual characteristics of words, within the supportive context of the reading of leveled text (K. Stahl, S. Stahl, & McKenna, 1999).

Text Predictability in the Earliest Phase in Development: Toward Visual Cueing

The earliest books a child uses tend to be highly predictable, in both language pattern and picture use. Often, they are no more than a few words labeling a picture. Early predictable books such as *Brown Bear, Brown Bear, What Do You See?* fit into this category. The purpose of these books is primarily to teach directionality, book talk, concept of a word, and one-to-one matching. Teachers may also begin teaching high-frequency words with these books.

In the early phases, this may be "pseudoreading" of a previously memorized text. What distinguishes "pseudoreading" from actual reading is the inability of the child to fingerpoint accurately. If children cannot fingerpoint, they cannot make the print-to-speech match that defines reading (Clay, 1991; Morris, 1993; Uhry, 1999). Without an accurate print-to-speech match, the child is engaging in pure memorization, something that can occur with or without the text. Fingerpointing is that developmental milestone that suggests the child is paying attention to the text itself.

With the exception of labeling books, even the simplest predictable books need to vary the pattern, so that the book will be interesting. An early predictable book, *Brown Bear, Brown Bear, What Do You See?* (Martin, 1967), maintains a consistent pattern until the end. Each pair of pages follows the pattern "[color] [animal], [color] [animal], what do you see? / I see a [different color] [different animal] looking at me" until the end, when the subject is either a teacher or mother (depending on the edition) and finally the children, who recapitulate all of the animals and end on "That's what we see." This book is more structured than most, but as is true of nearly all predictable books, it has violations of the pattern. These violations (such as the recapitulation at the end and the "we" rather than "I" at the end) are not predictable and require more graphic processing. An easy book might have one or two violations; more complex books have many more violations. As books become less predictable (Peterson, 1991), these violations become more common and the texts require more orthographic processing. Because children need to pay attention to these violations, they are more likely to use letter cues. Thus, these violations to the pattern may help children move from a purely visual cue reading to a partial alphabetic cue reading.

Children need to have some instruction in words and letters to learn more than basic print concepts from predictable texts. Johnston (1998, 2000) found that children absorb few words from merely reading them in predictable books. She had children who were reading at the preprimer level or below re-read three predictable books 10 times apiece in a 4-day period. Children learned an average of one word per week through re-reading alone, not significantly different from zero. In contrast, studying words in a word bank led to significantly more growth, although this condition led to only an average of a scant three words in a week. Johnston concluded that children pay little attention to the words in predictable books because they can "read" the story with minimal print cues. Unless children are motivated to learn the print, as many precocious readers are (Durkin, 1966), they can avoid the print, and thus avoid learning the words. In Johnston's studies, and in Bridge, Winograd, and Haley's (1983) study, predictable texts were useful for word learning only if supported by some teacher-directed word study. A large degree of the success of the Reading Recovery program is the result of book selection combined with focused word analysis instruction, both carefully matched to the child's awarenesses.

Picture cues can also lead to print avoidance. If the pictures in a text are too revealing, children will use those pictures to aid in story recall, allowing them to use minimal print cues in order to read the text. Singer, Samuels, and Spiroff (1973–1974) found that picture cues interfered with word learning by allowing the child to identify the word without focusing on its graphic characteristics.

Thus, excessive reliance on either text predictability or picture cues, or both, can interfere with the development of automaticity. If the non-orthographic cues are too salient, then children will not encode the word into short-term memory, and thus not develop the memory trace needed to develop automaticity.

Text Factors in the Second Phase of Development: Toward Partial Alphabetic Cue Reading

Consistent fingerpointing requires some knowledge of letters and sounds such as develops in the partial alphabetic phase (Ehri & Sweet, 1991; Morris, 1993; Uhry, 1999). Ehri and Sweet, for example, found that children could fingerpoint accurately in memorized text only when they had minimal phonological awareness. They found that children needed to be in at least a partial alphabetic cueing phase before they could accurately fingerpoint. Stahl et al. (in press) and Uhry (1999) found that children needed knowledge of *both* initial and final sounds in order to fingerpoint successfully. In an emergent literacy context, this is quite a bit of literacy knowledge, suggesting that fingerpointing is the result of learning about words rather than a significant source of learning words.

As children read more advanced predictable books such as *Ms. Wishy-Washy* that have two patterns or more complex patterns, they need to rely more heavily on the print. Pictures in these books are more theme-oriented rather than explicitly matching the words on the page. Children need to use some knowledge of letter sounds and individual words as "anchors" as they read these less predictable texts. The book *Who Is Tapping at My Window?* (Deming, 1994) begins with the question, "Who is tapping at my window?" and continues:

"It's not I," said the cat.

"It's not I," said the rat.

"It's not I," said the fox.

"It's not I," said the ox.

In this story, the rhyme encourages the child to use the initial letter to cue the word *rat* instead of "mouse," and *ox* instead of "cow." In addition, the book introduces the animal *cony*, a word/concept that is likely to be unfamiliar to most young readers. Many of these books originated in New Zealand and contain unfamiliar animal names. These unfamiliar names especially force children to rely on letters or the rhyming pattern instead of on pictures.

Although the story reading is still propelled by the story content and structure, the high-frequency anchor words enable the child to read the story precisely. Anchor words also act as clues that enable the child to figure out new words. The book *A Dark, Dark Tale* (Brown, 1981) provides children with opportunities to use anchors in these ways. Although the book follows a fairly predictable story pattern, each page has a slightly different pattern. It begins:

Once upon a time there

was a dark, dark, moor

On the moor there was

a dark, dark wood

In the wood there was

a dark, dark house (pp. 2–6)

The first page begins with a standard "Once upon a time." After this page, each sentence begins with a different preposition. These prepositions are not cued by the pictures and must be learned as units. In order to read this book accurately, the child must concentrate first on the initial preposition and then on the final word. Some of these are cued partially by pictures, but others, such as *moor* and *cupboard*, may not be known by all students. These words get more attention. The predictable words are the ones that do not get attention.

Text Factors in the Later Phase of Development: Toward Full Alphabetic Coding

At this phase, children need to concentrate on each of the letters in a word. This is a phase that seems to require some degree of instruction in sound–symbol relationships, at least for most children (Chall, 1996). Texts used at this phase become less predictable in terms of language patterns and more concerned with providing interesting stories.

Vocabulary Load.   At this phase, texts have a wider vocabulary. The amount of vocabulary control has varied considerably over the years. Chall (1996) reported that from the 1920s to 1962, new words per hundred running words increased slightly from 0.9 to 1.7 in basal readers. By the 1986/87 programs, the number of new words per hundred running words was at 5.6 and by 1993, it had ballooned to 13.7 (Hoffman et al., 1994). The number has dropped somewhat since then (Menon, Martin, & Hiebert, 2000) but remains considerably higher than the average to be found 100 years ago.

These shifts in numbers of new words represent different theories of the development of automatic word recognition. From 1920 to 1962, the underlying theory, explicit or implicit, was that children needed repetition in order to develop automaticity in word recognition. By the middle 1970s, there was an increased recognition of the need for phonics instruction, leading to books that contained more attention to words that reinforced the phonics lessons (Popp, 1975). With the advent of the whole language movement, educators believed that the importance of vocabulary control diminished, leading to the use of more interesting and authentic stories with little control of vocabulary difficulty, either within stories or across stories in the same basal reader. As the whole language movement has receded, textbooks again show a greater concern with vocabulary control and decodabilty.

What is the proper rate of introduction of new words? There really is no clear answer to this question. To say that it depends on the instruction and the text begs the question, but may be appropriate to do. Some have attempted to come up with a minimal number of exposures as for example, Reitsma (1983) who suggested that a child needs four exposures to a word. However, repeated exposure, in and of itself, does not seem to be useful in word learning, as evidenced from the lack of word learning from merely reading predictable texts. Instead, word learning comes from drawing attention to words, most powerfully from instruction or less powerfully from text features.

Decodability.   Another characteristic of texts used to develop full alphabetic coding is decodability. There is an assumption in code-emphasis programs that children need to practice the content of phonics lessons through reading of books that contain already-taught patterns. The notions of decodability are, of course, tied into the notion of what is regular and what is irregular in English (see Venezky, 1999). We define decodability in terms of the percentage of words in a text that represent patterns previously taught. As such, decodability is not a construct inherent in the text but in the relation between the text and previous instruction. If a child has only been taught the short "a," a text containing only short "o" words would be totally nondecodable. But if short "o" was taught, the text would be highly decodable.

In spite of the strong emphasis on decodable texts in the current basal reading programs (see Menon et al., 2000), there seems to be only one study in support of the use of decodable text, and the results of that study were equivocal (see Allington & Woodside-Jiron, 1998). Juel and Roper/Schneider (1985) compared the use of decodable text with text that contained fewer words decodable by the phonics instruction as adjuncts to a synthetic phonics program. They found no differences on measures of comprehension or general word recognition, but did find differences on measures of words taught in the lessons. As Allington and Woodside-Jiron (1998) pointed out, this is slim evidence for major policy directives.

Adams (1990) cautioned against the use of the previous incarnation of decodable texts, the linguistic texts of the 1960s (see Bloomfield & Barnhart, 1961, for an example). These texts, in their most extreme form, are barely meaningful concatenations of similarly looking words, such as "Dan is a man./ Dan can fan Nan./ Dan has a van./ Dan can fan Nan in a van." She asserted that these "visual tongue twisters" made learning to read excessively difficult. The First Grade studies (Bond & Dykstra, 1997) reported that linguistic approaches were more effective than basal readers at that time. Combining the three projects that used linguistic programs, Bond and Dykstra reported significant differences favoring the linguistic treatment on measures of word recognition and passage comprehension but not on measures of word study and spelling. This pattern is a bit surprising, given that the word recognition measure contains both regularly and irregularly spelled words but the word study measure contains only regularly spelled words. One would expect the linguistic treatment, with its repetition of regularly spelled words, to produce higher effects on measures of regularly spelled words than on measures of irregular words.

It is possible that, because many of the same words were repeated over and over (these books seem to have a greater population of people named *Dan* and *Nan* than the general population, and their preferred mode of transportation seems to be a *van* in the early readers, moving toward a *bus* later on), students see these regular words as predictable and do not analyze them. Instead, students may devote more of their attention to the irregular words, which are less predictable, and thus learn them better. Menon et al. (2000) have conducted an extensive examination of the 2001 copyright basal reading programs and expressed a concern about the number of "singletons" or words that appear only once in a book. These words are decodable but are less utile than more regular words and are not repeated. In text like that below, words such as "fins" and "hoses" are not repeated in other stories:

Tim made pictures of fish with fins.

"I like to make my fish with lots of colors, " said Tim. "I have five blue and white fish at home. I hope to buy a red fish."

Kate made fire trucks with big hoses. (Bottner, 2001, pp. 43–44)

We are not as concerned about the lack of repetition of individual words as Menon et al. (2000) were. Singletons are problematic only if you accept Logan et al.'s (1999) model that children develop automaticity through repetition of the exact stimulus. Instead, we feel that the overlap between words in reasonably written decodable text and the variety of patterns to which a child is exposed will force the child to examine words in a way that will help them internalize these patterns. Validation of the new texts is ongoing (Hoffman, Roser, Salas, Patterson, & Pennington, 2000) and this remains a hypothesis until new data are reported.

Given the model that suggests that children need to internalize orthographic patterns through analysis of new words, decodable text certainly should be part of the mixture that children read during first grade and possibly second grade. Through successive exposure to new words containing common patterns, children are forced to create the detailed representations in long-term memory necessary for automaticity. The value of decodable text is that it allows children to see orthographic patterns in dense concentrations that are not present in authentic text, forcing them to examine the patterns and helping them solidify the representations of the patterns in memory. This is especially true when children encounter different rimes, such as in the preceding example. The words *fish*, *five*, and *fin* present difficulties in discrimination that can only be resolved through analysis of the words.

We cannot stress enough that children need a diet of different types of text and that the recommendation that text be decodable not be interpreted to require texts similar to the linguistic texts of the 1960s. As noted earlier, these linguistic texts may lead to overanalysis because the task of reading a text in which all words are similar and the text is nonsensical becomes a discrimination task rather than a meaning-gathering task.

In all text encounters, comprehension should be the driving force behind reading. This is important not only for philosophical reasons but for reasons relating more closely to word recognition. According to Adams' (1990) model, and supported by numerous studies, words are not just learned in terms of their orthographic characteristics. Instead, orthographic representations are tied to the mental lexicon. When a word is learned, not only is its orthographic pattern stored in long-term memory, but the connections between that pattern and semantic memory are also stored. Not only do learners need to establish connections among letters to recall a word automatically, they need to establish connections between these patterns and word meanings (see Stahl, 1991). Although pseudowords (letter strings that are orthographically regular, but meaningless) are recognized faster than non-regular letter strings, they are not processed as quickly as known words.

In their own way, both highly predictable texts and early linguistic texts were not comprehensible. That is, in neither type of text could the reader easily create a message that could be summarized and conveyed to another person. To move from full alphabetic coding to consolidated word recognition, a person must practice reading comprehensible texts. To be comprehensible, a narrative should contain a beginning, a middle, and an end, roughly corresponding to a basic story. Much of the "new" decodable text is comprehensible, but not all. As the reader moves toward consolidated word recognition, the text should become less predictable and less decodable, and more comprehensible, containing a larger number of concepts that require the reader to connect more orthographic patterns to more semantic information.

Text Factors in Moving Toward Consolidated and Automatic Word Recognition

There are two important factors in the development of automatic word recognition from full alphabetic coding. First, children need to read connected text rather than isolated words. Second, the text must be difficult enough to force them to analyze words both in terms of orthographic patterns and semantic connections.

The Need for Connected Text. In the original formulations of automaticity, automatic word recognition was measured through the use of isolated word tasks such as the lexical decision task. In the general form of the lexical decision task, the participant is to decide whether a letter string is a valid word or not. Researchers have generally found that words are recognized more quickly than non-words and that a number of factors influence word recognition speed, including frequency, word length, and concreteness (see Adams, 1990, for review). It would seem that speeded practice in word recognition would improve children's automaticity of word recognition and thus, comprehension. The results of studies examining this hypothesis are mixed, at best. Roth and Beck (1987) found that computerized practice in identifying regularly spelled words led to improved speed in recognizing taught words but did not transfer to improved comprehension. Fleisher, Jenkins, and Pany (1979–1980) and Spring, Blunden, and Gatheral (1981) were unable to find that practice in speeded isolated word recognition transferred to passage comprehension. This does not mean that practice in reading words in isolation has no effect. Tan and Nicholson (1997) and Blanchard (1981) both found that training on flash cards did improve comprehension. However, over-training until recognition was automatic did not seem to have an effect on comprehension.

The effects of repeated readings are less clear. In the Method of Repeated Readings (Samuels, 1985), a child reads the same text until a desired level of fluency is obtained. The National Reading Panel (2000) conducted a meta-analysis on guided repeated reading. This included repeated reading with or without direct guidance, peer tutoring, the use of audiotapes, and so on. They found an effect size of 0.41, which was significantly different from zero and of moderate size. This is difficult to interpret, because the National Reading Panel included so many different instructional techniques, some of which involved repeated reading and some which did not, to calculate a single effect size.

In contrast, Kuhn and Stahl (2000, 2003), using published and unpublished studies, looked separately at a number of different approaches to building fluency. They used a vote-counting procedure, which allows the use of more studies, although it lacks the precision of meta-analysis. They found 15 studies of unassisted repeated reading that used a control group, in which the student reads the same passage over and over without teacher support. Of these studies, 3 comparisons found that the repeated-readings treatment produced significantly greater results than the control; 17 comparisons failed to find such an effect (note that some studies involved more than one comparison). This suggests that repeated readings do not have an effect on comprehension. When Kuhn and Stahl looked at Assisted Reading, in which a child reads along with a model provided by a tape or a more competent reader, they found that five of the seven studies used a control group to report significant treatment differences. These two approaches were used with individuals. When they looked at classroom treatments, they found only three studies that used a control group, too few from which to draw conclusions.

Effects of Text Difficulty on Fluency Development. With their larger database, Kuhn and Stahl (2000, 2003) were able to examine the effects of a number of variables on the development of fluency. One of these was relative difficulty of the text that children are practicing. Educators have made two different recommendations as to the optimal difficulty of texts used for repeated readings. Some (e.g., Samuels, 1985) recommend that the material be slightly difficult so that the child's reading is supported at a higher level. Others recommend that the material be easy so that the child can practice until automaticity is reached.

Kuhn and Stahl (2000, 2003) found that text difficulty influenced both fluency development and transfer to comprehension. For both types of measures,
studies in which children were given material that was easy for them and generally below their instructional level failed to find a difference between treatment
and control groups. There was a greater tendency for studies in which children
were given material at their instructional level to report an effect in favor of the
treatment. Studies in which children were given relatively difficult material,
generally above their instructional level, had the greatest tendency to report
treatment effects. This point is important because many have argued, Chall
(1979) being the classic example, that children should read easy material to develop fluency. We found the opposite (see Figs. 3.1 and 3.2).

The superiority of difficult material in repeated and assisted reading contexts
can be understood through a number of theoretical frames. First, these results
are in concordance with Vygotsky's (1978) notion of the Zone of Proximal Development (ZPD). Vygotsky suggested that assessments generally test the level
of performance that a child can demonstrate independently. He proposed assessing until one finds the level at which the child can perform the task with
maximum support and beyond which the child is unable to perform the task.
The space between the independent level and the level at which the child can
still do the task with maximum support is the ZPD and, Vygotsky suggested, this

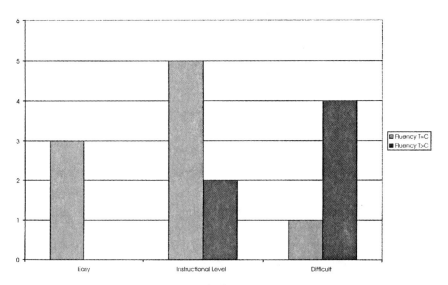

FIG. 3.1   Treatment/control comparisons for fluency measures.

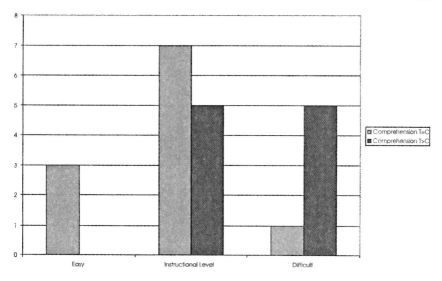

FIG. 3.2   Treatment/control comparisons for comprehension measures.

is where learning can take place. Others have suggested working with the child at the "top" of the zone, or by providing a great deal of support, gradually removing that support (e.g., Pearson & Gallagher, 1983; Pressley, 1998).

Although the notion of ZPD is most often applied to comprehension instruction, it seems compatible with the findings of Kuhn and Stahl (2000, 2003). Children seemed to benefit from material at or above their instructional level, with the support given by the repeated or assisted reading structure. Children did not benefit from reading material below their instructional level. Although not tested directly, it would make sense to predict that there is also a level at which children would no longer benefit from assisted reading support.

We have been using the conventional notion of instructional level, derived from the writings of Betts (1946), who suggested that children would benefit from instruction in material that they could read at between 95% and 99% accuracy. Johns (1997) reported that this level is not supported by research but only by convention and that children can use more difficult material if the circumstances warrant. Betts' notion of instructional level was based on Betts' Directed Reading Activity, in which children were given some support in reading, but not as much support as in the repeated reading or assisted reading approaches examined by Kuhn and Stahl (2000, 2003).

A better notion of "instructional level" may be based on the amount of instruction provided.[1] Stahl, Heubach, and Cramond (1997) found that children in their Fluency-Oriented Reading Instruction lessons were able to benefit from instruction using material they read initially with 85% accuracy. These lessons provided more support than a conventional Directed Reading Activity, allowing the teachers to use more difficult texts.

Another theoretical frame that might explain the effects of text difficulty found by Kuhn and Stahl (2003) is the one used to discuss the development of automatic word recognition used throughout this chapter. In this model, text with a high percentage of words that are known to the child would provide scaffolding for the child to analyze and encode the remaining words in long-term memory. In a Directed Reading Activity, the level of known words might well be 95%; in a repeated reading or assisted reading context, the level of known words might be as low as 85%. Of these known words, of course, some would be recognized automatically, others would be in the process of being learned. Of the unknown words, children will be able to analyze a certain number with each reading, one with a Directed Reading Activity, multiple readings with repeated approaches. When these previously unknown words are encountered again, they will be recognized. With each additional exposure in a different context, these words will move toward automaticity.

CONCLUSION: HOW TEXTS SUPPORT FLUENCY DEVELOPMENT

Fluency, of course, involves more than just automatic word recognition. But we know considerably more about how automatic word recognition develops than we know about prosody, another important component of fluency. Therefore we have stressed automatic word recognition in this chapter. Although we are talking about recognizing individual words, merely practicing words in lists does not seem to have the effects on children's learning that reading words in context does.

As we have reviewed various aspects of children's development, the same concepts appear repeatedly. First, in order for a word to be automatically recognized, the reader must first encode it well in long-term memory. This deep encoding seems to come from an analysis of the word through an examination of its constituent letters or spelling patterns. After a word is encoded in long-term memory, then it or its constituent spelling patterns need to be encountered in different contexts until the word is fully automatic. At the earliest phases in reading acquisition, such as the partial alphabetic phase,

---

[1]This suggestion was made by Jim Hoffman in an informal conversation a number of years ago.

children are learning to recognize letters automatically, rather than words, but the process is the same.

In order to support the acquisition of words, a text must be at an optimal level of difficulty. In any text, some of the words will not require any attention, others will be known but seen in a different context, and others will be unknown and need to be encoded. Again, in the earliest phases, when the child knows few if any words, the predictability of the text provides the support for many of the words, allowing the child to concentrate on using letter cues to recognize those words that are new. In later phases, this support is provided by already known words, again allowing the child to concentrate on new words. As more words are learned automatically, the child is able to concentrate on more new words, thus continuing the process.

As children develop to become fluent readers, they progress from the repetitive cadences of *Brown Bear, Brown Bear, What Do You See?* (Martin, 1967) to the complex, yet endearing, prose of *A Bear Called Paddington* (Bond, 1960). All along, the language of the text provides support for this development. First, this support is through repetition, later it is through the provision of an optimal level of difficulty, until the child is able to read fluently, not paying conscious attention to the words, focusing solely on the richness of the ideas.

REFERENCES

Adams, M. J. (1990). *Beginning to read: Thinking and learning about print.* Cambridge, MA: MIT Press.

Adams, M. J., & Huggins, A. W. F. (1985). The growth of children's sight vocabulary: A quick test with educational and theoretical implications. *Reading Research Quarterly, 20,* 262–281.

Allington, R. L., & Woodside-Jiron, H. (1998). What are decodable texts and why are policy makers mandating them? *Currents in Literacy, 1,* 21–22.

Betts, E. A. (1946). *Foundations of reading instruction.* New York: American Books.

Blanchard, J. S. (1981). A comprehension strategy for disabled readers in the middle school. *Journal of Reading, 24,* 331–336.

Bloomfield, L., & Barnhart, C. (1961). *Let's read: A linguistic approach.* Detroit: Wayne State University Press.

Bond, M. (1960). *A bear called Paddington.* Boston: Houghton-Mifflin.

Bond, G., & Dykstra, R. (1997). The cooperative research program in first grade reading. *Reading Research Quarterly, 2,* 5–142. (Original work published 1967)

Bottner, B. (2001). Yasmin's ducks. In *McGraw-Hill Reading Grade Book 4* (pp. 41–62). New York: McGraw-Hill

Bridge, C. A., Winograd, P. N., & Haley, D. (1983). Using predictable materials vs. preprimers to teach beginning sight words. *The Reading Teacher, 36,* 884–891.

Brown, R. (1981). *A dark, dark tale.* New York: Dial.

Chall, J. S. (1979). The great debate: Ten years later, with a modest proposal for reading stages. In L. B. Resnick & P. A. Weaver (Eds.), *Theory and practice of early reading* (Vol. 1, pp. 29–55). Hillsdale, NJ: Lawrence Erlbaum Associates.

Chall, J. S. (1996). *Learning to read: The great debate* (3rd ed.). New York: McGraw-Hill.

Clay, M. M. (1991). *Becoming literate.* Portsmouth, NH: Heinemann.

Cowley, J. (1980). *Mrs. Wishy-Washy.* Bothel, WA: The Wright Group.

Cowley, J. (1991). *The red rose.* Auckland, NZ: The Wright Group.

Deming, A. G. (1994). *Who is tapping at my window?* New York: Penguin.

Durkin, D. (1966). *Children who read early.* New York: Teacher's College Press.

Ehri, L. C. (1995). Phases of development in learning to read words by sight. *Journal of Research in Reading, 18,* 116–125.

Ehri, L. C. (1998). Grapheme-phoneme knowledge is essential for learning to read words in English. In J. L. Metsala & L. C. Ehri (Eds.), *Word recognition in beginning literacy* (pp. 3–40). Mahwah, NJ: Lawrence Erlbaum Associates.

Ehri, L. C., & Sweet, J. (1991). Fingerpoint-reading of memorized text: What enables beginners to process the print. *Reading Research Quarterly, 26,* 442–462.

Fleisher, L. S., Jenkins, J. R., & Pany, D. (1979–1980). Effects on poor readers' comprehension of training in rapid decoding. *Reading Research Quarterly, 15,* 30–48.

Fountas, I. C., & Pinnell, G. S. (1996). *Guided reading: Good first teaching for all children.* Portsmouth, NH: Heinemann.

Goodman, K. S. (1965). A linguistic study of cues and miscues in reading. *Elementary English, 6,* 126–135.

Hoffman, J. V., McCarthey, S. J., Abbott, J., Christian, C., Corman, L., Curry, C., Dressman, M., Elliott, B., Matherne, D., & Stahle, D. (1994). So what's new in the new basals? A focus on first grade. *Journal of Reading Behavior, 26,* 47–73.

Hoffman, J. V., Roser, N. L., Salas, R., Patterson, E., & Pennington, J. (2000). *Text leveling and little books in first-grade reading* (CIERA Report #1-010). Ann Arbor, MI: Center for the Improvement of Early Reading Achievement.

Johns, J. (1997). *Basic Reading Inventory.* Dubuque, IA: Kendall-Hunt.

Johnston, F. R. (1998). The reader, the text, and the task: Learning words in first grade. *The Reading Teacher, 51,* 666–675.

Johnston, F. R. (2000). Word learning in predictable text. *Journal of Educational Psychology, 92,* 248–256.

Juel, C., & Roper/Schneider, D. (1985). The influence of basal readers on first grade reading. *Reading Research Quarterly, 20,* 134–152.

Kuhn, M. R., & Stahl, S. A. (2000). *Fluency: A review of developmental and remedial practices* (CIERA Report 2-008) Ann Arbor, MI: Center for the Improvement of Reading Achievement.

Kuhn, M. R., & Stahl, S. A. (2003). Fluency: A review of developmental and remedial practices. *Journal of Educational Psychology, 95,* 3–22.

LaBerge, D., & Samuels, S. J. (1974). Toward a theory of automatic information processing in reading. *Cognitive Psychology, 6,* 293–323.

Leslie, L., & Calhoon, A. (1995). Factors affecting children's reading of rimes: Reading ability, word frequency, and rime-neighborhood size. *Journal of Educational Psychology, 87,* 576–586.

Logan, G. D. (1990). Repetition priming and automaticity: Common underlying mechanisms? *Cognitive Psychology, 22,* 1–35.

Logan, G. D., Taylor, S. E., & Etherton, J. L. (1999). Attention and automaticity: Toward a theoretical integration. *Psychological Research, 62,* 165–181.

Martin, B. (1967). *Brown bear, brown bear, What do you see?* New York: Holt, Rinehart, & Winston.

Menon, S., Martin, L. A., & Hiebert, E. H. (2000, April). *Teachers guides, and reading instruction: The interactions between teachers, texts, and beginning readers.* Paper presented at the meeting of the American Educational Research Association, New Orleans.

Morris, D. (1993). The relationship between children's concept of word in text and phoneme awareness in learning to read: A longitudinal study. *Research in the Teaching of English, 27,* 133–154.

Nicholson, T. (1991). Do children read words better in context or in lists: A classic study revisited. *Journal of Educational Psychology, 83,* 444–450.

National Reading Panel. (2000). *Report of the National Reading Panel.* Washington, DC: Author. <www.nationalreadingpanel.org>.

Pearson, P. D., & Gallagher, M. C. (1983). The instruction of reading comprehension. *Contemporary Educational Psychology, 8,* 317–344.

Perfetti, C. A. (1992). The representation problem in reading acquisition. In P. B. Gough, L. C. Ehri, & R. Treiman (Eds.), *Reading acquisition* (pp. 145–174). Hillsdale, NJ: Lawrence Erlbaum Associates.

Peterson, C. (1991). Children's literature in Reading Recovery. In D. E. DeFord, C. A. Lyons, & G. S. Pinnell (Eds.), *Bridges to literacy: Learning from Reading Recovery* (pp. 119–147). Portsmouth, NH: Heinemann.

Popp, H. M. (1975). Current practices in the teaching of beginning reading. In J. B. Carroll & J. S. Chall (Eds.), *Toward a literate society* (pp. 101–146). New York: McGraw-Hill.

Pressley, M. (1998). *Reading instruction that works: The case for balanced teaching.* New York: Guilford.

Reitsma, P. (1983). Printed word learning in beginning readers. *Journal of Experimental Child Psychology, 36,* 321–339.

Roth, S., & Beck, I. L. (1987). Theoretical and instructional implications of the assessment of two microcomputer word recognition programs. *Reading Research Quarterly, 22,* 197–218.

Samuels, S. J. (1985). Automaticity and repeated reading. In J. Osborn, P. T. Wilson, & R. C. Anderson (Eds.), *Reading education: Foundations for a literate America* (pp. 215–230). Lexington, MA: Lexington Books.

Singer, H., Samuels, S. J., & Spiroff, J. (1973–1974). The effect of pictures and contextual conditions on learning responses to printed words. *Reading Research Quarterly, 9,* 555–567.

Shankweiler, D., & Liberman, I. Y. (1972). Misreading: A search for causes. In J. F. Kavanaugh & I. G. Mattingly (Eds.), *Language by eye and by ear* (pp. 293–317). Cambridge, MA: MIT Press.

Share, D. L. (1995). Phonological recoding and self-teaching: *Sine qua non* of reading acquisition. *Cognition, 55,* 151–218.

Share, D. L., & Stanovich, K. E. (1995). Cognitive processes in early reading development: Accommodating individual differences into a model of acquisition. *Issues in Education, 1,* 1–57.

Spring, C., Blunden, D., & Gatheral, M. (1981). Effect on reading comprehension of training to automaticity in word-reading. *Perceptual and Motor Skills, 53,* 779–786.

Stahl, K. A. D., Stahl, S. A., & McKenna, M. C. (1999). The development of phonological awareness and orthographic processing in Reading Recovery. *Literacy, Teaching and Learning, 4,* 27–42.

Stahl, S. A. (1991). Beyond the instrumentalist hypothesis: Some relationships between word meanings and comprehension. In P. J. Schwanenflugel (Ed.), *The psychology of word meanings* (pp. 157–186). Hillsdale, NJ: Lawrence Erlbaum Associates.

Stahl, S. A., Heubach, K., & Cramond, B. (1997). *Fluency-oriented reading instruction.* Washington, DC: National Reading Research Center; U.S. Dept. of Education Office of Educational Research and Improvement Educational Resources Information Center.

Stahl, S. A, McKenna, M. C., & Kovach, J. (in press). *The concurrent development of word recognition, phonological awareness, and spelling.* CIERA Research Report series. Ann Arbor, MI: Center for the Improvement of Early Reading Achievement.

Stahl, S. A., & Murray, B. A. (1998). Issues involved in defining phonological awareness and its relation to early reading. In J. Metsala & L. C. Ehri (Eds.), Word recognition in beginning literacy (pp. 65–88). Mahwah, NJ: Lawrence Erlbaum Associates.

Tan, A., & Nicholson, T. (1997). Flashcards revisited: Training poor readers to read words faster improves their comprehension of text. *Journal of Educational Psychology, 89,* 276–288.

Uhry, J. K. (1999). Invented spelling in kindergarten: The relationship with finger-pointing. *Reading and Writing, 11,* 441–464.

Venezky, R. L. (1999). *The American way of spelling.* New York: Guilford.

Vygotsky, L. (1978). *Mind in society.* Cambridge, MA: Harvard University Press.

4

Children's Motivation to Read

Scott G. Paris
Robert D. Carpenter
University of Michigan

Adults read texts to learn new information, to solve problems, to relax, to do their jobs, and to have fun. So do children. Adults read a variety of genres including fiction, nonfiction, directions, lists, humor, music, poetry, and news reports. So do children. Adults read text in books, maps, product descriptions, captions, TV, video displays, and media reports; they often read for a minute or less and occasionally for hours. So do children. In many ways, children's motivation to read is not different from the reading goals, purposes, and activities of adults. These similarities allow us to understand children's motivation to read with reference to many research studies on motivation of adolescents and adults. The differences, though, are important. This chapter identifies some of the special motivational obstacles that confront children in their daily reading activities.

Most young children approach books eagerly, even before they can read them, because the pictures are appealing and joint book reading is usually an enjoyable social interaction. Many children sustain their motivation to read, in and out of school, through adolescence and adulthood. However, the ones who do not develop an appreciation for reading may become reluctant readers who avoid reading text in many formats and situations. Some reluctant readers do not develop the skills to read fluently and the strategies to comprehend easily, so the mental effort is taxing and the lack of success is frustrating. Other reluctant readers have the skill but not the will to read independently (Paris, Wasik, &

Turner, 1991). There are many underlying reasons why some children avoid reading. Both teachers and parents want to know how to help such children read more frequently and to feel better about their abilities. The first part of this chapter describes why some children develop into reluctant or avoidant readers, and the second part describes how teachers and parents can design more motivating opportunities for reading.

WHAT DOES IT MEAN TO BE MOTIVATED?

In casual conversations people might say that a child is "not motivated" or has "little motivation," but they mean more than a simple quantitative lack of energy. Relatively few children are "amotivated" (Deci & Ryan, 1995) in the sense that they are generally apathetic. Instead, children are motivated to approach or avoid specific activities and things. Their active or passive responses are the visible manifestations of motivation, revealed by the direction and strength of their behavior. Different motivational theories try (a) to explain why people strive to achieve or avoid a particular goal, object, status, or activity and (b) to describe the conditions that help or hinder their pursuits. We refer to these theories throughout the chapter, but we begin with a practical question that confronts teachers daily: "Why is this child not motivated to read?"

Teachers and parents generate similar answers to this question such as, "It is too hard," or "He does not have the basic skills." Others may say, "Reading is boring," or "The books are silly." Another answer is, "Her parents never read to her," or "She gets no support at home/school." A different answer might be, "He never pays attention in class," or "The assignments are dull." Do these responses sound familiar? Now consider the nature of the explanations, or what some might label as blame. Each pair of answers successively locates the "motivational problem" as mainly residing in the child, the text, the home, or the classroom. So we ask, where is the motivation to read and whose fault is it that some children avoid reading? We think that these are the wrong questions to ask in order to help children become better readers. Current research indicates that motivation is not a trait that children have in varying amounts and that, instead, a more useful view than casting blame is to restructure the environment. Our approach emphasizes a "situated" view of motivation. We believe that the motivation to read is the result of a complex interaction among the child's history and abilities, the properties of the text, the purpose for reading, and the social conditions and support surrounding the activity (Lave, 1991; Paris & Turner, 1994). Given a specific situation and text, any child might exhibit strong or weak motivation to read, so our focus is much more on the interplay among factors for an individual child. In the following sections, we discuss how characteristics of readers, texts, and contexts influence children's situated motivation to read.

The Reader

Is motivation in the reader? Yes, according to many teachers and theories of motivation. If children do not acquire enabling skills, such as decoding and phonological awareness, they may remain emergent readers who become frustrated with their inability to decode words. Older children who lack the requisite skills often become fluent decoders with few comprehension strategies. They remain word callers unable to understand the meaning of text. Arrested skill development may lead to decreased motivation to read because children recognize that their efforts do not lead to success and they cannot keep pace with their classmates. Some of these children simply give up trying, especially children 10 years old and older who recognize that high effort signals low ability (Nicholls, 1979). Thus, they avoid the attribution by others that they have poor abilities and the accompanying threat of diminished self-esteem by passively not trying or actively avoiding reading. This is the double-edged sword of effort and ability attributions noted by Covington (1984), who surmised that children who cannot succeed in school may prefer implicitly to appear lazy rather than stupid. The threat of trying when one knows one will fail is a powerful inhibitor of effort, and by fourth grade, many children realize that they cannot read well enough to succeed. Giving up to avoid failure is sometimes called *learned helplessness* because children learn not to try in order not to fail. They may become passive even when modest effort, such as reading a readily decodable text, might lead to success. Teachers and parents may think students are lazy, apathetic, or depressed because learned helplessness can become a pervasive handicap. This reinforces the view that strength of motivation is a personal trait.

Self-perceptions of competence engender motivation. Most children care what their peers and teachers think of them, which is based partly on attributions derived from their academic performance. However, there are some children who realize that they cannot make their self-esteem contingent on their demonstrated reading skills so they learn to base their self-perceptions on other skills or roles (Crocker & Wolfe, 2001). When students enact other roles, such as that of the rebel or class clown, they deflect attention from their academic difficulties. Unfortunately, these roles undermine academic performance and frustrate teachers who may not understand why children seem disinterested in reading. The rationalizations made by children in such circumstances, that "reading is boring," for example, are intended to hide their anxiety and their poor reading abilities by disconnecting academic achievement from valued goals. If a child is successful at disguising his or her low ability, the roles of rebel or clown may demand increasing time and self-regulated actions to enact this nonacademic identity and to shift attention away from the underlying reading problems (Paris, Byrnes, & Paris, 2001). Such behavior is highly motivated behavior, but behavior not aimed toward reading, and it requires a perceptive teacher to understand it.

Poor motivation for reading is a characteristic of the reader according to several other theories of motivation. For example, goal orientation theory suggests that some children seek to get the job done, to receive positive feedback for their performance, and to avoid negative evaluations; they have performance goals. In contrast, other children seek to improve their knowledge and abilities and to surpass their previous performance levels for their own satisfaction; they have mastery goals (Ames, 1992; Blumenfeld, 1992). Children with performance goals in reading engage texts superficially. They may skip parts of the text while reading. They may fill in worksheets mindlessly. They may hurry, cheat, copy, and take shortcuts that minimize effort yet complete the task. Understanding or enjoying the material being read is secondary to getting the job done. We have seen many children in Grades 3–6 turn to the worksheet questions before reading the text, answering as many questions as possible without reading, and only skimming the text for answers as a last resort. Ironically, some teachers actually teach children to follow this procedure when taking high-stakes achievement tests, a tactic that only reinforces a performance goal for reading *and* for high-stakes tests. Instead, most teachers want students to adopt mastery orientations because such students persevere in their efforts to learn and improve for their own intrinsic satisfaction.

Another variety of motivational theory is called expectancy-value theory. In this framework, motivation to read is a function of the reader's perceived value of the task and the child's subjective probability of success (Eccles, Wigfield, & Schiefele, 1998). Both variables pose problems for reluctant readers. If children devalue reading in general, or even the immediate reading task at hand, minimal effort can be expected. If children think their chances of success are low, they may not try hard or for a long time, either. Certainly, children with few effective reading skills and strategies may expect failure on difficult texts; however, many children overestimate task difficulty or underestimate their own abilities and hence, give up unnecessarily. This is exactly like learned helplessness but framed in other terms, such as children's perceived low probability of success or high fear of failure. When children have a history of failure and anxiety about reading, their perceptions of the difficulty of schoolwork and their perceptions of their abilities may become distorted and lead to passive helplessness or active resentment. Teachers find it difficult to cope with both kinds of responses.

Other motivational theories place the burden largely on children's self-perceptions, a slight variation on other theories. For example, if children feel that they do not have effective reading skills, they may have low self-efficacy for reading and fail to use strategies that they are capable of using (Schunk, 1991, 2001). Schunk and Swartz (1993) presented 20 lessons in children's classrooms that were designed to help the students write coherent paragraphs in multiple genres. The four different instructional conditions emphasized either product goals (i.e., the writing outcomes), process goals, process goals plus feedback about the individual's progress, or a general instruction that was a control condition. The researchers found that the best gains in writing achievement and self-efficacy occurred in the condition that emphasized process goals and feedback about progress. In other words, children worked harder, felt better, and were more successful when they focused on learning the strategies, understanding their importance for performance, and knowing that their progress was due to successful strategy use.

There are other motivational explanations based on self-perceptions, such as self-esteem and self-worth (Covington, 1992). The critical cognitive mediating link is that children who have poor skills usually have low opinions of their own competence and also worry that other people view them as incompetent. Of course, this presumes that children value reading and base their self-esteem on academic performance in the classroom (Crocker & Wolfe, 2001). This assumption seems more likely to be true for children younger than 10–11 years of age who often are optimistic and naïve about their actual reading abilities. The results of low self-worth perceptions for young children are embarrassment and reluctance to take on challenging tasks. Among older children, low self-worth about reading often is manifested in denial of the value of reading, blaming teachers and the materials for not helping or motivating them, or engaging in roles that are contrary to academic achievement. A quick and counterproductive reaction among adults is to point out the children's low reading abilities and attempt to remedy them. However, children engage in such coping strategies precisely to avoid the humiliation of being identified as poor readers. Thus, teachers and parents need to be careful in their reactions to the symptoms that reluctant readers exhibit.

Self-perceptions are fragile for young children. Children in primary grades base their self-perceptions on what parents and teachers say about their performance and abilities. They also use public comparative indicators such as the reading group of their friends, letter grades, oral reading fluency, the difficulty of the books read in class by different children, and the amount of help given to or needed by some children. There are three primary problems in the ensuing self-perceptions. First, the evidence that children use is fragmented and often not very reliable because teachers and parents do not want to signal low ability attributions to young children. Second, adults often try to prevent children from making comparisons among classmates so they give little information about a child's relative reading difficulties, or they may provide positive feedback to all students. Third, children from 5–9 years of age often exaggerate their self-perceptions, usually in an overly optimistic direction.

As an example, one study compared the academic self-perceptions of children who were learning disabled with the self-perceptions of children who were physically handicapped or mildly retarded (Halmhuber & Paris, 1993). The children with learning disabilities were most confused about their academic problems and had lower perceptions of control, efficacy, and esteem than the other children. Another example illustrates how malleable are the self-perceptions of young children. In a series of studies designed to change children's attributions for their past performance, Schunk (2001) demonstrated that children who are told that their past performance is due to good ability tend to have higher evaluations of their ability, self-efficacy, and achievement. Conversely, we can infer that children who surmise that they have low ability will have negative views about themselves. However, credibility of the feedback is important. Those children who have to work harder, such as low-achieving students, know that they need to give more effort, so effort attributions are credible for them. The difficult thing for teachers to do is to provide help to students appropriately, help them attribute their successes to effort and ability as warranted, and to cultivate children's trust in their opinions of their own learning in a positive manner. As most parents know, realistic evaluations of children's abilities may be less helpful for struggling achievers than an optimistic approach to the skills that need to be learned and the child's ability to master them.

Many of the negative self-perceptions, counterproductive goals, and maladaptive attributions are evident in the same children. That is, children who have less developed reading skills than their peers may feel less efficacious, less in control, less optimistic about their future achievement, less mastery oriented, and less competent. Avoiding reading tasks, pursuing performance goals, choosing easy books, taking shortcuts, cheating, and giving up prematurely are all manifestations of children who have little confidence in their abilities and increasing worries about the public display of their poor reading. In contrast, children who choose to read frequently for pleasure exhibit good comprehension and high achievement (Nell, 1988). Because the constellations of symptoms exhibited by avid and avoidant readers reflect cognitive, motivational, and affective characteristics of children, the problems may be framed in terms of children's self-regulated learning difficulties (Paris & Paris, 2001; Zimmerman & Schunk, 2001). This conceptual orientation embeds children's motivation for reading in a larger frame of reference, their general orientation to education. Children who have difficulty becoming and staying engaged in reading in school often have difficulty focusing their attention, applying learning strategies, avoiding distractions, and monitoring their own behavior, all symptomatic of poor self-regulation skills (Schunk & Zimmerman, 1997). The complexity of the problem conceptually is mirrored in the complexity of measuring children's motivation. Thus, there are many interviews, surveys, and observations designed to assess children's reading goals, attitudes, strategies, and self-perceptions. Because they are all predicated on explanations of motivation attributed to the child, we consider them next.

Assessing Children's Motivation for Reading

Most teachers use observations of children's behavior to gauge their motivation to read because these are daily and continuous indicators (Paris, Paris, & Carpenter, 2002). Teachers check children's willingness to read books in free time, they note the difficulty and variety of texts that children read, they observe children's enjoyment and reactions to reading, and they examine children's reactions to frustration or difficulty. In contrast, when researchers or teachers want to assess and record children's motivation more formally, they administer surveys and interviews (Baker & Wigfield, 1999; Gambrell, Palmer, Codling, & Mazzoni, 1996). For example, a popular motivational survey for elementary students is the Early Reading Attitude Scale (ERAS), more commonly referred to as the "Garfield Scale" (McKenna & Kear, 1990). The 20-item survey has two scales, one for recreational reading and the other for academic reading. It uses four graduated faces of frowning or smiling Garfield cartoon characters as response options for children to indicate their agreement or disagreement with statements such as, "I like to read on a rainy Saturday afternoon." McKenna, Kear, and Ellsworth (1995) used the ERAS to assess reading attitudes in a nationally representative sample of 18,000 children in Grades 1–6. Results indicated that children preferred recreational reading to academic reading, although both types showed declines as age increased. Additionally, girls had better attitudes toward reading than boys in both recreational and academic reading at all grade levels. Such surveys are quick to administer and score, and they permit quantitative analyses of data.

Another popular survey for elementary students is the Motivation for Reading Questionnaire (MRQ) created by Wigfield and Guthrie (1997). The MRQ includes questions related to 11 aspects of motivation (reading efficacy, reading challenge, reading curiosity, reading involvement, importance of reading, reading work avoidance, competition in reading, recognition for reading, reading for grades, social reasons for reading, and compliance). For example, self-efficacy beliefs are measured with questions such as, "I believe that I can succeed at reading," whereas reading curiosity was measured by, "I read to learn new information about topics that interest me." The MRQ is designed to assess the reading motivation of students in Grades 3–6. Surveys are also used with younger students by adapting surveys for older children (e.g., Young Children's Academic Intrinsic Motivation Inventory, YCAIMI; Gottfried, 1990) or designing formats specifically for students in K–2, such as the Reading Self-Concept Scale (RSCS) by Chapman and Tunmer (1995). The RSCS measures reading-related self-perceptions in young children (ages 5–7) who are asked to rate their self-perceptions on positively and negatively stated items using a 5-point Likert scale. It includes 30 items for three scales (perception of competence, perception of difficulty, and attitudes) that are measured by 10 questions each.

In our experience, we found that surveys of children's motivation to read have several fundamental problems. First, the content and response scales may be difficult for children to understand because of limited cognitive and psycholinguistic development. Sometimes the vocabulary and grammar are challenging, and sometimes the items are misinterpreted. For example, in the previous example from the ERAS, one little girl who was an avid reader pointed to the frowning Garfield and explained that she did not like it when it rained on Saturdays. In addition to the items, the Likert response scale requires children to make seriated and relativistic judgments that are unfamiliar at best. Second, young children tend to give exaggerated and optimistic ratings of their abilities, habits, and attitudes whereas older children give more negative, or realistic, responses. Perhaps that is why the average ERAS scores decline with increasing grade levels, not because older children are less motivated to read. Third, surveys and interviews with children often have modest reliability and validity or, in many instances, there are limited data to support the reliability and validity of the instruments.

These measurement problems are more troublesome for young children because older children are better able to assess their own abilities, to understand the items, and to respond to the survey response scales. We believe that most young children are eager to read and be read to, so observations of their daily literacy behaviors may be more informative than surveys. Motivational measures have stronger reliability and validity from Grade 3 on, partly because variations in reading achievement and motivation increase and partly because children become more accurate at responding to the surveys and interviews. Thus, we recommend observations and informal assessments of children's motivation to read until Grade 3 and careful use of surveys for older children that augment performance-based measures of motivation. From Grade 3 on, children's self-assessments of their work, skills, progress, and attitudes can provide opportunities for teachers to scaffold optimistic and motivated approaches to literacy.

The Text

Children's motivation to read is influenced by both the content and structure of text. Books for emergent readers usually present familiar activities, fairy tales, and stories in narrative form because the genre can be personal, humorous, and coherent. Expository texts, sparse as they are in primary grades (Duke, 2000), usually present information about familiar objects and events that help bridge children's oral language vocabulary to print. It is important for teachers to provide a variety of genre, content, and difficulty in the texts available for children at every grade level. Is motivation in the text? Yes, to some extent. Schallert and Reed (1997) claimed that considerate texts can "pull" readers into them so that readers become absorbed. Texts are considerate if they fit a reader's interests, present a challenging level of difficulty, satisfy the reader's curiosity, provide good stories, and yet are still comprehensible. Some people believe that children avoid reading because it is not as engaging as TV and video games (van der Voort, 2001). Some say children find reading slow, laborious, and boring. So the answer is yes, texts can pull readers in or push readers away, but we add some qualifications.

Text difficulty may pose more motivational obstacles than topic interest for beginning readers. Books for emergent readers usually have redundant pictures and text, they use familiar words, and they use rhyme and repetition to foster predictable reading. Books for beginning readers decrease these features and make greater demands for decoding unfamiliar words with fewer contextual supports. It is not simple to measure and codify this increasing complexity. One method is to use readability formulae to analyze and compare text, but the formulae have been criticized for measuring mostly sentence and word length and grammatical complexity (Bailin & Grafstein, 2001). Other methods have been based on decodability of words. However, it is clear that engaged readers understand text well and that comprehensible text maintains readers' attention, so the interaction between text and reader is crucial.

Hoffman (2002) showed that historical changes in basal texts have produced more complex texts for beginning readers, despite a century of efforts to control vocabulary. From the 1920s through the 1960s, there was a steady reduction in the number of unique words used in basal texts. The backlash to that trend produced texts that were authentic children's literature with more words and less controlled vocabulary. Hoffman et al. (1994) analyzed the first-grade texts in the 1987 basal readers and found that texts had become much more difficult for children to decode. One of the battles in the "reading wars" of the 1990s involved changes in basal readers to be more regular and systematic in their phonetic patterns to support children's learning of decoding rules. Hiebert (1999) analyzed the decodability of texts in the literature-based basal readers published in the 1990s to determine if texts had become more systematic. She found that the new texts contained more unique words than earlier versions, but there was no reduction in complex phonetic patterns or improvement in regularly decodable vocabulary. The "new" basal readers were not easier to read and did not provide more regular patterns in words to help children learn decoding rules. Thus, studies of text complexity and difficulty have shown that children in first grade today may face more novel words, longer texts, and less decodable and less predictable texts than children 20 or 50 years ago. It appears that the basal textbooks of the past 10 years traded the contrived simple text of early basal readers for more authentic but more difficult text. Whether this makes children better or more frustrated readers has yet to be determined.

We think that text affects children's motivation to read in three types of situations. First, when the content is unfamiliar and uninteresting, children are less likely to begin, engage, or sustain reading. Second, when text difficulty due to vocabulary or structure exceeds children's abilities, decoding becomes arduous and comprehension plummets, and so children lose interest or become distracted. Third, when children are given little help from others to overcome difficulty or boredom, they cannot apply effective reading strategies for long. As we discuss later, teachers who structure classrooms to avoid these situations have more motivated readers.

The Home

Certainly children's motivation to read is influenced by literacy practices at home. Parental literacy skills and practices vary widely in the formative preschool years with some parents providing few book experiences for their children before kindergarten. The lack of shared book reading at home is correlated with parental income, SES, education, and language skills so that families at risk economically and socially have children who begin school at risk for reading problems (Snow, Burns, & Griffin, 1998). The ensuing motivational risks are of two kinds. First, children with few shared book experiences may not develop excitement about the language and stories of books. They do not have a history of positive social interactions based on books that prepares them to read or to be read to. Baker, Scher, and Mackler (1997) reported that middle-class families may encourage their preschoolers to read for entertainment and to read independently more often than lower class families who place more emphasis on skill building when reading at home. Second, lack of book experiences in preschool years makes children unprepared for the social roles of dialogic book reading (Whitehurst & Fischel, 2000). Naivete may increase apprehension about reading, about revealing one's inadequacies to unfamiliar adults, and about reading publicly in front of other children. When reading is a mysterious cognitive and social activity, many children adopt performance goals to please the teacher, to finish the assignment, or to avoid public admonitions. Thus, children who have few preschool experiences with literacy begin formal schooling without fundamental reading skills and positive expectations for learning to read (Wigfield & Asher, 1984).

Studies among older children have been less conclusive about the importance of home experiences for children's reading, perhaps because the influences change as children get older. Greaney and Hegarty (1987) asked fifth graders to keep diary records of their leisure activities. Children who engaged in more frequent leisure reading had more positive attitudes toward reading, received more parental encouragement for reading, and were more likely to belong to a public library. Neuman (1986) also found that leisure reading habits of fifth graders were positively related to parental encouragement even after controlling for the influences of gender and SES. Rowe (1991) studied more than 5,000 Australian children between the ages of 5–14 years and concluded that reading at home and positive attitudes were significantly related to reading achievement at all ages. However, children's attitudes and leisure reading habits may account for a small amount of the variance in reading achievement, suggesting that enjoyment and achievement outcomes may be influenced by different factors.

The Classroom

Does motivation to read originate in the classroom? Yes, classroom activities often can enhance or impede children's engagement with text. Some children work hard for teachers' praise, parental approval of grades, and/or peer recognition, as well as to fulfill mastery goals. For many, reading is a task to do in school, and they may be reluctant or avoidant readers at home. Yet for other children, reading in school is boring, effortful, and unrewarding; they enjoy reading on their own terms, choosing what they like to read and when to read it. Teachers and parents recognize children who choose to read in one setting or the other, but they are often perplexed about what to do. Children who are successful, enthusiastic readers outside school, but not inside, are less at risk than children who read only in school under duress but not independently. How can these children be motivated to read?

To answer that question, we need to identify the features of daily literacy activities that can influence children's engagement with text. Consider the curriculum first. When all children are required to read the same texts at the same pace and respond similarly, the best readers are bored and the worst are frustrated. That is why teachers today prefer to use classroom libraries and leveled texts so that every child can read books at an appropriate level of difficulty. It also explains why publishers have designed curricula with leveled texts that accompany or replace basal reader anthologies (Hoffman, 2002). A wide variety of texts, genres, and complexity are needed at every grade level to provide a stimulating curriculum.

More important than the texts per se are the activities that teachers design to give purpose and meaning to the texts. When texts serve no other purpose than as vehicles for learning to read, children adopt performance goals. The lack of authentic purposes for reading inhibits motivation as much as contrived texts. Children are motivated to read when reading is the means to a valued end rather than an end arbitrarily imposed. That is why project-based learning and problem-based learning are so motivating (Blumenfeld et al., 1991). As children research, read, discover, and assemble new information, they apply it toward an authentic end such as a report, poster, oral presentation, or object that they create. Reading and writing, sometimes alone and sometimes in collaboration, are instrumental for learning and completing the project. This is much more creative and motivating than filling in workbooks.

The motivational importance of classroom activities was revealed in Turner's (1995) research in first-grade classrooms. She initially wanted to compare the motivation of children who were taught by basal methods with children taught by whole language methods. However, after she observed 20 teachers who had identified themselves as mostly following a basal or whole language approach, she discovered wide variation in their actual literacy practices. So, she decided to code classrooms according to whether teachers used mostly "open" or "closed" activities. Open activities included independent research, free reading, and searching for information as opposed to closed activities that usually were briefer, had correct answers, and allowed less creativity. Turner (1995) found that children who were in first-grade classrooms with many open-ended activities displayed more motivation for literacy than children in classrooms with mostly closed activities.

The complexity, variety, and difficulty of texts are important at all ages. So is the nature of open-ended classroom activities and project-based learning. Likewise, classroom assessment practices influence motivation at all grade levels. Formal assessment in grades K–2 is infrequent, but it is likely to increase across America with new pressures for school accountability at early grades. We highlight three main ways that assessment practices influence children's motivation. First, tests, quizzes, grades, and other assessments are public records of what counts and what is important in the classroom. Whether it is points for a pizza party or the number of books read that are charted on the wall, the visible signs of success are communicated through assessment, and these signs may engender pride or shame. Second, the results of assessment are often used to make comparisons of children by parents, teachers, and even the children themselves. Explicit comparisons are risky. For those children who do not measure up to their peers, assessment may be an embarrassing confirmation of their low ability and negative self-perceptions. Third, the higher the stakes, the more effort and importance are attached to the assessment. There is a danger that children may forego reading for pleasure if the assessments become the main reason for reading in school. Thus, assessment practices that emphasize normative, comparative, public use of performance data may undermine children's motivation to read for pleasure, mastery, and learning. The increasing emphasis on high-stakes testing may motivate children for the test, but the unintended consequences may be overwhelmingly negative for children's motivation to read, particularly for children already at risk (Paris & McEvoy, 2000).

WHAT CAN TEACHERS DO?

Children's motivation to read is influenced by many factors throughout childhood and educational experiences. Is motivation in the reader? Yes, but children are not born with a trait for more or less motivation to read. Is motivation in the text? Yes, but neither text difficulty nor interest is sufficient to explain why some children choose to read while others avoid it. Is motivation in the home? Yes, the values and shared reading experiences are established in the home, but neither SES nor parental education is the sole predictor of literacy success. Is motivation in the classroom? Yes, children's motivation to read in school is affected by the curriculum, instructional practices, and assessment activities in which they participate, but teachers alone do not determine children's orientation to reading. Although not satisfying, the answer is, "All of the above," and probably more factors need to be considered, because children's motivation for literacy is embedded in their lives and educational situations. Motivation should be expected to vary, maybe daily, certainly annually, as children read different texts for different purposes in different classrooms.

Yet, the situated nature of motivation does not make it unexplainable or resistant to intervention. On the contrary, we know more than ever how to help children become motivated for reading and writing. We discuss these ideas in the following sections.

Creating Engaging Activities in School

The heart of our approach to children's motivation to read is to blend cognitive skills and motivational will in the tasks that children do in school. This represents a convergence of cognitive and motivational research during the past 20 years as well as the recognition of the value of task engagement. When students are deeply engaged in meaningful tasks, they exhibit a motivational "flow" (Csikszentmihalyi, 1990) in which they lose track of time because they are so thoroughly immersed in the task. Flow is a satisfied state of consciousness associated with intense concentration, effortless control, and deep enjoyment. Schallert and Reed (1997) described "involvement" in reading in similar terms. Engaged or involved readers are not distracted easily; they sustain attention through difficulties and focus on making sense of what they read. Engaged readers are on "autopilot" with little metacognition or cognitive monitoring needed. Involved readers may have heightened emotional arousal and reactions to text, which only intensifies the experience (Nell, 1988). Not surprisingly, engaged or involved readers read more often for pleasure and have better comprehension. Most teachers and parents want children to be engaged, independent readers so they try to create opportunities for them to read texts for authentic purposes and with few distractions.

Engagement during reading, like flow experiences, depends on intrinsic motivation. Turner and Paris (1995) summarized some of the characteristics of engaged readers with reference to features of intrinsic motivation that have been supported by extensive research. As a mnemonic aid, the features were labeled with easy to remember words beginning with C. They noted that students who are engaged in learning and literacy activities frequently make *choices* of what they read and when they read and focus on *constructing* meaning from text. They choose *challenging* materials in terms of content and difficulty and exhibit *control* over their own learning and motivational strategies. Autonomy fosters positive attitudes and allows students to explore their own interests; challenging tasks encourage students to use strategies and to strive for self-improvement (Turner, 1997). Engaged readers often work *collaboratively* with peers and they derive *consequences* of their performance that enhance their own self-efficacy. We think these characteristics of engaged readers provide valuable guides for teachers and parents as they create oppor-tunities for students to read and learn.

Connell and Wellborn (1991) emphasized that engagement depends on the extent to which students' needs for competence, autonomy, and related-ness are satisfied. Their focus is on specific contextual factors to meet these needs, which include the provision of structure, autonomy support, and in-volvement. Behavioral, affective, and cognitive engagement are the out-comes when children have meaningful interactions in classrooms. Such an ecological approach emphasizes the "fit" between the environment and the child, an approach that is similar to "developmentally appropriate practice" in early childhood education. For example, Stipek, Feiler, Daniels, and Milburn (1995) found that child-centered classrooms encouraged peer in-teraction and gave children choices about a diverse set of activities and ma-terials that were meaningful to students. In contrast, teacher-directed classrooms focused on basic skills that were not embedded in meaningful ac-tivities and were controlled by the teachers. They also used external evalua-tions and rewards, and they emphasized performance goals and social comparisons.

Assessment as well as instruction can be organized by the principles de-scribed according to the Cs: constructing meaning with choice, control, col-laboration, challenge, and consequences that enhance self-efficacy. When assessment of students' reading reflects these characteristics, it is likely to be valued and effective. For example, teachers in Grades K–2 often use perfor-mance assessments such as book logs, writing journals, and daily observations of reading and writing to assess children's growth and motivation because they allow children to construct meaning, control their own learning, collaborate with others, and so forth. Teachers in Grades 3–6 gradually rely more on group-administered and standardized tests that compare children's perfor-mance to criteria and norms rather than previous individual benchmarks. There is often a corresponding decrease in assessment practices based on the Cs as students become older and assessment shifts from diagnostic functions to accountability and sorting functions. One way that teachers diminish the negative motivational impact that accompanies the shift to norm-referenced assessment is to use student portfolios and projects as the bases for classroom assessment. These collections of student work can be assessed by students to increase student pride and ownership (van Kraayenoord & Paris, 1997). They can also be used as the bases for parent–teacher–student conferences about progress that reinforce feelings of pride and self-efficacy (Paris & Ayres, 1994). In general, students' work samples, portfolios, self-assessment, and conferences include the motivational Cs in a positive manner, whereas high-stakes and norm-referenced tests do not.

Building Engaging Environments

The "engagement" perspective in literacy was popularized by researchers involved in the National Reading Research Center located at the Universities of Maryland and Georgia and is summarized in books by Guthrie and Wigfield (1997) and Guthrie and Alvermann (1999). These researchers describe engaging classrooms as intrinsically motivating because they are "hands-on" zones where students actively explore personally generated questions that are situated within a broader conceptual framework (Guthrie, Wigfield, & VonSecker, 2000). The focus of an engaging classroom is on general conceptual knowledge, but students are given room to pursue their own interests in subtopics related to the concepts. For example, in concept-oriented reading instruction (CORI), Guthrie et al. (1998) used hands-on science activities to teach general conceptual themes (e.g., weather, seasons, and climate) as students explored more specific personal questions (e.g., Why aren't sunny days all the same temperature?). When students generate their own questions, they are intrinsically motivated to find answers. These answers may come from a number of sources including conversation, observation, measurement, and text. It is important that classrooms, libraries, and homes have a variety of texts from different genres and with multiple levels of difficulty to provide information that is interesting, engaging, and accessible to all students. A literature-rich environment provides multiple avenues for students to explore alternative perspectives, to pursue conceptual questions, and to identify their own interests.

An activity-based learning environment provides multiple opportunities for direct instruction on strategies and skills necessary for learning (Winograd & Paris, 1989). The CORI program used a four-phase model of inquiry (observe and personalize, search and retrieve, comprehend and integrate, and communicate to others) as the basis of strategy instruction (Guthrie & Cox, 2001). For example, teachers used the "search and retrieve" phase in order to teach library research techniques (e.g., how to find relevant information, how to extract meaning from expository text, and how to use different genres to answer particular questions; Guthrie, Wigfield, & VonSecker, 2000). The instruction was embedded within a broader context of facilitating conceptual understanding, and it provided multiple opportunities for scaffolding to improve student learning.

One key component in an engaging classroom is collaboration with peers. Collaboration in the context of a community of learners provides a meaningful social discourse that is intrinsically motivating and personally meaningful (Brown, 1997). As students collaborate with peers, they engage in meaningful discussions that can bring out alternative thoughts, beliefs, ideas, or questions about the topic of inquiry. Collaboration in reading activities creates pressure for students to advance and defend their interpretations of text, often in writing and sometimes in group discussions.

Teachers in engaging classrooms use assessment as a window into students' cognitive processing and use continual informal evaluation to measure student progress rather than ability. Assessment is closely aligned with the curriculum because it provides a meaningful context in which to judge student learning. This on-going evaluation also provides a teacher with a good measure of what strategies need further instruction to ensure that students understand how and when to use a strategy or skill. Flexible assessment practices give students some choice in how they will be evaluated (e.g., posters, books, presentations) and provide a good model for later self-assessment. Portfolios and other cumulative records of student progress are good tools to measure student growth because they focus on where the students start and how they proceed through the learning activity.

An engaging classroom thoroughly integrates concept-oriented learning, real-world activities, interesting texts, strategy instruction, student autonomy, collaboration, and assessment to create a classroom ethos that is inquiry driven and intrinsically motivating to students (Guthrie & Cox, 2001). Cohesive classrooms that incorporate these practices take months to establish, but the result is intrinsically motivated students. For example, students in CORI classrooms were more curious and better strategy users than their peers in traditional classrooms (Guthrie, Wigfield, & VonSecker, 2000). The increased strategy use produced higher conceptual knowledge and transfer for students in concept-oriented classrooms. Finally, students in classrooms with an integrated curriculum driven by conceptual learning goals demonstrated higher text comprehension than students in a traditional curriculum (Guthrie et al., 1998).

Reading Beyond School

Many people today worry that children are not motivated to read because texts are becoming less attractive as leisure activities. Children have many nonacademic options at home that compete with recreational reading. A comparison of "time on task" reveals that most children read in school less than an hour a day and less than 10 minutes at home, yet they spend many hours watching television, playing video games, or practicing sports (Anderson, Wilson, &

Fielding, 1988). Imagine how much faster children might become skilled readers if they read 3–4 hours each day! The richest opportunities to increase the
time that children spend reading is to help them read more often beyond school
in the other 16 hours of the school day and the 150–170 days per year when they
are not in school.

When we consider where children read outside school, we usually think of
the home. Children read for many purposes at home. Young children share
books with social enjoyment as a main goal. When children can read independently, they often read and write for instrumental reasons such as playing games,
engaging in hobbies, assembling objects, following directions, and corresponding with family and friends (often on the Internet). Of course, doing research
and homework for school tasks occurs at home also for instrumental reasons.
Some children use their literacy skills to tutor siblings and neighbors at home,
but the most frequent use of literacy beyond school is simply for recreation. By 9
or 10 years of age, many children read alone regularly at bedtime, use their literacy skills on a computer, and surf the Web for leisure. It is the free-choice reading time that indicates the positive value that children place on reading for their
own enjoyment.

Parents and teachers need to create similar opportunities in other contexts.
Parents can encourage children to read text they encounter around the home and
on TV. They can encourage reading on weekends and vacations. Parents should
take children to community libraries, obtain library cards, and check out books
for children. They can model the process themselves and read for recreation at
home to reinforce the importance of reading beyond school requirements. There
are many opportunities for children to read as they explore museums, zoos, gardens, parks, aquaria, and other informal learning environments (Paris &
Hapgood, 2002). Parents can ask children to read labels and can help them learn
new vocabulary words. Reading for fun as well as learning should be done often by
families as they move through the community. Activities at churches, clubs,
Scouts, and community organizations are good venues for children to read but
only if adults encourage their active participation. Even shopping trips to malls
and stores can afford opportunities for children to practice reading. Sensitive
adults help children decode and interpret text wherever it appears.

CONCLUSIONS

Motivation is a difficult psychological construct to define and measure, and
there is no single way to view or assess children's motivation for reading. We

have described a situational model in which motivation does not reside only in the child, the text, the task, the home, or the classroom. Instead, we think that children can be more or less motivated for reading depending on the interactions of all these factors. The challenge for teachers and parents is to create interesting literacy activities and environments with many opportunities for children to engage with a rich variety of texts for meaningful purposes. The six features denoted by the Cs (i.e., constructing personal meaning with choice, challenge, control, collaboration, and positive consequences for self-efficacy) provide some guidance about how to design those activities.

The fluctuating nature of what it means to be motivated applies equally to the situational view of successful reading. When reading is viewed as work to be done and skills to be mastered, children may not get excited about reading. Yes, they can be prodded to read by authority, rewards, and threats, but these methods are not what we use when trying to improve children's talents in art, music, or sports. If reading is to be regarded as worthwhile and interesting, it must be validated as fun, relaxing, instrumental, and useful, independently of one's personal ability to do it and independently of the work value of achievement. Adults who read for pleasure are not encumbered by how fast or accurately they decode or how deeply they comprehend the text. Children need the same freedom from ability and work attributions if they are to become independent readers.

Teachers and parents need to understand successful reading as enjoyment as well as skill development; motivation and self-regulated reading must be as important as test scores. They need to be as concerned with children's feelings about reading, their affective responses to text, and their self-perceptions as readers. Both skill and motivation change developmentally, so the benchmarks of parental expectations and children's satisfaction will change. Kindergarten children are motivated to recite the alphabet, whereas first graders want to display the ability to decode unfamiliar words. Second graders may want to answer teachers' questions correctly, and third graders may want to question the author. Older children raise their standards for demonstrations of competence and motivated reading, so adults must be sensitive to the ways that children respond to increasingly higher standards of reading success. When children rise to these successive challenges, they become skilled and independent readers who display both skill and will while reading. They are also likely to demonstrate their motivated reading beyond homework, beyond grades, beyond compliance, and beyond school. In this way, they become truly motivated and successful readers for life.

REFERENCES

Ames, C. (1992). Classrooms goals, structures, and student motivation. *Journal of Educational Psychology, 84*, 261–271.

Anderson, R. C., Wilson, P. T., & Fielding, L. G. (1988). Growth in reading and how children spend their time outside of school. *Reading Research Quarterly, 23*, 285–303.

Bailin, A., & Grafstein, A. (2001). The linguistic assumptions underlying readability formulae: A critique. *Language & Communication, 21*, 285–301.

Baker, L., Scher, D., & Mackler, K. (1997). Home and family influences on motivations for reading. *Educational Psychologist, 32*, 69–82.

Baker, L., & Wigfield, A. (1999). Dimensions of children's motivation for reading and their relations to reading activity and reading achievement. *Reading Research Quarterly, 34*, 452–477.

Blumenfeld, P. (1992). Classroom learning and motivation: Clarifying and expanding goal theory. *Journal of Educational Psychology, 84*, 272–281.

Blumenfeld, P. C., Soloway, E., Marx, R. W., Krajcik, J. S., Guzdial, M., & Palincsar, A. S. (1991). Motivating project-based learning: Sustaining the doing, supporting the learning. *Educational Psychologist, 26*, 369–398.

Brown, A. (1997). Transforming schools into communities of thinking about serious matters. *American Psychologist, 52*, 399–413.

Chapman, J. W., & Tunmer, W. E. (1995) Development of young children's reading self-concepts: An examination of emerging subcomponents and their relationship with reading achievement. *Journal of Educational Psychology, 87*, 154–167.

Connell, J., & Wellborn, J. (1991). Competence, autonomy, and relatedness: A motivational analysis of self-system processes. In M. Gunnar & L. A. Sroufe (Eds.), *Self processes and development* (Vol. 23, pp. 43–77). Hillsdale, NJ: Lawrence Erlbaum Associates.

Covington, M. V. (1984). The self-worth theory of achievement motivation: Findings and implications. *Elementary School Journal, 85*, 5–20.

Covington, M. V. (1992). *Making the grade: A self-worth perspective on motivation and school reform*. Cambridge: Cambridge University Press.

Crocker, J., & Wolfe, C. T. (2001). Contingencies of self-worth. *Psychological Review, 108*, 593–623.

Csikszentmihalyi, M. (1990). *Flow: The psychology of optimal experience*. New York: Harper Collins.

Deci, E. L., & Ryan, R. M. (1995). Human autonomy: The basis for true self-esteem. In M. H. Kemis (Ed.), *Efficacy, agency, and self-esteem* (pp. 31–49). New York: Plenum.

Duke, N. K. (2000). 3.6 minutes per day: The scarcity of informational texts in first grade. *Reading Research Quarterly, 35*, 202–224.

Eccles, J. S., Wigfield, A., & Schiefele, U. (1998). Motivation to succeed. In N. Eisenberg (Ed.), *Handbook of child psychology* (Vol. IV, 5th ed., pp. 1017–1095). New York: John Wiley.

Gambrell, L. B., Palmer, B. M., Codling, R. M., & Mazzoni, S. A. (1996). Assessing motivation to read. *The Reading Teacher, 49*, 518–533.

Gottfried, A. E. (1990). Academic intrinsic motivation in young elementary school children. *Journal of Educational Psychology, 82*, 525–538.

Greaney, V., & Hegarty, M. (1987). Correlates of leisure-time reading. *Journal of Research in Reading, 10*, 3–27.

Guthrie, J. T., & Alvermann, D. A. (Eds.). (1999). *Engaged reading: Processes, practices, and policy implications*. New York: Teachers College Press.

Guthrie, J. T., & Cox, K. E. (2001). Classroom conditions for motivation and engagement in reading. *Educational Psychology Review, 13*, 283–302.

Guthrie, J. T., Van Meter, P., Hancock, G., Alao, S., Anderson, E., & McCann, A. (1998). Does concept-oriented reading instruction increase strategy use and conceptual learning from text. *Journal of Educational Psychology, 90*, 261–278.

Guthrie, J. T., & Wigfield, A. (1997). *Reading engagement: Motivating readers through integrated instruction.* Newark, DE: International Reading Association.

Guthrie, J. T., Wigfield, A. & VonSecker, C. (2000). Effects of integrated instruction on motivation and strategy use in reading. *Journal of Educational Psychology, 92*, 331–341.

Halmhuber, N. L., & Paris, S. G. (1993). Perceptions of competence and control and the use of coping strategies by handicapped children. *Learning Disabilities Quarterly, 16*, 93–111.

Hiebert, E. H. (1999). Text matters in learning to read. *Reading Teacher, 52*, 552–566.

Hoffman, J. V. (2002). Words (on words in leveled texts for beginning readers). *National Reading Conference Yearbook, 51*, pp. 59–81. Oak Creek, WI: National Reading Conference, Inc.

Hoffman, J. V., McCarthey, S. J., Abbott, J., Christian, C., Corman, L., Dressman, M., Elliott, B., Matherne, D., & Stahle, D. (1994). So what's new in the new basals? A focus on first grade. *Journal of Reading Behavior, 26*, 47–73.

Lave, J. (1991). Situating learning in communities of practice. In L. B. Resnick, J. M. Levine, & S. D. Teasley (Eds.), *Perspectives on socially shared cognition* (pp. 63–82). Washington, DC: American Psychological Association.

McKenna, M. C., & Kear, D. J. (1990). Measuring attitude toward reading: A new tool for teachers. *The Reading Teacher, 43*, 626–639.

McKenna, M. C., Kear, D. J., & Elsworth, R. A. (1995). Children's attitudes toward reading: A national survey. *Reading Research Quarterly, 30*, 934–956.

Nell, V. (1988). The psychology of reading for pleasure: Needs and gratifications. *Reading Research Quarterly, 23*, 6–50.

Neuman, S. B. (1986). The home environment and fifth grade students' leisure reading. *Elementary School Journal, 86*, 333–343.

Nicholls, J. G. (1979). Development of perception of own attainment and causal attributions for success and failure in reading. *Journal of Educational Psychology, 71*, 94–99.

Paris, S. G., & Ayres, L. J. (1994). *Becoming reflective students and teachers with portfolios and authentic assessment.* Washington, DC: American Psychological Association.

Paris, S. G., Byrnes, J. P., & Paris, A. H. (2001). Constructing theories, identities, and actions of self-regulated learners. In B. Zimmerman & D. Schunk (Eds.), *Self-regulated learning and academic achievement: Theoretical perspectives* (2nd ed., pp. 253–287). Mahwah, NJ: Lawrence Erlbaum Associates.

Paris, S. G., & Hapgood, S. (2002). Children's learning with objects in informal learning environments. In S. Paris (Ed.), *Perspectives on object-centered learning in museums* (pp. 37–54). Mahwah, NJ: Lawrence Erlbaum Associates.

Paris, S. G., & McEvoy, A. P. (2000). Harmful and enduring effects of high-stakes testing. *Issues in Education, 6*, 145–159.

Paris, S. G., & Paris, A. H. (2001). Classroom applications of research on self-regulated learning. *Educational Psychologist, 36*, 89–101.

Paris, S. G., Paris, A. H., & Carpenter, R. D. (2002). Effective practices for assessing young readers. In B. Taylor & P. D. Pearson (Eds.), *Teaching reading: Effective schools and accomplished teachers* (pp. 141–160). Mahwah, NJ: Lawrence Erlbaum Associates.

Paris, S. G., & Turner, J. C. (1994). Situated motivation. In P. Pintrich, D. Brown, & C. Weinstein (Eds.), *Student motivation, cognition, and learning: Essays in honor of Wilbert J. McKeachie* (pp. 213–237). Hillsdale, NJ: Lawrence Erlbaum Associates.

Paris, S. G., Wasik, B. A., & Turner, J. C. (1991). The development of strategic readers. In R. Barr, M. Kamil, P. Mosenthal, & P. D. Pearson (Eds.), *Handbook of reading research* (2nd ed., pp. 609–640). New York: Longman.

Rowe, K. J. (1991). The influence of reading activity at home on students' attitudes toward reading, classroom attentiveness and reading achievement: An application of structural equation modeling. *British Journal of Educational Psychology, 61,* 19–35.

Schallert, D. L., & Reed, J. H. (1997). The pull of the text and the process of involvement in reading. In J. Guthrie & A. Wigfield (Eds.), *Reading engagement: Motivating readers through integrated instruction* (pp. 68–85). Newark, DE: International Reading Association.

Schunk, D. H. (1991). Self-efficacy and academic motivation. *Educational Psychologist, 26,* 233–262.

Schunk, D. H. (2001). Social cognitive theory and self-regulated learning. In B. Zimmerman & D. Schunk (Eds.), *Self-regulated learning and academic achievement: Theoretical perspectives* (2nd ed., pp. 125–151). Mahwah, NJ: Lawrence Erlbaum Associates.

Schunk, D. H. & Swartz, C. W. (1993). Goals and progress feedback: Effects on self-efficacy and writing instruction. *Contemporary Educational Psychology, 18,* 337–354.

Schunk, D. H., & Zimmerman, B. J. (1997). Developing self-efficacious readers and writers: The role of social and self-regulatory processes. In J. T. Guthrie & A. Wigfield (Eds.), *Reading engagement: Motivating readers through integrated instruction* (pp. 34–50). Newark, DE: International Reading Association.

Snow, C. E., Burns, S., & Griffin, P. (1998). *Preventing reading difficulties in young children.* Washington DC: National Academy Press.

Stipek, D., Feiler, R., Daniels, D., & Milburn, S. (1995). Effects of different instructional approaches on young children's achievement and motivation. *Child Development, 66,* 209–223.

Turner, J. C. (1995). The influence of classroom contexts on young children's motivation for literacy. *Reading Research Quarterly, 30,* 410–441.

Turner, J. C. (1997). Starting right: Strategies for engaging young literacy learners. In J. Guthrie & A. Wigfield (Eds.), *Reading engagement: Motivating readers through integrated instruction* (pp. 183–204). Newark, DE: International Reading Association.

Turner, J. C., & Paris, S. G. (1995). How literacy tasks influence children's motivation for literacy. *The Reading Teacher, 48,* 662–673.

van der Voort, T. H. (2001). Television's impact on children's leisure-time reading and reading skills. In L. Verhoeven & C. Snow (Eds.), *Literacy and motivation: Reading engagement in individuals and groups* (pp. 95–119). Mahwah, NJ: Lawrence Erlbaum Associates.

van Kraayenoord, C. E., & Paris, S. G. (1997). Children's self-appraisal of their worksamples and academic progress. *Elementary School Journal, 97,* 523–537.

Whitehurst, G. J., & Fischel, J. E. (2000). A developmental model of reading and language impairments arising in conditions of economic poverty. In D. Bishop & L. Leonard (Eds.), *Speech and language impairments in children: Causes, characteristics, intervention and outcome* (pp. 53–71). East Sussex: Psychology Press.

Wigfield, A., & Asher, S. R. (1984). Social and motivational influences on reading. In P. D. Pearson, R. Barr, M. L. Kamil, & P. Mosenthal (Eds.), *Handbook of reading research* (Vol. 1, pp. 423–452). New York: Longman.

Wigfield, A., & Guthrie, J. T. (1997). Relations of children's motivation for reading to the amount and breadth of their reading. *Journal of Educational Psychology, 89,* 420–432.

Winograd, P., & Paris, S. G. (1989). A cognitive and motivational agenda for reading instruction. *Educational Leadership, 46,* 30–36.

Zimmerman, B. J., & Schunk, D. (Eds.). (2001). *Self-regulated learning and academic achievement.* New York: Springer-Verlag.

II

Considering the Forms
of Texts in Classrooms

5

Choosing Fiction to Support Young Children's Literacy Development

Susan Keehn
Miriam G. Martinez
University of Texas at San Antonio

William H. Teale
University of Illinois at Chicago

Primary grade teachers are well aware of the importance of a classroom filled with good literature. Baumann, Hoffman, Moon, and Duffy-Hester (1998) surveyed teachers throughout the United States, finding strong evidence that teachers are committed to using children's literature. Over 80% of first-grade teachers who responded to the survey reported using big books and trade books. Almost all prekindergarten–Grade 2 teachers (97%) said they regularly read aloud to their students. Of the teachers responding, 94% held the goal of developing readers who are "independent and motivated to choose, appreciate, and enjoy literature" (p. 641). Furthermore, the majority of the teachers agreed that children must be immersed in literature if they are to become fluent readers.

Although clearly committed to using authentic children's literature, teachers nonetheless face a seemingly overwhelming number of choices when deciding *what* literature to use in their programs. Approximately 5,000 new children's book titles per year have been published in the United States for the past decade, and currently more than 70,000 children's books are in print (Huck, 1996). Additionally, in recent years, publishers have produced a large number of trade books designed to foster young children's reading development, that is, to move children into beginning reading, sustain and expand beginning readers, and help them make the transition from easy-to-read picture books to longer and more complex chapter books (Martinez & McGee, 2000). So, one of the challenges for teachers of young children is selecting from this cornucopia of literature the books that best nurture children's literacy and literary development.

This chapter focuses on the qualities of fiction that support various facets of young children's literacy learning. In examining the topic of fiction and young children, it was helpful for us to begin by thinking about the nature, value, and purposes of literature. Certainly, entire books have been written on this topic, and perhaps we risk too much in offering a simple explanation. Still, in our view, fiction for 5- to 7-year-old children is aimed at connecting with their emotions, educating their imaginations, providing ways of exploring issues that matter to them, entertaining, promoting insight into other people's ways of thinking and living, developing lifelong reading habits, and affording aesthetic experiences. Just as is the case with fiction for adults, some books for children present good yarns whereas others offer deeper literary experiences. We find these different types of fiction valuable in developing young children's literacy, language, and thinking.

We also thought about the nature of the reading/language arts curriculum in the primary grades. Many K–2 teachers include the following three instructional components in their programs: a read-aloud component, an independent reading component, and a reading/writing instruction component. We have organized the discussion of appropriate book choices in terms of these three components. Although there are many connections across these components, we believe that each contributes in unique ways to children's literacy development and hence to the kinds of literature needed for each of them varies in certain respects.

In discussing appropriate literature for these three aspects of the instructional program, we center on book choices related to the aspects of literacy development that each component seems best suited to foster. So, for example, even though some teachers may, through their book choices and ways of reading, effectively use reading aloud to develop in children everything from comprehension to alphabet knowledge and phonemic awareness, in addressing the read-aloud component, we focus on a limited number of facets of literacy development that reading aloud is especially well suited to develop. Nevertheless, there are overlaps that we have chosen to preserve and discuss with respect to more than one component.

READ ALOUD COMPONENT

In its influential 1985 report, *Becoming a Nation of Readers*, the Commission on Reading declared, "There is no substitute for a teacher who reads children good stories" (Anderson, Hiebert, Scott, & Wilkinson, 1985, p. 51). Teachers of young children recognize the contributions of the storybook read-aloud experience. In a survey of read-aloud practices, Hoffman, Roser, and Battle (1993) found that 84% of kindergarten teachers read to their students on a given day. Yet the impact of a read-aloud program depends on what, why, and how teachers read to children in the classrooms. In other words, reading aloud is no magic solution for early childhood literacy instruction, and one of the factors critical to its impact is the teacher's selection of books that constitute the read-aloud repertoire.

Another factor for primary-grade teachers to consider can be seen in a second finding from the Baumann et al. (1998) study. They found a decline in the percentage of teachers reading aloud as the grade levels rose. This decline may occur because teachers believe that, as children learn to read, they should read on their own. Of course they should; however, this does not mean that there is no place for read-alouds once children become independent readers themselves, which for most children occurs during the latter half of kindergarten or in first grade. Read-alouds are an essential instructional activity for children of all ages. Nonetheless, as children acquire skill in reading, the contributions of the read-aloud begin to shift, and teachers must read aloud different types of books and shift the main reason for reading aloud to a focus on developing higher level skills.

Books That Support Children's Literacy Development

Reading aloud to young children nurtures their literacy development in a wide variety of ways. It motivates them to learn to read. It stretches their language and builds their store of knowledge about the world. It provides a context for fostering children's comprehension and literary development. Reading aloud can even support children's independent reading and writing. Because read-alouds contribute to children's literacy development in a whole host of different ways, books with different characteristics have the potential to support different facets of this development. Furthermore, because kindergartners, first graders, and second graders are typically at different points in their literacy development, children at different grade levels may need to hear different kinds of books read to them. Some books, of course, easily stretch across grade levels, but not all do. In this section we explore the different types of books that teachers can use to support different facets of children's literacy development through reading aloud. Table 5.1 lists the features of books that support various facets of children's development.

Books That Motivate a Love of Reading.   Reading aloud whets children's appetite for reading. When we read to young children, they discover the rewards of reading and are motivated to learn to read. In fact, books that are read aloud to young children are frequently the ones they pick up to read themselves when they visit the classroom or school library (Hickman, 1981; Martinez, Roser, Worthy, Strecker, & Gough, 1997; Martinez & Teale, 1988). (See Fig. 5.1 for a list of books that motivate a love of reading).

Teachers can tell they are succeeding in motivating a love of reading when children ask for a book to be read again and again. Stories with strong, prob-

TABLE 5.1
Features of Read-Aloud Fiction That Support Children's Literacy Development

Facet of Literacy Development	Book Features
Motivation	• Strong plot line
	• Humor
	• Unusual formats
	• Distinctive illustrations
	• "Invitations to move"
	• Multicultural literature
Language development	• Rich vocabulary with strong clues to meaning
	• Evocative language
Comprehension	• Diverse patterns of organization
	• Lengthier texts
	• Strong story lines
	• "Gaps" that require inferences
World knowledge	• Interesting pieces of information about the world woven into story
Literary understandings	• Diverse genres
	• Distinctive literary elements
	• Stories in which characters grapple with dilemmas

Buttons	By Brock Cole
Henny-Penny	By Jane Wattenberg
Joseph Had a Little Overcoat	By Simms Taback
Louella Mae, She's Run Away!	By Karen Alarcon
Office Buckle and Gloria	By Peggy Rathman
Petunia	By Roger Duvoisin
Small Green Snake	By Libba Moore Gray
Suddenly!	By Colin McNaughton
The Ghost-Eye Tree	By Bill Martin, Jr.
The Three Sillies	By Steven Kellogg
The Wolf's Chicken Stew	By Keiko Kasza
Too Many Chickens!	By Paulette Bourgeois

FIG. 5.1   Books that motivate a love of reading.

lem-centered plot lines are especially likely to be winners. On a first reading of a book with a strong plot line, children are likely to be on the edge of their seats, wanting to know what happens next. When children listen to books such as *Doctor DeSoto* (Steig, 1982), they can be caught up in predicting just how the mouse dentist will outwit the patient (a fox) who is determined to eat him. When they hear *Too Many Tamales* (Soto, 1993), they enjoy making guesses about whether the missing ring really is lost in the tamales and who is likely to find it.

Stories featuring humorous situations are also likely to be winners. Children delight in *The Emperor's Old Clothes* (Lasky, 1999) in which a silly farmer finds the finery discarded by the emperor (the one who wore no clothes) and dresses in his new apparel to do the barnyard chores. Stories with unusual formats and distinctive illustrations also engage children. For example, they love to linger over *The Napping House* (Wood, 1984) as they search for all the creatures in each illustration of the book or seek to discover how the visual perspective changes from illustration to illustration.

Young children also relish books that invite movement. As they listen to *We're Going on a Bear Hunt* (Rosen, 1989/1997), each and every one wants to join that bear hunt and splash splosh though the river and swish swash through the long, wavy grass. They also want to assume the role of the peddler or a monkey as their teacher reads aloud *Caps for Sale* (Slobodkina, 1940/1999).

Including multicultural literature in the read-aloud program is also critical if we want to motivate all children to become readers. A Latino child once said to one of us, "They don't have people like us in books." That child needed to hear books like Soto's *Chato's Kitchen* (1995) or Mora's *Pablo's Tree* (1994). We believe it is the responsibility of every teacher to ensure that students have ample opportunities to meet characters like themselves in literature. For young children, the read-aloud may be the component of the literacy program in which this is most likely to happen because the predictable books that emergent and beginning readers may favor for reading on their own are typically not multicultural in nature.

Books That Stretch Language Development.   Reading aloud to children is one of the best ways of nurturing their language development. Well-written literature is filled with evocative language that children typically do not encounter in their everyday, face-to-face interactions. Where else but in a read-aloud of *Where the Wild Things Are* (Sendak, 1963) will kindergartners come upon the word "gnash." Perhaps only in *Amos and Boris* (Steig, 1972) will second graders hear rich descriptions such as the "phosphorescent sea." The language of literature has the potential to nurture children's vocabulary and their ear for the patterns and rhythms of written language.

To find books that stretch children's language, we recommend that teachers look for ones written by authors who do not talk down to children, who choose just the right word, even if it is a "big" word, and place that word in a context rich with clues to the word's meaning. William Steig is just such a writer. In *Doctor DeSoto*, he tells readers that Doctor DeSoto (a mouse dentist) was "hoisted" up to his patients' mouths. We learn that when Doctor DeSoto stepped inside the fox's mouth to work, the fox's jaw began to "quiver" because he had a tasty "morsel" in his mouth. Doreen Cronin is another writer who challenges young children with words while simultaneously providing them support in figuring out their meanings. Before listening to *Click, Clack, Moo—Cows That Type* (Cronin, 2000), children may not know the meaning of "ultimatum," but after seeing the note that Farmer Brown writes to his cows and hens demanding that they produce milk and eggs, they will likely gain insight into the meaning of the word.

Children's language can also be stretched by listening to books with evocative language. Yolen's *Owl Moon* (1987) is filled with rich imagery. She wrote that "… the moon was so bright the sky seemed to shine" and "… a train whistle blew, long and low, like a sad, sad song." Typically, second graders enjoy books filled with idiomatic language. After listening to Stanley's *Saving Sweetness*

(1996) and *Raising Sweetness* (1999), they will likely want to start a list of their favorite idioms from the book: "I was feelin' like somethin' that was chewed up and spit out." "She was as mean as an acre of rattlesnakes."

Books That Foster Comprehension Development. Read-alouds can also support children's development as comprehenders. In fact, we feel that for kindergartners and first graders (and perhaps to a lesser extent for second graders), the read-aloud component *is* the comprehension component of the reading program. This is because the texts beginning readers can handle on their own are typically so simple that they offer few, if any, comprehension challenges. To move young children forward in their comprehension development, teachers should take advantage of reading aloud to children on an ongoing basis.

Children must develop schemata for the ways in which stories are organized. These schemata enable them to integrate story information and provide the basis for anticipating and predicting story events. During read-alouds, children encounter and begin to internalize the diverse patterns that writers use to organize fiction. In selecting stories to read to their students, teachers need to seek out stories organized in diverse ways: the problem-centered pattern of *Strega Nona* (de Paola, 1975), the circular pattern of *If You Give a Mouse a Cookie* (Numeroff, 1985), the repetitive pattern of *That's Good! That's Bad!* (Cuyler, 1991), or the cumulative pattern of *Shoes from Grandpa* (Fox, 1992). Familiarity with these and other organizational patterns supports children's development as readers and writers.

Fiction becomes increasingly complex as children begin to move from picture books to chapter books. In first and second grades, teachers can begin to read aloud simple chapter books to help their students learn to navigate in this more complex fiction format that they will be expected to move into on their own in second and third grades. Good "start-up" chapter books are short ones like *Frog and Toad Together* (Lobel, 1979), in which individual chapters each feature a story about Frog and Toad but whose plot lines are not connected. Somewhat more complex chapter books are those in the Mr. Putter and Tabby series written by Cynthia Rylant (e.g., Mr. *Putter and Tabby Paint the Porch*, 2000). These are also short books, but their chapters are tied together through a common plot line. Longer chapter books in which characters deal with different facets of a single problem are good read-alouds for second graders. *The Grand Escape* (Naylor, 1993), in which two house cats make a grand escape to the outside world where challenges and opportunities abound, would be just such a chapter book. By reading aloud these longer and more complex books, teachers can ensure that developing readers have the opportunity to encounter books they enjoy but do not have the skill to read on their own.

In addition to promoting a knowledge of story structures, primary grade teachers have the opportunity to impact another facet of children's comprehension development through read-alouds: reading strategies such as activating background knowledge, making predictions, asking questions, and drawing inferences. This can be achieved by modeling and guiding children during read-alouds. Books such as *Borreguita and the Coyote* (Aardema, 1991) that have strong story lines are the kind most likely to elicit predictions. To encourage children to ask questions and make inferences, teachers can find books that provide challenges to young children. For example, in *The Pig Who Ran a Red Light* (Johnson, 1999), George the pig imitates everything Gertrude the cow does—always with disastrous results. When Gertrude takes up flying, George launches himself off the porch only to land in the petunias. When Gertrude drives the tractor, George swipes the car, only to wreck it. No matter what Miss Rosemary tells George, he does not stop imitating Gertrude. Finally, Miss Rosemary has a heart-to-heart talk with Gertrude. The reader must infer just what she tells the cow in light of the subsequent changes in Gertrude's behavior. Books like this one demand that readers/listeners be strategic.

Books That Build World Knowledge   Most often we think about nonfiction as the genre that builds children's world knowledge, but children learn about the world through fiction as well. In fact, fiction can be a rich source of the real-world knowledge that is critical for success in school and supports achievement in reading comprehension throughout the school years. For example, in Carle's *The Very Hungry Caterpillar* (1983), children learn about the life cycle of the butterfly, and Kellogg's *The Mysterious Tadpole* (1972/1997) helps them find out about the life cycle of the tadpole. Steven's *Tops and Bottoms* (1995) affords children the opportunity to develop insights about the edible (and nonedible) portions of vegetables.

Books That Foster Literary Understandings   Read-alouds support children's literary development as well as their literacy development. Through read-alouds, children are introduced to literary devices (e.g., conventional story openers like "Once upon a time") and literary motifs such as the enchanted journey. They meet stock characters like the sly fox and the wicked witch. Read-alouds can also introduce students to a variety of literary genres. Finally, as part of the read-aloud experience, teachers can invite children to think in response to literature, and when discussion is a part of the read-aloud, even very young children learn how to participate in literary conversations.

Teachers should select the very best fiction to promote children's literary growth—stories that "sparkle" and have some "meat" to them. We suggest looking for stories that are distinctive in terms of one or more literary elements. McKissack's *Flossie and the Fox* (1986) is a book that delights because of the humorous plot line that develops through unexpected twists and turns and because of the wonderfully rich characters of Flossie (as clever a protagonist as is likely to be found in children's literature) and the Fox (an arrogant creature who has the misfortune of coming face-to-face with Flossie). Gray's *Small Green Snake* (1994) has wonderful language that is filled with alliteration and repetition. Demi's *The Empty Pot* (1990) has important themes that provide plenty of interesting ideas for primary grade children to discuss. All of these stories sparkle because of powerful literary elements.

It is also important to share diverse genres of fiction with young children. More than ample numbers of titles appropriate for primary-grade children exist in the genres of fantasy, realistic fiction, and traditional literature. Historical fiction appropriate for young children is not as plentiful, but increasing numbers are being published. One such book is *Mailing May* (1997), Tunnell's story about a young girl who longs to visit her grandmother. Her parents cannot afford a train ticket, but they can afford to put stamps on May and send her on the mail train.

INDEPENDENT READING COMPONENT

We use the term *independent reading* to refer to the child's reading the printed words of a book and, in conjunction with whatever illustrations are included, comprehending what was read well enough to be able to provide a retelling of the story or answer comprehension questions about it. Having adopted this definition of independent reading, we also wish to be clear that, for primary-grade children, the beginnings of independent reading are manifested as *emergent readings* (Sulzby, 1985). When children read books emergently, they interact independently with books that have been previously (and most likely repeatedly) read to them, but the children do not read the books conventionally. In early phases of reading emergently, children attend almost exclusively to the illustrations and recreate the story as if they were telling it. Later, they use a reading prosody but still rely on the pictures. In still later phases, they pay attention to the print but construct a reading that focuses only on one of the three aspects of processing involved in conventional reading: comprehension, sight word recognition, or decoding. These ways of reading are typical of prekindergartners and kindergartners. Conceptualized this way, independent reading involves a considerable range of reading behaviors and reflects significant developmental change across the primary-grade years.

In essence, most children go from emergent readers who are not capable of reading the words in the simplest predictable books to readers who can fluently read and understand sophisticated picture books and simple chapter books. Such progress typically results from a number of factors, but independent reading plays a key role in the process. It provides the practice that is an essential part of virtually every primary literacy curriculum framework and theoretical model of reading (e.g., Ruddell, Ruddell, & Singer, 1994; Stanovich, 2000). Furthermore, scores of correlational studies suggest that the more that children read connected discourse, the better their fluency, vocabulary, and comprehension achievement will be. Thus, spending time reading connected discourse is positively related to reading achievement (Pearson & Fielding, 1991). In essence, curling up with a good story is not only fun for children, it also improves their ability to read.

During the primary-grade years, then, the fiction for independent reading stretches across a considerable range in difficulty and content in order to meet the diverse levels of reading development and diverse interests of children from ages five to eight. In discussing the types of literature that can be beneficial for independent reading, we found it helpful to consider each of the three phases of early literacy learning in turn, and thus, in what follows, we focus on books for emergent readers, books for early readers, and books for developing readers. That is not to imply that these phases of reading development are linear; they are not. For instance, on occasion, developing readers do and should choose literature that is "easy" (and may be thought of as better suited to emergent readers) because they want to kick back with a simple book. Or a kindergarten child may struggle with a "second grade" book because she is particularly interested in the main character in the story. Also, it is important to remind ourselves that literature is worth revisiting across the years. For example, a kindergartner may read emergently Lester's *Hooway for Wodney Wat* (1999) because she enjoys the way Rodney talks and may also find in second or third grade that it is a book that helps her think about bullying and peer relations. Or, a child may rely on the detailed illustrations of Barrett's *Cloudy with a Chance of Meatballs* (1978) to "read" it when young and enjoy it in second or third grade as a book that contains examples of rich description.

School-based independent reading should also be thought of as a "hands-on" time for the teacher. Although students benefit from occasionally seeing teachers modeling their love of reading and habit of reading, Teale and Bean (2002) argued it is also important for the teacher to spend time and effort keeping on top of who is reading what, as well as encouraging and scaffolding students' written, artistic, and oral responses to books in order to build a true community of readers in the classroom.

Finally in this introductory discussion, we emphasize important connections between the readaloud component and independent reading. A number of researchers found that children were especially likely to select books for independent reading that had been introduced or read to them (Hickman, 1981; Martinez et al., 1997; Martinez & Teale, 1988). Children across the primary grades are often attracted to other books by the same illustrator or author as those that were read to them. Finally, in primary grade classrooms that use thematic or topical units, children gravitate toward independently reading other books about animals, changes, transportation, community helpers, or whatever is the unit focus when the teacher reads aloud as a central activity for the unit. Thus, by considering both what is read aloud and what is made available to the children for their self-selection, the teacher can help create conditions that heighten the independent reading experience, creating enthusiasm for rereading books, reading more extensively on the same topic, and promoting author and illustrator awareness.

Books for Independent Reading: Emergent Readers

Predictable Books That Support Emergent Reading. As young children engage in emergent readings, they draw on picture clues and their memory of the story to recreate the basic storyline and try out the language of literature. Through these readings, they learn what reading is, experiment with their developing understandings about reading, and build confidence in themselves as readers. When emergent readers attempt to read on their own, books with familiar sequences and elements of predictability fuel their risk taking and help them succeed (Peterson, 1991; Rhodes, 1981). There are numerous elements of predictability, including repetitive, cumulative, and rhyming patterns that assist children in remembering stories and that increase the likelihood that they will read them independently (Bridge, Winograd, & Haley, 1983; Rhodes, 1981). Of course, the children's familiarity with a text, most typically through the teacher's repeated reading of the book, also helps make the text predictable.

Kindergartners are especially likely to engage in emergent readings of highly predictable books like *Do Donkeys Dance?* (Walsh, 2000) or *Let's Go*

Visiting (Williams, 1998). Or, when children have chanted the jump rope rhyme "Teddy Bear, Teddy Bear" many times, the book *Teddy Bear, Teddy Bear* (Hague, 1993), with its clear illustrations, becomes a text they can successfully read. Books like *Hush!* (Ho, 1996) or *I Heard a Little Baa* (MacLeod, 1998) offer a repetitive sequence as well as rhyming couplets. The illustrations of *Hush!*, a Caldecott honor book, make it especially appealing to children, and *I Heard a Little Baa* has the added attraction of being a flip book so that as children read the final word on the pattern page, they can flip the next page to confirm their predictions. Barnes-Murphy's *One Two, Buckle My Shoe* (1987) offers multiple elements of predictability: counting sequence, rhyming words, familiar text, and simple illustrations that match the text. Such books are not intended to stretch children's comprehension abilities or evoke insightful literature discussion, but rather to encourage children to do emergent readings.

Books for Independent Reading: Early Readers

Easy Reader Stories. When children have learned how to decode and have also developed a basic sight vocabulary for reading, one of the most important things they can do to continue their reading trajectory is to get comfortable orchestrating the various aspects of their developing reading skills such as decoding, word recognition, and comprehension skills into a coordinated reading activity. This phase of reading development is especially focused on achieving fluency. Practicing reading is the best way to achieve fluency, and books known as "easy readers" are especially well suited for helping beginning readers extend their development in this area.

Easy readers are an identifiable genre put out by virtually all of the major children's trade book publishers. Easy readers help promote fluency development because they typically have controlled vocabularies and a low comprehension load (plots that are easy enough so that children who can read the words usually have little trouble understanding the book). The format of easy readers is smaller than that of a picture book, with illustrations ranging from the functional to the more aesthetic, depending on the series and publisher.

There are many easy readers and easy reader series available today, with most publishers assigning a level to each of their books. It is important to recognize that (a) there is no standard in the industry or the profession for the various levels (Publisher A's level 2 may be similar in difficulty to Publisher B's level 3), and (b) many of the easy reader trade books on the market are just plain boring to children. Thus, teachers should think of using easy reader trade books in the classroom as a classic case of "let the buyer beware." Happily, there are a number of well-written easy readers that children enjoy (see Fig. 5.2).

Picture Books That Promote Fluency.   Picture books that have vocabulary simple enough for beginning readers to read independently are more difficult to find, but the search is worth it. Compared to easy readers, such books typically have more complex or subtle story lines, higher quality and more nuanced illustrations, and greater attention to overall book design in their production. Young children enjoy the opportunities these books afford for "really reading" while also being able to savor multifaceted characters, experience complex plots, and engage with the books' rich illustrations.

Some picture books that promote fluency have been around for quite a while. The works of Robert Kraus (often illustrated by José Aruego and Ariane Dewey) serve as one example. *Leo the Late Bloomer* (Kraus, 1971), well loved by kindergarten and first-grade teachers, is also a book that children of these ages can read independently. Children also seem to enjoy stories of his like *Come Out and Play, Little Mouse* (Kraus, 1987) or *Herman the Helper* (Kraus, 1974) even more. Other

Amanda Pig Series	By Jean Van Leeuwen
Arthur Series	By Lillian Hoban
Aunt Eater Series	By D. Cushman
Commander Toad Series	By Jane Yolen
Fox Series	By Edward Marshall
Frog and Toad Series	By Arnold Lobel
The Golly Sisters Series	By Betsy Byars
Henry and Mudge Series	By Cynthia Rylant
Little Bear Series	By Else Holmelund Minarik
Messy Bessey Series	By Patricia McKissack
Minnie and Moo Series	By Denys Cazet
Mr. Putter and Tabby Series	By Cynthia Rylant
Pinky and Rex Series	By James Howe
Poppleton Series	By Cynthia Rylant
Zelda and Ivy Series	By Lisa Kvasnosky

FIG. 5.2   Easy-to-Read Series.

books that are well suited to children's early independent reading are being written by the current generation of authors. Keiko Kasza is an accomplished au-
thor/illustrator whose books work well as independent reading material for
beginning readers. *The Wolf's Chicken Stew* (1987) is already a well-loved standard, and others of her more recent books like *A Mother for Choco* (1992) and
Don't Laugh, Joe (1997) are also good selections. In addition, the Little Bear books
by Martin Waddell (e.g., *Can't You Sleep, Little Bear?*, 1994; *Let's Go Home, Little
Bear*, 1991; *Good Job, Little Bear*, 2002) are greatly enjoyed by some children and
provide a "just right" level of challenge that also supports beginning independent
reading.

Books for Independent Reading: Developing Readers

By the end of the primary-grade years, many children (but by no means all) have
moved into a stage of reading in which they can easily decode unknown words
and read text fluently. Now, of course, reading can be rewarding in a way that
more closely approximates the pleasure reading of adults. The real reward of
reading comes not from merely understanding what is happening in the book
but from the new insights about characters, inventive twists of plot, evocative
language, or information the book provides.

First Chapter Books.   Chapter books contain relatively few illustrations
and more extended story lines than are typical of picture books. Although picture books continue to be appropriate even into the intermediate grades, chapter books carry a certain aura for young children, marking the passage into more
mature reading. Once children begin to read chapter books, they are regarded
by their teacher and peers—as well as by themselves—as having advanced beyond the beginning reader phase.

Many children enjoy reading series chapter books at this stage. A number of
first and second graders enjoy reading works like the George and Martha books
(Marshall, 1972, 1978) when they get into short chapter books. Also, ones like
the Junie B. Jones (Park, 2002), Ronald Morgan (Giff, 1988, 1995), and Flatfoot
Fox books (Clifford, 1990, 1997) or the Mud Flat series by Stevenson, (e.g.,
1997, 1999) are attractive to numerous children. The key seems to be books
that have a set of characters who continue from one book into another, offering
beginning readers something familiar from book to book.

More Advanced Chapter Books.   At the upper end of the difficulty spec-
trum of books for most primary children are ones like *Just Juice* by (Hesse, 1998),
Gooseberry Park (Rylant, 1995), the widely popular Magic Tree House books

(e.g., *Dinosaurs Before Dark*, Osborne, 1992; *Stage Fright on a Summer Night*, Osborne, 2002), Julian books by Cameron (*The Stories Julian Tells*, 1981; *Julian, Dream Doctor*, 1990), and even Danzinger's books featuring Amber Brown (e. g., *Amber Brown Is Not a Crayon*, 1994; *Get Ready for Second Grade, Amber Brown*, 2002). Such books often run to 100 pages or more and provide reading challenges for primary age children because of their vocabulary load, considerable number of multisyllabic words that require capable decoding skills, and more complex plots.

LITERACY INSTRUCTION COMPONENT

Huck (1989) observed, "We don't achieve literacy and then give children literature; we achieve literacy through literature" (p. 258). Children's books offer a viable, rich source for teaching reading and writing (Temple, Martinez, Yokota, & Naylor, 2002). Effective teachers understand how to use books to promote children's development of reading skills and strategies while simultaneously fostering their love of literacy. As instruction helps children move from initial learning about print to the challenge of decoding and on to growing independence and fluency, different kinds of books are needed to nurture progress. Knowledgeable teachers select books based on the scaffolding they provide: "... using particular types of texts at particular times in readers' development is a material way to support their progress" (Brown, 1999/2000, p. 293).

Having discussed the read-aloud and independent reading components, we now explore how books can support the small group, whole class, and one-on-one instruction the teacher provides in the primary classroom. We examine books appropriate for emergent readers as they learn how print works and about sounds and letters, we identify the characteristics of books that help early readers master sight words and strengthen their decoding skills, and we also discuss the features of texts that can support the growing independence and fluency of developing readers. In addition, we look at how books can support another important facet of the early literacy curriculum: writing.

Books That Support Emergent Readers

Emergent readers are learning how to handle books and are developing concepts about print such as directionality. They are also discovering how print and pictures function in books, what a title is, who an author is. They are learning to hear sounds within words and discovering how those sounds map onto letters. There are many books that support young children during this phase of literacy development.

Books That Help Children Learn About Print.   An excellent way to help emergent readers construct concepts of print is the shared book experience (Holdaway, 1979). Shared reading enables large groups of children to participate in the reading of a book under the guidance of a teacher. Big books are typically used because their oversized format allows all the children to see the pictures and to observe the teacher as she points to the words while reading, thus demonstrating directionality of print and voice-to-print matching. Many narrative trade books are now available in big book format. The best ones for emergent readers have limited text on a page, illustrations that support the text, and repetitive or predictive elements that invite children to chime in with the teacher during subsequent readings of the book. *The Chick and the Duckling* (Ginsburg, 1992) is one example of such a book that works well with kindergartners. Its repetitive narrative structure and "Me, too" refrain from the chick, as well as an engaging story line, make it a book that is enjoyed, easily read, and repeatedly accessible for shared readings. Such shared reading allows children's early reading experiences to be successful and fun.

Books That Foster Phonemic Awareness.   Phonemic awareness, the ability to hear the separate sounds of words, is an important precursor to learning phonics to read (Adams, 1990; National Reading Panel, 2000). Children who are phonemically aware can segment individual sounds within words as well as blend sounds together. One way to help children develop phonemic awareness is through the use of children's literature that encourages children to "play" with the sounds of language (Griffith & Olson, 1992; Opitz, 2000).

Rhyme, alliteration, and sound substitutions are all features that can foster phonemic awareness, and these features characterize the language of many books for young children. To get toes tapping and hands clapping, the teacher should look for books that combine rhythm and rhyme. *Chugga-Chugga-Choo-Choo* (Lewis, 1999) is a rhyming story that describes a day in the life of a freight train in a rhythmic pattern that mimics the wheels of the train on a track. To ensure that children learn to attend to rhyming words, the teacher should seek out books that tell a story and have engaging pictures so that the context and illustrations offer support as children "fill in" the rhyming word. When Mrs. Brown has to go to the hospital in *Mrs. Brown*

Went to Town (Yee, 1996), the animals on the farm take over the house and engage in mischievous behavior that delights children: "In the bathroom they played for hours; Putting on makeup and taking long showers." Children giggle at the illustration that depicts the cow putting on lipstick and the yak using a blow dryer. Alliteration is a third linguistic feature that promotes phonemic awareness. A book like *Four Famished Foxes and Fosdyke* (Edwards, 1995) lets children enjoy a funny story laced with a cornucopia of words beginning with the initial /f/ sound. An extensive bibliography of books that promote children's phonemic awareness can be found by clicking on "phonemic awareness booklist" at http://www. edci.uconn.edu/ctell/archive/links.htm. Also, Fig. 5.3 presents a selection from this list of good books that promote phonemic awareness.

Books That Support Alphabet Knowledge. To become readers, young children must discover the alphabetic principle. That is, they must understand that words are composed of sounds and that these individual sounds are represented by specific letters. We know that children who master let-

The Beastly Feast	By Bruce Goldstone
Boo to a Goose	By Mem Fox
Clickety Clack	By Rob and Amy Spence
Cock-a-Doodle-Moo	By Bernard Most
Down by the Bay	By Raffi
"Fire! Fire!" Said Mrs. McGuire	By Bill Martin Jr.
Four Famished Foxes and Fosdyk	By Pamela Duncan Edwards
Goodnight Moon	By Margaret Wise Brown
"I Don't Care!" said the Bear	By Colin West
Mice Squeak, We Speak	By Tomie dePaola
Monkey Do!	By Allan Ahlberg
Old Black Fly	By Jim Aylesworth
One Monkey Too Many	By Jackie French Koller
Sheep in a Jeep	By Nancy Shaw
To Market, To Market	By Anne Miranda

FIG. 5.3   Books that promote phonemic awareness.

ter–sound relationships are better readers than children who do not (Adams, 1990). Thus, another goal of early reading instruction is to teach children the names of the alphabet letters and their corresponding sounds, and alphabet books are one of the invaluable tools teachers can use to achieve this goal. Although only a few quality alphabet books contain a true narrative storyline, we include alphabet books here because of their powerful instructional potential.

Alphabet books that feature a single letter and an accompanying illustration on each page are ideal for children working to learn letter names. *ABC Kids* (Williams, 2000) is such a book. It offers a single word illustrated with large, colorful photographs of children, so the word *clown* on the C page shows a child in clown makeup and wig, and the child on the W page is biting into a big slice of watermelon. Likewise, *Action Alphabet* (Rotner, 1996) offers wonderful photographs of children engaged in activities such as eating, floating, giggling, and hugging.

To help children learn letter–sound associations, it is ideal to have alphabet books that offer multiple objects whose names begin with each letter. *ABC Discovery* (Cohen, 1998) invites the reader to identify many objects in each illustration and includes a list of the object names under the letter. Additional challenge is presented in alphabet books using alliterative text, such as *Miss Spider's ABC* (Kirk, 1998). Each of Miss Spider's guests prepares for a birthday party in such a way that the guests' names and the words describing their actions begin with the same letter (e.g., "Bumblebees blow balloons.") In *A My Name is Alice* (Bayer, 1992), each letter introduces a female animal and her "husband," both of whose names begin with the letter. The alliterative text is repetitive, and Steven Kellogg's illustrations are humorously engaging. Children will be eager to create alliterative text innovations using their own names after enjoying *A My Name is Alice*. In *Goblins in Green* (Heller, 1995), the goblins dress themselves in clothing of a color that corresponds to the first letter of their names. So while Clara clowns in cranberry dungarees, Desmond has donned denim earmuffs. The wide range of challenge in alphabet books affords fun opportunities for emergent readers to apply their growing knowledge of letters and their sounds to figure out the book's pattern and organization.

Books That Support Early Readers

Once young readers have grasped the alphabetic principle, they use their knowledge of letter–sound relationships and context to decode printed words. At this point in their development, "easy reading" books are very helpful to use for instructional activities because they afford children ample opportunity to apply their developing skills. They also allow early readers to work on automatic recognition of high frequency words. When early readers can recognize the most frequently occurring words, "all their attention is freed for decoding less frequent words, and, more important, for processing of meaning" (Cunningham, 2000, p. 54). We have already discussed the use of such books in conjunction with independent reading. Trade books are valuable tools for reading lessons.

Predictable Books That Support the Acquisition of Sight Words.
Teachers of young children are always looking for suitable materials for beginning readers whose sight vocabularies are in the early stages of developing. Fiction selections provide a good source for children to extend their sight vocabularies in reading. Many high frequency words are difficult to decode and have no meaning in and of themselves. We know that the more abstract a word is, the more association and practice is required to learn it (Cunningham, 2000). A story offers a context in which the early reader can associate the abstract word with meaning. Repeatedly encountering these words in a meaningful context promotes children's instant recall of them. Predictable books feature many high frequency words and, through naturally occurring repetition in the text, children encounter the words over and over. Indeed, Bridge, Winograd, and Haley (1983) found that struggling readers in first grade learned sight words in the context of predictable trade books better than in basal reader series. As children read the words over and over in meaningful, patterned structures, the words gradually become part of the sight vocabularies. (See Fig. 5.4 for a list of predictable books that feature high frequency words.)

Decodable Trade Books. A number of researchers (e.g., Ehri, 1998; Hiebert, 1999; Juel, 1994) have argued for texts that provide early readers with words that follow common sound–letter patterns. In selecting books to support children in their decoding efforts, we must give attention to the consistency of phonetic elements in the words, as well as to the number of times the child sees a word within the text and thus has the opportunity to identify it. The primary function of decodable texts is to provide children with the practice they need to become fluent decoders.

Additionally, early readers can learn to decode words by using known word patterns (also called rimes, word families, or phonograms; Adams, 1990; Cunningham, 2000). Because the brain is a pattern seeker, proficient readers recog-

A Beasty Story	By Bill Martin, Jr.
"Buzz, Buzz, Buzz," Went Bumblebee	By Colin West
The Chick and the Duckling	By Mirra Ginsburg
Do Pigs Have Stripes?	By Melanie Walsh
Here Are My Hands	By Bill Martin, Jr. & John Archambault
Let's Go Visiting	By Sue Williams
Where's Spot?	By Eric Hill
Who Ate It?	By Taro Gomi
Who Hoots?	By Katie Davis
Who Is Tapping at My Window?	By A. G. Deming
Who Took the Cookies from the Cookie Jar?	By Bonnie Lass & Philemon Sturges
Z-Z-Zoink!	By Bernard Most

FIG. 5.4   Predictable books that feature high-frequency sight words.

nize unfamiliar words by analogy to similar parts in known words. When we provide texts based on phonogram patterns, we help early readers learn this word recognition strategy that mature readers use. For example, *Zoo Looking* by Fox (1996) contains many words that use the *-ack* pattern. *How Do Dinosaurs Say Good Night?* (Yolen & Teague, 2000) is filled with humor and familiar good-night antics performed by dinosaur children while it also offers words based on the *-ight*, *-ide*, and *-out* phonograms. (See Fig. 5.5 for additional decodable fiction.)

Books That Support Developing Readers

Often by second grade (and sometimes even earlier), young readers master sight words and learn to identify unknown words, thus growing in independence. Their decoding becomes more automatic, and they are increasingly able to attend to meaning as they read. The instructional goal at this point turns to helping these children develop fluency. Fluency involves reading at a good pace with a high degree of accuracy and appropriate phrasing and expression. We know that fluency correlates highly with comprehension and that students who do not move beyond robotic, word-by-word reading subsequently struggle in reading (Allington, 1983). It is important to seek out books that nurture children's reading fluency.

Can You Find It?	By Bernard Most
The Fat Cat Sat on the Mat	By Nurit Karlin
Little Dogs Say "Rough!"	By Rick Walton
Lulu Crow's Garden	By Lizi Boyd
Sheep in a Jeep	By Nancy Shaw
Silly Sally	By Audrey Wood
Tog the Dog	By Colin and Jacqui Hawkins
Zoodles	By Bernard Most

FIG. 5.5   Decodable fiction.

Because at this developing stage readers are ready for more challenge, teachers should select books that are longer and more complex. The sentences can be more complicated and lengthier, and a wider range of words can be used, including more difficult high-frequency words.

Predictable Books That Support Developing Readers.   Most often we think of predictable books as tools to use with emergent and early readers, but more sophisticated predictable books can offer a fine combination of support and challenge to developing readers as well. *The Grouchy Ladybug* (Carle, 1977/1996) offers a predictable hourly time sequence as well as repeated elements such as "Hey you, want to fight?" *Bringing the Rain to Kapiti Plain* (Aardema, 1981) offers challenging new vocabulary, but the cumulative pattern of the book means that the new words are repeated many times, ensuring that they are manageable. Teachers need to seek out good fiction that both promotes children's growing ability to identify new words and offers scaffolding in the form of predictable, repetitive elements.

Books That Promote Fluency Growth.   Children's repeated readings of the same piece of text aloud makes them sound better. Indeed, studies confirm that as students repeatedly read a passage, their reading rate and accuracy improve (e.g., Dowhower, 1987; Samuels, 1979), and their reading confidence grows. Children who lack fluency typically read only when they have to and thus do not gain the ability to identify words automatically that develops from wide reading. The prescription for developing fluency is extensive and repeated reading of easy books (Allington, 1983). Such fluency work can easily become a part of guided reading with small groups in the classroom.

Series books are particularly useful for building fluency, because they offer characters and situations that are familiar to the child. For first-grade readers, Lobel's *Frog and Toad* series is appropriate and popular, as is Marshall's *Fox* series. For second grade readers, Brown's *Arthur* series and Marshall's *Cut-Up* series work well. Such series books can also become powerful instructional tools for building fluency when they are adapted for Readers Theater (e.g., Martinez, Roser & Strecker, 1998/1999) or cross-age reading (e.g., Labbo & Teale, 1990). Readers Theater and cross-age reading build in motivation to read a text repeatedly because each rereading is a rehearsal for a performance, either to an audience of peers or to a younger or older "reading buddy." (See Fig. 5.2 for a list of easy-to-read series books.)

Books To Support Writing

Rich exposure to children's literature nurtures children's development as writers (e.g., Dahl & Freppon, 1995; Fitzgerald & Teasley, 1986). Children frequently use the stories they read or hear read aloud as models for their own writing (Calkins, 1983; Morrow, 2001). To encourage young writers to use literature in this way, teachers can guide children in the creation of class-authored books. The teacher serves as scribe, and children collaboratively create personalized versions of familiar stories. For example, the class can brainstorm together to produce their own scary version of *A Dark, Dark Tale* (Brown, 1992). One group of young writers produced a fun, creative version of "I Know an Old Lady Who Swallowed a Fly":

> I know an old lady who swallowed a bee.
>
> Don't ask me why she swallowed a bee.
>
> We'll have to see.

Predictable, patterned books are particularly useful as foundations to foster growth in written language. They seem to invite writing. The structure and language used by the author are used by the children to write their own innovations with delightful, satisfying results. Even children with limited English language skills can write their own books by substituting different words into a basic sentence pattern. Patterned books also provide powerful models for emerging and developing readers and writers. The simple, predictive *Brown Bear, Brown Bear* (Martin, 1967/1998) was used by a group of second graders to culminate their learning about food chains within the ocean, beginning:

Bright sun, bright sun
What do you see?
I see plankton looking at me....

and ending:

Whale, whale
What do you see?
I see an Eskimo looking at me.

Reading and writing rhyming patterned books also provide opportunities
for children to work with the common word families in an engaging and creative way. The language is natural and the meanings accessible as they come
from the children themselves. Two first-grade collaborators used their knowledge of word patterns to produce their own version of *Green Eggs and Ham*
(Seuss, 1960):

Will you eat them wearing a coat?
Will you share them with a goat?
Will you catch them as they float
And scoop them up into your boat?

Figure 5.6 offers a list of predictable books that promote writing.

The Best Friends Book	By Todd Parr
The Book of Bad Ideas	By Laura Huliska-Beith
Do Donkeys Dance?	By Melanie Walsh
The Great Big Enormous Turnip	By Alexei Tolstoy
The House that Jack Built	By Rodney Peppe
It Looked Like Spilt Milk	By Charles Shaw
Over in the Meadow	By Ezra Jack Keats
Rosie's Walk	By Pat Hutchins
Teeny Tiny Woman	By Margot Zemach
Underwear Do's and Don't's	By Todd Parr
Whose Mouse Are You?	By Robert Kraus

FIG. 5.6   Predictable books that promote writing.

CONCLUSION

A rich world of children's fiction trade books awaits teachers as they plan early literacy curricula and select materials to make available for read-alouds, children's independent reading, and literacy instruction. Different books contribute to the various dimensions of early literacy development. Ultimately, the teacher has responsibility for selection of the trade books used in the classroom. Fundamental to this decision making is the teacher's knowledge of the books that interest his or her students and address their needs. Teachers should select books that support students' changing literacy development as they move from learning about print and how it works to decoding to increased independence and fluency. At all levels of development throughout the primary grades, many kinds of books support reading and writing instruction. Happily, there are so many good books for so many different children.

REFERENCES

Adams, M. J. (1990). *Beginning to read: Thinking and learning about print*. Cambridge, MA: MIT Press.

Allington, R. L. (1983). Fluency: The neglected goal. *The Reading Teacher, 35,* 556–561.

Anderson, R C., Hiebert, E. H., Scott, J. A., & Wilkinson, I. A. G. (1985). *Becoming a nation of readers*. Champaign, IL: University of Illinois Center for the Study of Reading.

Baumann, J. F., Hoffman, J. V., Moon, J., & Duffy-Hester, A. M. (1998). Where are teachers' voices in the phonics/whole language debate? Results from a survey of U.S. elementary classroom teachers. *The Reading Teacher, 36,* 636–650.

Bridge, C. A., Winograd, P. N., & Haley, D. (1983). Using predictable materials to teach beginning reading. *The Reading Teacher, 35,* 884–891.

Brown, K. J. (1999/2000). What kind of text—for whom and when? Textual scaffolding for beginning readers. *The Reading Teacher, 53,* 292–307.

Calkins, L. M. (1983). *Lessons from a child: On the teaching and learning of writing*. Exeter, NH: Heinemann.

Cunningham, P. M. (2000). *Phonics they use* (3rd ed.). New York: Longman.

Dahl, K. L., & Freppon, P. (1995). A comparison of inner-city children's interpretations of reading and writing instruction in the early grades in skills-based and whole language classrooms. *Reading Research Quarterly, 30,* 50–74.

Dowhower, S. L. (1987). Effects of repeated reading on second-grade transitional readers' fluency and comprehension. *Reading Research Quarterly, 22,* 329–406.

Ehri, L. (1998). Grapheme-phoneme knowledge is essential for learning to read words in English. In J. Metsala & L. Ehri (Eds.), *Word recognition in beginning literacy* (pp. 3–40). Mahwah, NJ: Lawrence Erlbaum Associates.

Fitzgerald, J., & Teasley, A. B. (1986). Effects of instruction in narrative structure on children's writing. *Journal of Educational Psychology, 78,* 424–433.

Griffith, P., & Olson, M. (1992). Phonemic awareness helps beginning readers break the code. *The Reading Teacher, 45,* 516–523.

Hickman, J. (1981). A new perspective on response to literature: Research in an elementary school setting. *Research in the Teaching of English, 15,* 343–354.

Hiebert, E. H. (1999). Text matters in learning to read. *The Reading Teacher, 52,* 552–566.

Hoffman, J. V., Roser, N. L., & Battle, J. (1993). Reading aloud in classrooms: From the modal toward a "model." *The Reading Teacher, 46,* 496–503.

Holdaway, D. (1979). *The foundations of literacy.* Portsmouth, NH: Heinemann.

Huck, C. S. (1989). No wider than the heart is wide. In J. Hickman & B. E. Cullinan (Eds.), *Children's literature in the classroom: Weaving Charlotte's Web* (pp. 252–262). Needham Heights, MA: Christopher-Gordon.

Huck, C. S. (1996). Literature-based reading programs: A retrospective. *The New Advocate, 9,* 23–33.

Juel, C. (1994). *Learning to read and write in one elementary school.* New York: Springer-Verlag.

Labbo, L. D., & Teale, W. H. (1990). Cross-age reading: A strategy for helping poor readers. *The Reading Teacher, 43,* 362–369.

Martinez, M. G., & McGee, L. M. (2000). Children's literature and reading instruction: Past, present, and future. *Reading Research Quarterly, 35,* 154–169.

Martinez, M., Roser, N. L., & Strecker, S. K. (1998/1999). "I never thought I could be a star": A readers theater ticket to fluency. *The Reading Teacher, 52,* 326–335.

Martinez, M. G., Roser, N. L., Worthy, J., Strecker, S., & Gough, P. (1997). Classroom libraries and children's book selections: Redefining "access" in self-selected reading. In C. K. Kinzer, K. A. Hinchman, & D. J. Leu (Eds.), *Inquiries in literacy theory and practice: 46th Yearbook of the National Reading Conference* (pp. 265–272). Chicago: National Reading Conference.

Martinez, M., & Teale, W. H., (1988). Reading in a kindergarten classroom library. *The Reading Teacher, 41,* 568–572.

Morrow, L. M. (2001). *Literacy development in the early years* (4th ed.). Boston: Allyn & Bacon.

National Reading Panel. (2000). *Teaching children to read.* Washington, DC: National Institute of Child Health and Human Development.

Opitz, M. (2000). *Rhymes and reasons: Literature and language play for phonological awareness.* Portsmouth, NH: Heinemann.

Pearson, P. D., & Fielding, L. (1991). Comprehension instruction. In R. Barr, M. L. Kamil, P. Mosenthal, & P. D. Pearson (Eds.), *Handbook of reading research* (Vol. 2, pp. 815–860). White Plains, NY: Longman.

Peterson, B. (1991). Selecting books for beginning readers. In D. DeFord, C. Lyons, & G. Pinnell (Eds.), *Bridges to literacy: Learning from Reading Recovery* (pp. 119–147). Portsmouth, NH: Heinemann.

Rhodes, L. K. (1981). I can read! Predictable books as resources for reading and writing instruction. *The Reading Teacher, 34,* 511–518.

Ruddell, R. B., Ruddell, M. R., & Singer, H. (Eds.). (1994). *Theoretical models and processes of reading.* Newark, DE: International Reading Association.

Samuels, S. J. (1979). The method of repeated readings. *The Reading Teacher, 32,* 403–408.

Stanovich, K. E. (2000). *Progress in understanding reading: Scientific foundations and new frontiers.* New York: Guilford.

Sulzby, E. (1985). Children's emergent reading of favorite storybooks. *Reading Research Quarterly, 20,* 458–481.

Teale, W. H., & Bean, K. (2002, March). *Of SSR, AR, and the notion of independent reading: What's a teacher to do?* Paper presented at the Illinois Reading Conference, Springfield, IL.

Temple, C., Martinez, M., Yokota, J, & Naylor, A. (2002). *Children's books in children's hands: An introduction to their literature* (2nd ed.). Boston: Allyn & Bacon.

CHILDREN'S LITERATURE CITED

Aardema, V. (1981). *Bringing the rain to Kapiti Plain.* New York: Dial.

Aardema, V. (1991). *Borreguita and the coyote.* Illustrated by P. Mathers. New York: Knopf.

Barnes-Murphy, R. (1987). *One two, buckle my shoe.* New York: Simon & Schuster.

Barrett, J. (1978). *Cloudy with a chance of meatballs.* Illustrated by R. Barrett. New York: Atheneum.

Bayer, J. (1992). *A my name is Alice.* Illustrated by S. Kellogg. New York: E. P. Dutton.

Brown, R. (1992). *A dark, dark tale.* New York: E. P. Dutton.

Cameron, A. (1981). *The stories Julian tells.* Illustrated by A. Strugnell. New York: Pantheon.

Cameron, A. (1990). *Julian, dream doctor.* Illustrated by A. Strugnell. New York: Random House.

Carle, E. (1983). *The very hungry caterpillar.* New York: Philomel.

Carle, E. (1996). *The grouchy ladybug.* New York: Harper Collins. (Original work published 1977)

Clifford, E. (1990). *Flatfoot Fox and the case of the missing eye.* Illustrated by B. Lies. Boston: Houghton Mifflin.

Clifford, E. (1997). *Flatfoot Fox and the case of the missing schoolhouse.* Illustrated by B. Lies. Boston: Houghton Mifflin.

Cohen, I. (1998). *ABC discovery!* New York: Dial.

Cole, B. (2000). *Buttons.* New York: Farrar, Straus & Giroux

Cronin, D. (2000). *Click, clack, moo—cows that type.* Illustrated by B. Lewin. New York: Simon & Schuster.

Cuyler, M. (1991). *That's good! that's bad!* Illustrated by D. Catrow. New York: Henry Holt.

Danziger, P. (1994). *Amber Brown is not a crayon.* Illustrated by T. Ross. New York: Putnam's.

Danziger, P. (2002). *Get ready for second grade, Amber Brown.* Illustrated by T. Ross. New York: G. P. Putnam's.

Demi. (1990). *The empty pot.* New York: Holt.

de Paola, T. (1975). *Strega Nona.* New York: Prentice-Hall.

de Paola, T. (1997). *Mice squeak, we speak.* New York: Puffin.

Edwards, P. D. (1995). *Four famished foxes and Fosdyke.* Illustrated By H. Cole. New York: HarperCollins.

Fox, M. (1992). *Shoes from grandpa.* Illustrated by P. Mullins. New York: Orchard.

Fox, M. (1996). *Zoo looking.* Illustrated by Candace Whitman. New York: Mondo.

Galdone, P. (1984). *The teeny tiny woman.* Boston: Houghton Mifflin.

Giff, P. R. (1988). *Ronald Morgan goes to bat.* Illustrated by S. Natti. New York: Viking.

Giff, P. R. (1995). *Ronald Morgan goes to camp.* Illustrated by S. Natti. New York: Viking.

Ginsburg, M. (1992). *The chick and the duckling.* Illustrated by J. & A. Aruego. New York: Macmillan.

Gray, L. M. (1994). *Small green snake.* Illustrated by H. Meade. New York: Orchard.

Hague, M. (Illus.) (1993). *Teddy bear, teddy bear.* New York: Scholastic.

Heller, N. (1995). *Goblins in green.* Illustrated by J. A. Smith. New York: Mulberry Books.

Hesse, K. (1998). *Just juice.* Illustrated by R. A. Parker. New York: Scholastic.

Ho, M. (1996). *Hush!* New York: Orchard Books.

Johnson, P. B. (1999). *The pig who ran a red light.* New York: Orchard.

Kasza, K. (1987). *The wolf's chicken stew.* New York: G. P. Putnam's Sons.

Kasza, K. (1992). *A mother for Choco.* New York: G. P. Putnam's Sons.

Kasza, K. (1997). *Don't laugh, Joe.* New York: G. P. Putnam's Sons.

Kellogg, S. (1997). *The mysterious tadpole.* New York: Dial. (Original work published 1972)

Kirk, D. (1998). *Miss Spider's ABC*. New York: Scholastic.

Kraus, R. (1971). *Leo the late bloomer*. Illustrated by J. Aruego & A. Dewey. New York: Greenwillow.

Kraus, R. (1974). *Herman the helper*. Illustrated by J. Aruego & A. Dewey. New York: Greenwillow.

Kraus, R. (1987). *Come out and play, little mouse*. Illustrated by J. Aruego & A. Dewey. New York: Greenwillow.

Lasky, K. (1999). *The emperor's old clothes*. Illustrated by D. Catrow. San Diego: Harcourt Brace.

Lester, H. (1999). *Hooway for Wodney Wat*. Illustrated by L. Munsinger. Boston: Houghton Mifflin.

Lewis, K. (1999). *Chugga-chugga choo-choo*. Illustrated by D. Kirk. New York: Hyperion Books.

Lobel, A. (1979). *Frog and toad together* (An I-Can-Read Book). New York: Harper Trophy.

MacLeod, E. (1998). *I heard a little baa*. Illustrated by L. Phillips. Toronto: Kids Can Press.

Marshall, J. (1972). *George and Martha*. Boston: Houghton Mifflin.

Marshall, J. (1978). *George and Martha: One fine day*. Boston: Houghton Mifflin.

Martin, B., Jr. (1998). *Brown bear, brown bear, what do you see?* Illustrated by E. Carle. New York: Holt. (Original work published 1967)

McKissack, P. (1986). *Flossie and the fox*. Illustrated by R. Isadora. New York: Dial.

Mora, P. (1994). *Pablo's tree*. Illustrated by Cecily Lang. New York: Macmillan.

Naylor, P. R. (1993). *The grand escape*. New York: Atheneum.

Numeroff, L. J. (1985). *If you give a mouse a cookie*. Illustrated by F. Bond. New York: Harper.

Osborne, M. P. (1992). *Dinosaurs before dark*. Illustrated by S. Murdocca. New York : Random House.

Osborne, M. P. (2002). *Stage fright on a summer night*. Illustrated by S. Murdocca. New York: Random House.

Park, B. (2002). *Junie B. Jones*. New York: Random House.

Rosen, M. (1997). *We're going on a bear hunt*. Illustrated by H. Oxenbury. Boston: Little Simon. (Original work published 1989)

Rotner, S. (1996). *Action alphabet*. New York: Athenuem.

Rylant, C. (1995). *Gooseberry Park*. Illustrated by A. Howard. San Diego: Harcourt Brace.

Rylant, C. (2001). *Mr. Putter and Tabby paint the porch*. Illustrated by A. Howard. San Diego: Harcourt Brace.

Sendak, M. (1963). *Where the wild things are*. New York: Harper & Row.

Seuss, Dr. (1960). *Green eggs and ham*. New York: Beginner Books.

Slobodkina, E. (1999). *Caps for sale*. New York: HarperCollins. (Original work published 1940)

Soto, G. (1993). *Too many tamales*. Illustrated by E. Martinez. New York: Putnam.

Soto, G. (1995). *Chato's kitchen*. Illustrated by S. Guevara. New York: Penguin Putnam.

Stanley, D. (1996). *Saving Sweetness*. Illustrated by G. B. Karas. New York: Putnam.

Stanley, D. (1999). *Raising Sweetness*. Illustrated by G. B. Karas. New York: Putnam.

Steig, W. (1972). *Amos and Boris*. New York: Farrar, Straus & Giroux.

Steig, W. (1982). *Doctor DeSoto*. New York: Farrar, Straus & Giroux

Stevens, J. (1995). *Tops and bottoms*. San Diego: Harcourt.

Stevenson, J. (1997). *Heat wave at Mud Flat*. New York: Greenwillow.

Stevenson, J. (1999). *Mud Flat April fool*. New York: Greenwillow.

Tunnell, M. O. (1997). *Mailing May*. Illustrated by T. Rand. New York: Greenwillow.

Waddell, M. (1991). *Let's go home, Little Bear*. Illustrated by B. Firth. Cambridge, MA: Candlewick.

Waddell, M. (1994). *Can't you sleep, Little Bear?* Illustrated by B. Firth. Cambridge, MA: Candlewick.

Waddell, M. (2002). *Good job, Little Bear.* Illustrated by B. Firth. Cambridge, MA: Candlewick.

Walsh, M. (2000). *Do donkeys dance?* Boston: Houghton Mifflin.

Williams, L. E. (2000). *ABC kids.* New York: Philomel Books.

Williams, S. (1998). *Let's go visiting.* San Diego: Harcourt Brace.

Wood, A. (1984). *The napping house.* Illustrated by D. Wood. San Diego: Harcourt.

Yee, W. H. (1996). *Mrs. Brown went to town.* New York: Houghton Mifflin.

Yolen, J. (1987). *Owl moon.* Illustrated by J. Schoenherr. New York: Philomel.

Yolen, J., & Teague, M. (2000). *How do dinosaurs say good night?* New York: Blue Sky Press.

6

Leveled Texts for Beginning Readers: A Primer, a Test, and a Quest

James V. Hoffman
Nancy L. Roser
The University of Texas at Austin

Misty Sailors
The University of Texas at San Antonio

The texts used for beginning reading instruction have changed in remarkable ways over the last half of the 20th century. Traditional "Look–Say" basal texts, challenged by literature-based advocates of the 1980s and early 1990s, gave way to literature-based anthologies. Challenged by phonics advocates in the mid-1990s, these "real literature" texts soon yielded to more "decodable" texts (see Hoffman, Sailors, & Patterson, 2002). Caught in the middle of these changes were (and are) the teachers and students who come daily to schools to teach and learn. Teachers must continue to instruct, even in the absence of consensus, and children must continue to become literate, even as adults squabble over the materials and methods to teach them. In this chapter, we offer a perspective on the leveled texts used for beginning reading instruction that attempts to separate the political rhetoric from the research. We focus our discussion specifically on *leveled texts*, texts written and designed with the goal of fostering early reading development. Leveled texts are organized around some sequence or progression of difficulty level for the reader. Traditional basal readers are an example of leveled texts, as are the *little books* and *leveled libraries* that are common in schools today. Our goal is to provide a principled perspective on the texts for beginning readers that can inform and support classroom teachers in their decision making. We hope that this perspective might also inform policymakers as they continue to struggle with issues of quality instruction.

A PRIMER ON LEVELED TEXTS

The instructional needs of beginning readers in America were once served by alphabet letters, syllables, and a prayer—all on a paddle-shaped board covered with transparent horn. Henderson (1990) marveled at how astonishingly complete and effective an instructional text the hornbook was:

> It covers every base that contemporary theory would require and through its application many children learned to read. Even so no serious educator today would be tempted to limit materials of instruction to a single hornbook. (p. 78)

Following the hornbook, most young colonialists would have as their primary reading text *The New England Primer*, with its alphabet and "innovative" couplets (in addition to its syllables, prayers, and catechism):

In Adam's fall,

We sinned all.

Thy life to mend

God's book attend.

With its tiny woodcuts matched to the couplets, and its attempt at rhyme, *The New England Primer* may have done an even *better* job than the hornbook of covering (as Henderson put it) every aspect of contemporary theory.

This tidy tandem of hornbook and *New England Primer* catapulted rather than baby-stepped children toward literacy during the period of our nation's founding. That is, the gaps in reading materials from the basic words and syllables of the hornbook, to the moral and religious platitudes of *The New England Primer* packed in verse, to the ultimate challenge of reading *The Bible* must have been a formidable challenge. When Webster introduced his *Blue-Back Speller*, he provided a bit more of a stile in the pathway from the study of shorter to longer words. And McGuffey, along with the authors of other "progressive" reading series introduced in the mid-1880s, provided still more ladder rungs by introducing reading selections in graded books.

The basal readers that flourished in the first half of the 20th century offered even more carefully sequenced steps designed to support reading progress through the elementary grades. These leveled texts consisted of preprimers, primers, and texts identified with grade levels. Eventually, the adventures of Sally, Dick, and Jane introduced millions of Americans to literacy through the various iterations of the Elson-Gray and the New Basic Readers. Even into the early 1970s, basal texts were crafted to control for difficulty level primarily through the rate of introduction and repetition of key vocabulary. They became the mainstay of American reading instruction, representing the formula for success in teaching reading and a consensus about beginning reading instruction (Chall, 1967).

The confidence surrounding this consensus began to unravel in the second half of the 20th century as both educators and the public gave greater scrutiny to the success of students in schools. Concerns over the progress of the children of ethnic minorities and children from economically disadvantaged homes ushered in a period of rapid change and innovation in instructional materials and methods. Consensus turned into controversy and conflict. The debates over whole language versus phonics, code versus meaning, synthetic versus analytic, top-down versus bottom-up, and literature versus skills raged on in academia, in print journalism, in political arenas, and across communities. (For a more comprehensive description of this historical context, see Hoffman, 2002.)

There has been no shortage of opinions, mandates, and materials for teaching beginning reading. What may be less prevalent are sets of principles or guidelines that teachers can rely on as they make decisions about meeting the instructional needs of their beginning readers. Our stance in this chapter is straightforward: We argue that quality leveled texts are invaluable to teachers in making decisions and delivering instruction to beginning readers. We contend that every classroom serving beginning readers should have access to a rich supply of quality leveled texts. Finally, we suggest that the quality of the leveled texts now available in the marketplace varies enormously, ranging from the outstanding to the appalling. We are less concerned here with the strategies teachers use to match these texts with readers. Neither do we address the instructional support that teachers offer alongside these texts. We are less concerned with the packaging (e.g, whether big books, little books, or anthologies), the labeling (e.g., whether basals, systems, kits, libraries), the formatting (size and contrast of font, location of print on the page, number of pages, etc.), or the arraying of levels (by grade, by letters, by numbers, or by labels). Rather, we are primarily concerned in this chapter with the qualities of the texts themselves. We focus on the selection and inclusion of these "baby-step" texts in the literacy environment. Our goal is to provide teachers with a critical consumer framework they may apply to identify or recognize the qualities of instructional texts constructed or gathered for the purpose of teaching young children to read.

We ground our position in available empirical research. There are gaps in this research base and places where there is much more to learn, but we take considerable guidance from this literature that informs principled decision making.

Compare the excerpts presented in Table 6.1 from Dr. Seuss's (1963) *Hop on Pop* with similar word patterns taken from a 1960s "linguistic" basal program *Let's Read: A Linguistic Approach* (Bloomfield & Barnhart, 1961). Beyond the obvious conclusion that both these texts were expressly designed for beginning readers, there are still other similarities. For example, both texts rely on and even exploit the "-op" rime as a recurring feature. There are also ways in which these texts in their original formats are different (e. g., the variation in fonts, the use of rhyme, the presence or absence of illustrations).

How do we begin to approach the question of quality when it comes to making choices among texts like these to support beginning readers? It is probably not enough to argue, "I know it when I see it." We posit three major principles that teachers should consider in selecting leveled texts for the classroom. Leveled texts for beginners should be inspected and held accountable for their attention to (a) engaging qualities, (b) accessibility, and (c) instructional design.

TABLE 6.1
Comparing the Language of Two Texts Intended for Young Readers

From Hop on Pop by Dr. Seuss	From Let's Read: A Linguistic Approach by Bloomfield and Barnhart
HOP	Hop mop pop sop top
POP	Cop fop lop
	A hop a mop a pop a top
We like to hop.	Sam had pop. Yum, yum!
We like to hop on top of Pop.	Mum got a mop. Ed got a top.
	If Dan can hop, Pat cannot tag him.
STOP	Bob had pop in a cup.
	Did Bob tip it? Yes, Bob did.
You must not	Did Sis hop? Did Sis get a mop?
hop on Pop.	Did Sis mop it up? Did Sis get mad at Bob?
	Sis did not get mad.
	Sis let Bob sip pop.
	Cop hop lop mop sop top
	Cap hap lap map sap tap

THE ENGAGING QUALITIES PRINCIPLE

Leveled texts for beginners should invite readers in through their appealing content, language, and formats. The construct of *engaging* qualities draws on a conception of reading that emphasizes its psychological and social aspects (Guthrie & Alvermann, 1999). Texts with the potential to engage readers intellectually, socially, affectively, and personally have rich appeal in content, language, and format. *Content* refers to what the text offers, and what the author has to say. Does the text develop a character, story line, and/or theme? Does it entertain or inform? Are the ideas worthwhile? Does the text stimulate thinking and response? Is there the potential that many children can "find themselves" in the texts, that is, characters are diverse and situations may be personally, socially, or culturally relevant? *Language* refers to the way in which the author presents the content. Is the language playful, clear, enlisting, fresh? Is the text challenging but appropriate? Is the structure clear? Will beginners find it manageable as well as fun to read and reread? Does it lend itself to oral interpretation? *Format* refers to the visual presentation of the text. Do the illustrations/art enrich and extend the text? Is the layout imaginative and does it enhance the text? Do the illustrations and text work together?

Using the principle of engaging qualities to compare the two examples of reading materials presented in Table 6.1, we argue that the Bloomfield and Barnhart "linguistic" text is nearly devoid of meaning and coherence. The sequence of sentences could confound any reader's attempt to uncover or make sense of its unstructured litany. The absence of appealing illustrations or design leaves readers to their own devices to conjure images that might enhance understanding. There is no joy intended or associated with this text. It lies as flat as will the likely response of its readers. In contrast, the Seuss text is spirited and fanciful. Its rhythms sweep the reader along. *Hop on Pop*, like many good reads intended for young children, does not offer complex characterization or layered themes. Instead, it offers jolly images and fixable dilemmas with a spirit, a playfulness, and a sound that draws the reader in to engage again and again. In summary, the engaging qualities of the Seuss text are far greater than those offered by the "linguistic" text.

THE ACCESSIBILITY PRINCIPLE

Leveled texts for beginners should carefully balance the challenges and demands for skillful decoding with the support of predictable features and text format. The accessibility principle addresses such important questions as: How challenging is the text in terms of the decoding demands it places on the reader?

How supportive is the text of a reader's word recognition through its provision of predictable features? How does the print array make reading easier or more difficult? The construct of accessibility seems tied to three factors: decodabilty, predictability, and legibility. *Decodability* is concerned with text at the word level and reflects the degree to which individual words are drawn from a corpus of highly frequent words as well as representative of simple or regular spelling/sounding patterns. The evidence for the critical role of decodability in ensuring that texts are accessible for developing readers seems irrefutable. *Predictability* refers to the surrounding language patterns and contextual support for the identification of challenging words (e.g., rhyme, repeated phrases, predictable language structures—and more broadly, picture clues). The evidence for the substantial contribution of predictability to word recognition and fluency is also irrefutable (Goodman, 1984), despite the fact that "context" has been tainted by accusations that children have been taught over-reliance on its use (to the detriment of their ability to decode). Claims that context exerts less influence on word recognition, though, are referenced almost entirely to studies of skilled readers. The evidence that "poor" readers who struggle with decoding attempt to use context for support is less a trait of the struggling reader's process than it is a failure to provide that reader with accessible text. No aspect of word recognition should be abandoned simply because struggling readers do not use it as effectively as more skillful readers. Any principle for selecting accessible texts for beginners is not primarily concerned with skilled readers. Rather, our principles address developing readers, and for them, context is an important source of support for literacy development. Decodability and predictability work together for readers within a text. The balance of these factors helps determine the accessibility of the text.

Finally, the attributes of the text's *legibility* may support or inhibit its accessibility for beginners. This is an area in which research has been lacking. We are curious about the basis for highly prescriptive mandates for the formats of beginners' books. For example, some criteria for leveling books for beginners specify the exact location of text on the page (most often threading across the bottom), speak with certainty about the necessity for uniform font sizes, indicate the particular numbers of words per page, and make other legibility specifications that seem to have little documentation or supporting research. In early studies of legibility, Tinker (1965) investigated accessible font sizes, ink shades, and ink/paper contrast, all in an effort to understand legibility and perception. We know of no recent efforts, however, to test the prescriptions for leveled texts with its users, beginning readers. We wonder if prescriptions born of consensus rather than evidence restrict creative design considerations that would leave such innovative and best-loved authors and illustrators of books for beginners as Bill Martin, Jr., Denise Fleming, Keith Baker, and Lois Ehlert floundering under the constraints. Before a field goes too far in asserting and specifying what features and formats confuse or support young readers, we need more research.

In comparing the Seuss and the Bloomfield & Barnhart texts for accessibility, we argue that the decodability of the words seems comparable for the two selections. The "-op" rime is frequently repeated in both. Both rely on a few function words. In each, single syllables and consonant–vowel–consonant patterns dominate. However, the two texts contrast in the predictable structures that can support reading. *Hop on Pop* builds on rhyme, rhythm, and repetitions, whereas the linguistic text does not. Seuss provides illustrations that support; the linguistic text does not (arguing that readers can be distracted by illustrations). Seuss offers text that is clever in construction and layout, an engaging factor, as well as a print size that seems easily accessible to young readers. In summary, the accessibility of the Seuss text is greater than the Bloomfield text.

THE INSTRUCTIONAL DESIGN PRINCIPLE

Leveled texts for beginners should reflect an underlying instructional design principle that bridges one text to the next, or one level of text to the next level. Furthermore, the instructional design principle must be compatible with the goals and purposes of the instructional program in which the leveled texts will be used.

Instructional design addresses the issue of how the leveled texts reflect an underlying philosophical base and instructional plan for helping young readers become skillful readers. Clymer (1963/1996), through his examination of the phonics "rules" that were taught in beginning reading programs, was one of the first to introduce the notion of "utility" or usefulness into our professional conversations. His work helped us think about the match between what children are taught about the rules of written language contrasted with the patterns they encounter in the texts they read. Certainly, the work of Beck (1981), Juel (1994), and Stein, Johnson, and Gutlohn (1999), as well as recent mandates for decodable texts for beginners in Texas, California, and other states, reflect a concern for utility that is tied to instructional design.

Attention to the close match between the skills taught and the words read, however, is not the only perspective we could adopt in considering utility. For example, we could emphasize the value of repetition and frequency over regularity, taking a *sight word* or memorization stance. An attention to selection and repetition of high frequency words was at the heart of the instructional design for the "Look–Say" basal era.

Still another view can be found in the work of Hiebert (1998), who argued for the importance of beginners' texts that provide practice with words and within-word patterns referenced to a developmental perspective. According to Hiebert, text that has high utility for beginning readers provides for repeated exposure to these patterns, beginning with the simplest, most common, and most regular patterns and building toward the more complex, that is, less common, and less regular words. Instantiations of recurring words and spelling patterns in a variety of contexts lead to automatic recognition.

Skill and strategy instruction, as offered, for example, in Reading Recovery, is yet another interpretation of instructional design and leveling. In focused programs such as these, the teacher selects texts that can be used easily and efficiently to guide particular children to meaning (Fountas & Pinnell, 1999). The arrangement, introduction, and repetition of the leveled texts reveal an instructional design.

There are likely other perspectives one could take in advocating for instructional designs that map texts with teaching. The key to evaluating leveled texts from this perspective is to examine the underlying philosophy of the instruction being offered to children as it is manifested in what students are offered to read. For example, why are certain word level features presented at a particular point in a reader's development? How does the leveling of the text reflect and support the instructional emphasis? How do the texts match with what the children are trying to accomplish? The exploration of these questions should not stop with superficial "noticings." Rather, deep inspection of the underlying instructional design may be necessary to appreciate all aspects of leveled text quality. To make informed judgments about the value of an instructional design feature, then, requires considerations of the goals, perspectives, and consequences of reading experiences for particular readers.

To apply this broadened perspective to an inspection of Bloomfield and Barnhart's *Let's Read* linguistic series reveals an instructional design that features repeated practice with carefully introduced rhyme patterns and increasingly complex internal words structures. There is no explicit phonics instruction or sound isolation, and comprehension and thought are actively discouraged in this instructional design. Despite the low engaging qualities of the Bloomfield and Barnhart text and the problems associated with accessibility, the segment is consistent and congruent in its representation of the instructional design (repeated practice with rhyme/word family patterns). In contrast, it could be argued that the Seuss text, with no explicit instructional design features or progression of difficulty across other books in this series, is not strong in this area. Looking across the various *I Can Read Books* associated with Dr. Seuss, there is little sense of sequencing or even an attempt at careful leveling.

Our point in applying the principles of engaging qualities, accessibility, and instructional design to these two texts is not to prove Seuss better for beginning readers than Bloomfield and Barnhart, but rather to argue that a careful

analysis of any leveled texts must become the important basis for teacher decision-making regarding use.

A TEST

We have offered a "three-principled" view of leveled texts that stands in stark
contrast with some of the extreme positions taken in the recent "whole language" versus "phonics" debates. We have offered a position that conflicts as
well with many of the current mandates regarding texts for beginning readers.
To clarify further our own position on leveled texts, and in the spirit of inviting
you into the conversation, we constructed a "true–false test" that explores current issues. In constructing this test, we compiled (and sometimes constructed)
a series of statements that have appeared in the professional and popular literature surrounding the texts for beginning reading. Examine your own notions by
identifying the following statements as true or false. Our responses and comments follow each statement.

1. *Leveled texts are contrived. You can't expect both attention to skills and good literature.* False, you can. It is possible to have leveled texts that are accessible, engaging, and reflective of an instructional plan. Trends over the past two decades
suggest falsely that these are antithetical constructs. Even though decodability
appeared to decline when engaging qualities increased in the literature-based
series published in 1993, and engaging qualities seemed to diminish when
decodability increased in the 2000 basals (Hoffman et al., 2002), this may simply be a case of publishers responding to shortsighted, simplistic mandates. In
examining the Texas adoption of 2000, Hoffman and his colleagues (2002)
found texts that were high on instructional design, showing a high degree of
consistency between the skills taught and the words encountered, and yet low
in accessibility. Yet, there were also highly engaging texts that were high in both
accessibility and instructional design.

2. *Beginning readers should not be encouraged to use context to recognize words.*
False, they should. Our conception of leveled texts rests in part on the notion
that the decoding demands of the text should be balanced with support features
that encourage the use of the context to support recognition. All readers use
context as they are developing automaticity and fluency. Context may become
less necessary as a support for word recognition as readers reach higher levels of
automaticity and fluency, but this is not typically the case for beginners.

3. *Basals are bad, bad, bad.* False. Basals are neither good nor bad. Basals are an organizational plan, and they continue to evolve in response to market demands.
Innovations in education seem to require a demonizing of the opposition. To advocate for the use of quality literature in beginning reading meant bashing basals

generally rather than criticizing specifically. Some basal programs do offer leveled texts for students that meet the criteria for quality we are proposing. Just because these texts are associated with a particular organizational scheme does not diminish their potential value for beginners. We argue for the need to apply the same set of lenses and principles presented here to evaluate any leveled text.

4. *Leveled texts means labeled readers.* False. No students should be labeled by the leveling value assigned to a text they are reading. The consequences of labeling, ability grouping, and tracking of students are well known, and they are mostly negative. Instead of a one-level moniker ("she's a 16"), the same reader may require different levels of "text fit" for different purposes. For example, a child developing fluency may be zooming through many independent level texts, but while developing word recognition strategies, the same reader may be working in more challenging texts.

5. *A good readability formula can be used to scientifically determine the level of a text.* False. Readability formulas are notoriously flawed in providing useful estimates of the success a student will have with a text. Much of the research with these formulas suggests that they are reliable within an error range of plus or minus a year. This broad estimate is not helpful to a teacher when other tools are available. Furthermore, readability formulas tend to focus only on those factors that challenge the reader, such as vocabulary load, rather than the elements that might support the reader, such as predictable structures.

6. *The consumer (teacher) does not shape the market. The marketplace shapes the teacher.* False. Publishers are very responsive to shifts in the marketplace when the marketplace forces are free to operate. There is ample evidence that publishers are willing to provide the quality of product demanded by the consumer. If the standards for quality shift, the publishers seem to respond with text that matches the demand.

7. *You can legislate quality leveled texts.* False. Here again, the evidence is clear from past experience. Efforts by policymakers to mandate improvements in reading texts have failed to produce texts that are effective in the classroom. Sometimes it becomes a matter of policy and legislation misunderstanding good ideas, as with the zeal with which literature anthologies were interpreted in 1990s. Under a strict mandate to publishers to offer only prereleased tradebooks, the quality of the literature rose, but the accessibility waned. We have evidence for the shortcomings of mandates again in the early 2000s when policy statements requiring "engaging and decodable" texts specified what standards for "decodable" were to be, but failed to interpret "engaging." As a result, the texts have been strained.

8. *Quality leveled texts are easy to find.* False. The proliferation of big books and little books produced over the past decade might suggest a wealth of material

from which to choose. The fact is that the quality varies enormously. Too many of these texts are being produced today following simplistic formulas (e.g., number of lines on a page, text-wrapping patterns) that give them "the look" of texts for beginners. Yet, closer inspection for their engaging qualities, accessibility, and instructional design reveals many for what they are: poor imitations of quality texts.

9. *We need to level texts all the way through the elementary grades and perhaps even higher.* False. Although our focus in this chapter has been on beginning reading and teaching beginning reading, we cannot ignore the fact that there are text-leveling systems sweeping the country that promote the use of text–reader matching through the elementary grades and even into secondary schools. Many of these programs are computer-based in their assessment of reading abilities and in the assessment of text difficulty. We are troubled by the fact that such systems take decisions out of the hands of teachers and, more importantly, out of the hands of readers when it comes to choices and options in the selection of reading materials as readers become more proficient. The careful kind of leveling that *may* be necessary to support the early steps in reading should not be taken as a license or a mandate to assign all texts to all children.

10. *Quality leveled texts are an answer to all the challenges we face in reading instruction.* False. A good supply of quality leveled texts in a classroom can make a significant contribution to an instructional program, but are only a part of a large array of texts that should be available for browsing, listening to, reading, talking about, and learning from. The impact of quality leveled texts will always rest on the skilled and timely use of these texts with beginning readers.

11. *There is scientific evidence that "decodable" texts work best in promoting reading achievement.* False. There is not yet scientific evidence in the research literature for this assertion. Not only is this assertion a blatant overstatement, but its widespread acceptance has reduced research and debate over the qualities of leveled text that may be important to consider. The traits of quality leveled texts are too complex ever to be reduced to a single factor such as "decodability."

12. *All beginning readers need leveled texts.* False. Many readers are able to make the transition from emergent to fluent reading without the "baby steps" of leveled texts. However, all teachers of beginners can make use of quality leveled texts as a resource in their classroom. The decisions teachers make are shaped, in part, by the tools they have available. If we subscribe to the position that teachers must be flexible and responsive to all students, then it is important to provide the full range of texts/tools that give instructional options. It is simply wrongheaded to argue that *all* students must work through all levels of a program even if they do not need them.

A QUEST

Leveled texts have an important place in classrooms serving beginning readers. What was largely intuitive in texts like *The New England Primer* has been both validated and refined through research. We know a great deal today about the ways in which the features of leveled texts work to support beginning readers. Recognizing this, we believe firmly that the place of leveled texts in the teaching of beginning reading is one of those arenas in which practice is ahead of research. There are primary grade teachers across this country who have risen to the challenge of using leveled texts in their classrooms. These teachers assess and teach their students using collections of leveled books in combination with trade books and other texts to promote reading achievement. These teachers negotiate and adapt basal programs in ways that fit the needs of their students. These teachers choose texts carefully and do not simply accept mandated texts as appropriate. It is time for the research community to step into these classrooms and study effective practices. It is time for the research community to document and study the variations in practice in ways that contribute to our scientific knowledge base on effective teaching. Policymakers and publishers must actively serve effective teachers as they work to help children make sense of and take pleasure in literacy learning.

REFERENCES

Beck, I. L. (1981). Reading problems and instructional practices. In G. E. MacKinnon & T. G. Waller (Eds.), *Reading research: Advances in theory and practice* (Vol. 2, pp. 53–95). New York: Academic Press.

Bloomfield, L., & Barnhart, C. (1961). *Let's Read. A Linguistic Approach.* Detroit: Wayne State University Press.

Chall, J. (1967). *Learning to Read: The Great Debate.* Fort Worth, TX: Harcourt Brace.

Clymer, T. (1963/1996). The utility of phonics generalizations in the primary grades. *The Reading Teacher, 50,* 182–187. (Original work published 1963)

Fountas, I. C., & Pinnell, G. S. (1999). *Matching books to readers: Using leveled books in guided reading, K–3.* Portsmouth, NH: Heinemann.

Goodman, K. S. (1984). On the wording of texts: A study of intra-text word frequency. *Research in the Teaching of English, 18,* 119–145.

Guthrie, J. T., & Alvermann, D. E. (1999). *Engaged reading: Processes, practices, and policy implications.* New York: Teachers College Press.

Henderson, E. H. (1990). *Teaching spelling* (2nd ed). Boston: Houghton Mifflin.

Hiebert, E. H. (1998). *Early literacy instruction.* Fort Worth, TX: Harcourt Brace.

Hoffman, J. V. (2002). Words (on words in leveled text for beginning readers). *National Reading Conference Yearbook, 51,* pp. 59–81. Oak Creek, WI: National Reading Conference.

Hoffman, J. V., Sailors, M., & Patterson, E. U. (2002). Decodable text for beginning reading instruction: The Year 2000 basals. *Journal of Literacy Research, 34*(3), 269–298.

Juel, C. (1994). *Learning to read and write in one elementary school.* New York: Springer-Verlag.

Seuss, Dr. (1963). *Hop on Pop.* New York: Beginner Books.

Stein, M., Johnson, B., & Gutlohn, L. (1999). Analyzing beginning reading programs: The relationship between decoding instruction and text. *Journal of Remedial and Special Education, 20,* 275–287.

Tinker, M. A. (1965). *The basis for effective reading.* Minneapolis, University of Minnesota Press.

7

Nonfiction Texts
for Young Readers

Nell K. Duke
Cathy Tower
Michigan State University

Meat-eating plants, all kinds of bugs, crafts to make and do, the life of E. B. White, the eruption of Mt. St. Helens, science experiments for all ages, colors, numbers, shapes, why people sneeze … This chapter concerns nonfiction texts for young readers. In the sections that follow, we begin by addressing some preliminaries: (a) should we even be talking about nonfiction for *young* readers? (b) what is nonfiction? (c) recognition of quality nonfiction, and (d) finding nonfiction texts for *young* readers. We then consider five types of nonfiction in more depth: informational text, concept books, biography, procedural text, and reference materials. For each, we discuss the purpose and some key features of this type of text, research on young readers' interactions with this type of text, and some considerations in selecting these texts for use in the classroom. Throughout our discussion, we reference some outstanding nonfiction texts for young readers and suggest resources for finding more.

PRELIMINARIES

Should We Even Be Talking About Nonfiction for *Young* Readers?

With some exceptions, in the history of American reading instruction nonfiction has had little place among texts for young readers (Duke, Bennett-Armistead, & Roberts, 2002, 2003). Many theorists and educators apparently believe that only

narrative, and in particular fictional narrative, is appropriate for our youngest learners. Indeed, a common pattern in American schools has been to wait until fourth
grade before providing children with significant opportunities to read to learn—a
common purpose for nonfiction—not just learn to read (Chall, 1983). One study
found that first-grade students were provided with an average of only 3.6 minutes
per day of experience with informational text forms throughout the entire school
day (Duke, 2000), and less than that with many other key nonfiction genres.

So is the banishment of nonfiction from preprimary and primary-grade classrooms well justified? More than a decade of research now answers that question
with a resounding no (e.g., Newkirk, 1989; Pappas, 1993; Read, 2001; Tower,
2002; see Duke, 2003, for a review). At least with respect to informational text,
perhaps the prototypic form of nonfiction and the form on which there has been
the most research, young children are highly capable. Many young children also
show a high degree of interest in nonfiction texts (e.g., Kletzien, 1999), suggesting not only that they *can* interact successfully with such text, but that they
should be given opportunities to do so (e.g., Caswell & Duke, 1998).

Perhaps most noteworthy is research suggesting important educational opportunities presented by nonfiction texts for young readers. Some research indicates
that informational texts, for example, can play a role in building children's knowledge about the world around them (e.g., Duke & Kays, 1998), and certainly concept books, such as those about letters, numbers, and shapes, have that potential
as well (Dowd & Lyday, 1991). Dreher (2000) built an argument that informational and other nonfiction texts have promise for developing vocabulary, an important area for growth, particularly for children who struggle with beginning
reading (Snow, Burns, & Griffin, 1998). Research by Smolkin and Donovan
(2000) suggested that informational texts provide a particularly important locus
for building comprehension skills. A teacher they studied focused more on comprehension in the context of informational texts than she did in the context of
storybook reading. There is even research suggesting that when parents read informational texts to their young children, they are more likely than with other
forms of text to discuss text content, ask questions, and introduce vocabulary
(Lennox, 1995; Pellegrini, Perlmutter, Galda, & Brody, 1990). Thus although research on a wider variety of nonfiction genres is needed, and unanswered questions with respect to even informational text remain, all indications are that we
should indeed be talking about nonfiction texts for even young learners.

What Is Nonfiction?

So what is nonfiction? In its most basic sense, nonfiction is anything that is not
fiction, that is, anything that is true or at least promotes the expectation of being

true (an informational text that contains some error of fact would nonetheless be considered by most people to be nonfiction). However, by that definition nonfiction could include texts as functional as bus schedules, menus, coupons, or shopping lists. So definitions of nonfiction often specify that nonfiction is *literature* of fact (e.g., Longman, 1984), thus eliminating texts, such as bus schedules, that are true but that would not be considered literature. By this narrower definition, and depending on how one defines literature, nonfiction includes such texts as "true stories," biographies, autobiographies and profiles, informational and some narrative-informational texts, diaries and journals, persuasive texts of various kinds, "how to" or procedural texts, and others. In this chapter, we discuss reference books such as dictionaries, encyclopedias, and field guides as well, although many would not consider those to be literature.

Nonfiction is sometimes referred to as a genre (e.g., Bamford & Kristo, 2000). However, whether you define genre by specific linguistic features of a text, or by purpose and context of text use (Miller, 1984), nonfiction is not a genre but rather is comprised of a number of different genres, such as those previously listed. In this chapter, we discuss several nonfiction genres, but by no means all that exist. We refer to both purpose and linguistic features of several genres, but do not attempt to provide an exhaustive account of either, or take up in any depth the question of whether there are narrower genres or subgenres within categories such as biography or informational text. Our position is that it is far more important to adhere to general principles of variety, quality, and appropriateness in texts for young readers than to be definitive or exact in categorizing these texts.

Recognition of Quality Nonfiction

There is no question that the latter decades of the 20th century saw an explosion in the publication of nonfiction texts for children. Where once there were few quality and engaging nonfiction texts for children, there are now countless such texts, many of high quality and great interest (Freeman & Person, 1992). Although there remains a need for more quality nonfiction texts that very early readers can read themselves, the situation today is certainly vastly improved over decades ago.

Appropriate to its more prominent role in the world of children's literature, there are now more awards for nonfiction for children than ever before. For example, the Orbis Pictus Award for nonfiction, begun in 1990, is bestowed each year by a committee of the National Council of Teachers of English (www.ncte.org). The committee also identifies "honor books" and "recommended titles." A recent book published by NCTE is devoted to the first 10 years of the award (Zarnowski, Kerper, & Jensen, 2001). The Washington Post/Children's Book

Guild also presents an award to an author or author-illustrator whose total work has contributed significantly to the quality of nonfiction for children (www.childrensbookguild.org). Several other publications and organizations now bestow awards for nonfiction (see Duke & Bennett-Armistead, 2003).

Awards for titles related to science and social studies also often go to nonfiction. For example, the National Council for the Social Studies presents the Carter G. Woodson Book Award for outstanding social science books for young readers that deal sensitively and accurately with topics related to ethnic minorities (www.ncss.org). The New York Academy of Sciences bestows the Children's Science Book Awards for books of high quality in the field of science for children (www.nyas.org). Nonfiction can also be among the awardees of more general awards such as the Golden Kite Award of the Society of Children's Book Writers (www.scbwi.org) and even the Newbery, which in 1988 was awarded to the nonfiction work *Lincoln: A Photobiography* (Freedman, 1987).

There are a number of other organizations and publications that regularly print reviews of nonfiction titles for children. These include:

- *Appraisal: Science Books for Young People*, published four times a year by the Children's Science Book Review Committee,
- *Book Links*, published six times a year by the American Library Association (http://www.ala.org/BookLinks),
- *Booklist*, published twice a month by the American Library Association (http://www.ala.org/Booklist),
- *Horn Book Magazine*, published six times a year (www.hbook.com),
- *School Library Journal*, published monthly (www.slj.com),
- *Science and Children*, published by the National Science Teachers Association includes a monthly column that reviews books and nonprint materials (www.nsta.org), and
- *Science Books and Films*, published four times a year by the American Association for the Advancement of Science (www.aaas.org).

There are also books that list recommended nonfiction titles for children, such as:

- *Beyond fact: Nonfiction for children and young people* (Carr, 1982),
- *Checking out nonfiction K–8: Good choices for best learning* (Bamford & Kristo, 2000),
- Children's literature textbooks, such as *Children's Literature in the Elementary School* (Huck, Hepler, & Hickman, 1993) and *Through the Eyes of a Child: An Introduction to Children's Literature* (Norton, 1995),

- *Eyeopeners: How to choose and use children's books about real people, places, and things* (Kobrin, 1988),
- *Eyeopeners II: Children's books to answer children's questions about the world around them* (Kobrin, 1995),
- *Making facts come alive: Choosing quality nonfiction literature K–8* (Bamford & Kristo, 1998), and
- *Using nonfiction trade books in the elementary classroom from ants to zeppelins* (Freeman & Person, 1992).

Finding Nonfiction Texts for *Young* Readers

Unfortunately for the teacher of young readers, none of the resources or awards listed are specifically devoted to nonfiction for very young readers. On the contrary, the vast majority of award-winners and other recommended titles are more appropriate for upper elementary students and beyond. Only a fraction are appropriate for reading aloud to children before third grade, and even fewer could be used in guided or independent reading in the early grades. This is not to say, of course, that there is no quality nonfiction appropriate for young readers to read themselves, simply that it is less common and, perhaps, more difficult to find.

For the most part, the teacher committed to using nonfiction will need to sift through resources like the ones listed earlier to find those texts that are appropriate for young readers. Several of the resources do specify ages or grade levels, and this can help, although often these refer to the text's appropriateness for reading aloud to this age group, rather than whether they are likely to be readable by the children themselves. Some books and articles focused on strategies for developing young readers' nonfiction literacy do list some books that might be used in that effort. For example, Duthie's (1996) book *True Stories: Nonfiction Literacy in the Primary Classroom* includes reference to a number of nonfiction titles, including many that her first-grade students read on their own (and see Table 7.1 of this chapter for our own list of some such titles). Stead's (2002) book *Is That a Fact? Teaching Nonfiction Writing K–3* also contains several lists of nonfiction books at Reading Recovery Levels 1 through 20 and above. Notably, many of the books Stead lists are not what would be considered trade books. Rather, they are books written specifically for the school setting, often as part of a reading series designed for guided and independent reading. There are a growing number of such book sets focused on nonfiction (see Table 7.2 for lists of some such sets). Although naturally these series, and individual titles within them, vary in quality, they do provide a substantial source of nonfiction materials for young readers.

TABLE 7.1
Fifteen Nonfiction Trade Books for Guided or Independent Reading in Grades K and 1

Alphabet City by Stephen Johnson (1995)

Buzz! A Book About Insects by Melvin Berger (2000)

Diggers and Dump Trucks by Angela Royston (1991)

Dinosaurs, Dinosaurs by Byron Barton (1989)

Do Monkey's Tweet? By Melanie Walsh (1997)

I Am Rosa Parks by Rosa Parks and Jim Haskins (1997)

I Read Signs by Tana Hoban (1983)

Let's Find Out About Ice Cream by Mary Reid (1996)

Let's Visit Some Islands by Allan Fowler (1998)

Nature for Fun Projects by Sally Hewitt (2000) (selected procedures from)

On the Go by Ann Morris (1990)

Pretend soup and other real recipes: A cookbook for preschoolers and up by Mollie Katzen and Ann Henderson (1994) (selected procedures from)

Starfish by Edith Thacher Hurd (1990)

Wonderful Worms by Linda Glaser (1992)

A Girl Named Helen Keller by Margo Lundell (1995)

TYPES OF NONFICTION

Thus far we have established that it is appropriate to talk about nonfiction texts even for young readers—young children can interact successfully with nonfiction texts if given the opportunity, and there are nonfiction texts available for young children. We have identified some resources for locating quality nonfiction and we have attempted to define nonfiction. By our definition nonfiction is not a single genre but rather comprises many genres. In this section we discuss five types of nonfiction: informational texts, concept books, biography, procedural texts, and reference materials. These are certainly not all the types of nonfiction that exist, but they are some types that may play particularly important roles in early literacy instruction.

Informational Texts

We define informational texts as texts intended to convey information about the natural and social world, typically from someone presumed to know that in-

TABLE 7.2
*Fifteen School-Directed Nonfiction Series Written for Guided
or Independent Reading in Grades K and 1*

Capstone Press' *Pebble Books* series (www.capstone-press.com)

Dominie Press' *Factivity Series* (www.dominie.com)

Mondo Publishing's *BookShop* series (www.mondopub.com) (certain theme and genre packs)

National Geographic *Windows on Literacy* (www.NationalGeographic.com)

Newbridge *Discovery Links Science and Discovery Links Social Studies* (www.newbridgeonline.com)

Rigby Educational Publishers *Discovery World* and *PM Nonfiction* series (www.rigby.com)

Scholastic *Science Emergent Readers* and Social Studies Emergent Readers (www.Scholastic.com)

Shortland Publications' *Storyteller Nonfiction* (www.WrightGroup.com)

Sundance's *Little Green Readers* (www. Sundancepub.com)

The Wright Group's *Twig Books* Nonfiction and *Wonder World* (www.WrightGroup.com)

Benchmark Education *Early Childhood Connection Nonfiction* series (www.benchmarkeducation.com)

Please note: Exclusion or inclusion on this list is not intended to be a judgment of quality. For an expanded list See Duke and Bennett-Armistead, 2003.

formation to someone presumed not to (Duke, 2000). Perhaps the key feature of informational texts as we define them is a generalizing quality: talking about whole classes of things and in a timeless way (e.g., *Fish live in water*) as opposed to talking about one specific thing and in a timed way (e.g., *That goldfish lives in my fishbowl* or *One day the fish swam too far*). Other common features of informational texts include presentation and repetition of a topic or theme, descriptions of attributes and characteristic events, comparative/contrastive and classifactory structures, technical vocabulary, realistic illustrations or photographs, labels and captions, navigational aids such as indexes, page numbers, and headings, and various graphical devices, such as diagrams, tables, and charts (Duke & Kays, 1998; Purcell-Gates & Duke, 2001; Pappas, 1986, 1987). These features differ markedly from those of many other genres, including fictional and personal narrative. Learning to understand, use, and appreciate these features may be a challenge, but, as discussed earlier in this chapter, it also accrues many benefits for even young readers.

There is a growing body of research on how young readers learn to interact with informational texts and what we can do to aid them in that process. Based on research available at this point (see Duke, Bennett-Armistead, & Roberts, 2002, 2003; and Duke & Bennett-Armistead, 2003, for reviews), it appears that informational texts can be fruitfully incorporated into several instructional routines in primary-grade classrooms. Studies suggest that read-aloud of informational text teaches young children both language and content of informational text. Studies show that young children can write informational and emergent informational forms if given the opportunity. Some work suggests that young children can engage in research using informational text as one source of data. Other studies indicate that young children can engage in discussion of and response to informational texts, for example by making connections between different informational texts and their own personal experiences. And encouragingly, given the many potential benefits of informational text for young readers (see our first section discussing whether young readers should be exposed to nonfiction), recent research suggests that teachers can promote independent reading of nonfiction texts by making such texts a significant portion of the books available to young readers in their classroom libraries and by including these books in their read-aloud routines (Dreher & Dromsky, 2000).

There are many factors to consider when selecting informational texts for young readers (in addition to the kinds of general readability issues one would consider with reference to any text for young readers). Some evaluate the content of the book, including the degree to which that content is actually informative. In some cases, in an effort to make a text easier for young readers, authors provide very little actual information. This is a violation of the purpose of the genre and poses the danger of turning the child off of (or at least failing to turn the child on to) this genre of text. Good informational texts for young readers convey at least some information that children may not already know, but would like to. Others factors to consider when selecting informational texts for young readers regard accuracy and perspective. Authors and teachers alike have a responsibility to provide children with information that they believe to be accurate, or to discuss with them when content is inaccurate, suspect, or unknown. At the same time, many believe that no text, including informational text, is without perspective. Helping students to recognize the author's perspective is an important part of teaching reading, in the strong sense of that word. Another set of factors to consider in selecting informational texts regards the clarity of the text. As we well know from our own experiences attempting to learn from text, informational texts can vary tremendously in their level of clarity. Carefully chosen explicit language, well-designed informative graphics, and truly supportive navigational devices are all characteristic of high quality informational text. A fourth set of factors to consider in selecting informational text relates to the text's appeal. Gone are the days when nearly all of the informational texts available for young children were dry and monochromatic. With such a wide array of informational texts available today, there is little excuse for overlooking issues of appeal. And importantly, what appeals to one child may not appeal to another, underscoring the need to consider not only the text, but the reader, when selecting informational texts, or any texts, for young readers.

Fortunately, more so than with other genres of nonfiction discussed in this chapter, there are many resources that help with evaluating the quality of informational texts, including those for young readers. Perhaps most notable are those resources in which subject matter specialists participate in evaluating the quality of the informational texts. These specialists bring their expertise to bear on assessing the accuracy and perspective of the text in ways that those of us without such expertise cannot. At the same time, it is important to bear in mind that such reviewers may not be as attuned as the teacher of young children to the constraints posed by young readers' still limited literacy skills. Meeting the demands of both readability and content is indeed a challenge in evaluating as well as creating informational texts for young readers.

Concept Books

The term *concept books* generally refers to a broad array of texts that have in common the purpose of introducing fundamental yet abstract concepts to young children. Common topics for concept books include numbers, letters, shapes, and colors. In some cases, these topics are addressed in such a way as to have many features of informational text, such as in the book *Let's Look at Shapes* (Lorenz Books, 1996) that includes prototypical informational book language like "A triangle has three straight sides." In other cases, the topics are addressed without generalization, as in the book *Shapes Galore* (Dorling Kindersley, 2000) that includes the name of a shape, and pictures and names of individual items with that shape, but does not describe the shape or talk in any general way about that shape or objects of that shape. Concept books can even be largely fiction, as in the book *Miss Spider's ABC* (Kirk, 2000), in which "Ants await," "Bumblebees blow balloons," and so on, until all are gathered for "Surprise!" Miss Spider's birthday. Clearly, concept books are a broad and diverse category. For this reason, it is difficult to talk with much specificity about features of concept books. One characteristic that does prove true of many concept books is that they carry a great deal of information in their illustra-tions—a book about colors, for example, must rely on the illustrations to con-vey much of the meaning. The structure of concept books is often what Newkirk (1989) simply called "the list," in which an overall topic or category is given, perhaps through the title, and then the remainder of the text presents instantiations or examples of that topic or category. For the young reader, comprehending concept books involves recognizing and understanding the larger category or concept depicted, as well as decoding and comprehending the text on a more micro-level. In essence, this is both a challenge and a bene-fit of concept books for young readers.

We are aware of no research on whether or how young children come to un-derstand concept books as a genre. One simply anecdotal observation we might offer is that concept books seem to have promise in fostering reading–writing connections among primary-grade children. We have several times seen teach-ers reading aloud a concept book, or series of concept books, and then leading students to create class or individual concept books based on that model. Children seem to respond well to this sort of literacy activity, perhaps because of the built-in structure that the concept books afford. Indeed, Yopp and Yopp (2000) suggested having students create their own concept books as a good af-ter-reading activity. They show pages of an alphabet book one first grader cre-ated after hearing *Eating the Alphabet: Fruits and Vegetables from A to Z* (Ehlert, 1989) read aloud. Pages included "A is for apple," "E is for egg," and so on. Ac-tivities such as this may help encourage children to revisit the text read to them, and become attuned to features and patterns of the text. Writing the books for a real audience, such as younger siblings or schoolmates, will likely enhance the motivational dimension of the writing.

Because concept books comprise such a broad category, it is difficult to pro-vide general guidelines for selecting them. As with any texts, but perhaps even more so with this genre, it is important to have in mind your purpose or purposes for the text when selecting it. If your intention is really primarily to teach a con-cept, you will want to select a book that seems largely focused on that concept, rather than using that concept primarily as a device. If, on the other hand, you are equally or more interested in some other benefit of the concept book, then your selection would look different. For example, *The Spice Alphabet Book: Herbs, Spices, and Other Natural Flavors* (Pallotta, 1994) does show an upper and lower case version of each letter of the alphabet and names a spice beginning with each letter, but with text like the following, the primary intention of the book does not seem to be to teach alphabet knowledge, but rather to convey in-formation about spices:

A *a*

A is for Anise. Anise is a spice that comes from a seed and tastes like licorice. *What is a spice?*

A spice is the section of a plant that has the flavor. The spice flavor could be from the bark, the stem, the flower, the bean, the nut, the oil, the sap, the seed, the leaf, or the root of the plant.

Even simpler concept books may have dual purposes. For example, the book *Museum Numbers* (Voss, 1993) seems to be designed to teach or reinforce number knowledge, with numbers one through ten displayed prominently throughout the book along with clear line drawings of that number of objects (e.g., nine birds). At the same time, for each number there is a work of art in which that same number of objects is depicted (e.g., for nine birds there is a photograph of a Japanese robe with nine flying cranes embroidered on it). It appears that the purpose of this book is not only to teach or reinforce number concepts but also to expose children to works of art. Books like these help underscore the need to attend to purpose when selecting concept books for use with young readers.

Biography

Another important genre of nonfiction is biography. Fundamentally, the purpose of biography is to convey information about an individual's life and experiences. Biographies for children, as for adults, are often, although not always (cf. Fritz, 1981), written about people who have overcome seemingly great obstacles and made significant contributions to society. We do not know of any formal analyses of common features of biographies for children, but some that seem likely include largely chronological organization, multiple narrative passages focused on particular events or experiences in the person's life, third person and past tense, and some explanation, either implicit or explicit, of the importance of the person's life for society today. Young readers learning to read biography will have to grapple with all of those features to learn how to learn about another's life, and to connect what they learn to larger social and historical issues or principles. In turn, experience with these books can provide many important lessons for students. For example, reading biographies may help students develop empathy by demonstrating that other people also have needs much like theirs; they can expose children to other cultures, societies, and religions, thus helping them to understand and appreciate diversity in its many forms; and they can help children to understand historical and other content knowledge in a way that is often more intimate and memorable than through textbooks alone (Huck, Hepler, & Hickman, 1993).

To our knowledge, there has been no research on how young children develop the ability to read or write biography, or even to understand biography read to them. Duthie (1996) did provide an account of how she worked with first-grade students around biography. She explained that she structured lessons that would "help children begin to recognize the term 'biography' and associate it with interesting, informative books about human experience" (p. 87). In one such lesson, after identifying several biographies the children had read (or heard read aloud), she focused on a biography of Schubert (Gofstein, 1989), and a tape of a few of Schubert's waltzes. (One student commented that the waltzes sounded like music she had heard at ice skating, and this inspired Duthie to pass out paper plates on which the students could "skate" on the tile floor to the waltzes.) After many such experiences, Duthie guided her students as they generated a list of characteristics that describe biographies and engaged in writing biographies themselves. By combining wide reading of biographies with engaging experiences and explicit discussion of the genre, Duthie was able to help her students recognize and understand this nonfiction genre.

In selecting biographies to share with young readers, there are a number of criteria to consider. Five that seem particularly important are: accuracy and authenticity, aspects of the subject, style, characterization, and theme. Accuracy is an essential feature of good biographical writing for children. Authors of biography have a responsibility to their readers to conduct careful research and to make sure that both the writing and the illustrations are accurate and truly reflect the historical and social contexts. In addition, authors should take care not to diminish the accuracy and authenticity of their texts by omitting important aspects of their subjects' lives in an effort to protect children from controversial topics (such as the fact that Washington and Jefferson owned slaves). Other criteria to consider in the selection of biography are aspects of the subject. Children can benefit from reading about a wide range of biographical subjects, including famous persons, less-well-known figures whose accomplishments are highly specialized, and even subjects who are known for their misdeeds. Norton (1995) offered the following question regarding subject selection: "Has the subject made a significant impact on the world—for good or ill—that children should be aware of?" (p. 651).

Another consideration in the selection of biography for young children is style. The language of a biography should be engaging and lively. The illustrations should be appropriate to the subject as well as to the author's tone. The illustrations in *Duke Ellington* (Pinkney, 1998) are an outstanding example of this, seeming to capture the essence of both the subject and the author's approach to him. Characterization of the subject in biographies should be true to life and neither adulatory nor demeaning in tone (Huck, Hepler, & Hickman, 1993). Authors of biography have a responsibility to present the subject in a three-dimensional way while remaining true to the facts of the person's life and the historical and social setting. Finally, high quality biographies often present an underlying theme that serves to provide a structure and to unify the facts of the subject's life. For example, in *One Giant Leap: The Story of Neil Armstrong* (Brown, 1998), an underlying theme regards focusing on a dream and working hard—Armstrong is depicted mowing lawns and cleaning mixing vats—in service of that dream. In *Wilma Unlimited: How Wilma Rudolph Became The World's Fastest Woman* (Krull, 1996), there are repeated examples of exceeding expectations, doing more than others believe that you can.

Finding biographies that meet these criteria and yet that young children can read themselves is difficult. A few authors, such as David Adler, or publishers, such as Heinemann (www.heinemann.com) have developed series of biographies geared specifically toward at least relatively early readers. Some publishers also include some biographies within broader series, such as in the Puffin *Easy to Read* Series (www.puffin.co.uk) and Cartwheel/Scholastic *Hello Reader!* series (www.scholastic.com). If we consider biographies that children can listen to read aloud, if not read themselves, there are many more quality titles available. In fact, there are awards and resources that provide bibliographies of biography titles. Examples include the Jefferson Cup Award, presented by the Virginia Library Association for a distinguished book in American history, historical fiction, or biography (www.vla.org), and the *Index to Collective Biographies for Young Readers* (Breen, 1988). Biographies certainly can be included among texts for young readers.

Procedural Texts

Put simply, procedural texts are texts whose primary purpose is to tell how to do something. Procedural texts are found in a wide range of domains—science (experiments), cooking (recipes), crafts (how to make …), and others. Across these domains, however, procedural texts have a number of common components (Derewianka, 1990; Purcell-Gates & Duke, 2001). These typically include an indication of what the procedure is to accomplish or result in, a section for materials needed for the procedure, a set of steps to go through to carry out the procedure, and photographs or illustrations depicting the final result and/or steps along the way. Headings and subheadings, letters or numbers to indicate the order of steps, and other features may be used to organize the text. Text language is often imperative (Put … Sift … Paste …), with either an understood or explicit second person pronoun, and uses temporal terms, such as *first* and *after*. Effective procedural texts are sufficiently detailed and explicit to allow the reader to carry out the procedure successfully, and the reader must have knowledge of this genre to process the text successfully. Indeed, the unique purpose and features of procedural texts make errors in decoding and comprehension especially costly (resulting in being unable to carry out the procedure successfully). At the same time, success at decoding and comprehending procedural text can give the young reader a very tangible reward—a sweet dessert, a desired craft, an intriguing experiment.

We know of no published research on how children acquire the ability to read written procedures (we are currently involved in a study in this area, but it is still in progress). However, we have at least some evidence that young children can interact with and enjoy procedural texts. Duthie (1996) included "how to" books as one of the genres she taught with her first graders. She presented a minilesson in which she began by identifying cookbooks (a type of procedural text likely to be familiar to students) as how-to books, and then went on to explain that there are many more things that this type of nonfiction can teach people. Together the class read a number of procedural texts and eventually, students wrote their own how-to books. We, the authors, have also observed young children interacting with procedural texts. One of us (Duke) worked with a first-grade student who read the procedural text *How to Make Salsa* and actually made salsa. The child delighted in sharing the finished product with teachers in the school. The other (Tower) observed a second-grade class in which the teacher challenged students to determine whether or not they could put a paper towel under water without it getting wet. Students were presented with procedural text that outlined the steps involved in accomplishing just that, and they eagerly followed the steps in order to see if the claim (that the paper towel would stay dry) was true. Those students who were not careful in following the steps ended up with soggy paper towels. Regardless of outcome, all of the students were engaged with this experience, and motivated to try to explain the results of their experiment. Indeed, it is difficult to imagine that young children would not enjoy carrying out the kinds of procedures in books like Ardley's *The Science Book of Things That Grow* (1991), while at the same time learning valuable scientific process and content.

In selecting procedural texts for young readers, teachers should look for texts that present clear, straightforward instructions and that include visuals to support students in following the procedure. The procedures should be broken down into steps of manageable size for young children, and they should be clearly ordered and visually separated. Where appropriate, procedural texts such as cookbooks and science experiments should include adequate warnings about the safe use of tools and equipment.

Procedural texts for children are available on a variety of topics, including cooking, crafts, knitting, origami, sandcastles, calligraphy, quilting, sculpting, jewelry making, science experiments, music, and many others. Often, these texts are written above the reading level of primary-grade students, but supportive graphics or a rewrite from a sensitive teacher can put them within reach. Procedural text series that are written with the young reader in mind include Mondo Publishers' (www.mondopub.com) how-to series (in their theme and genre packs) and Williamson Publishing (www.williamsonbooks.com) "Kids Can!," "Kaleidoscope Kids," and "Little Hands" series, all featuring how-to books on a variety of topics.

Reference Materials

Perhaps more so than the other categories discussed so far, reference materials are probably best characterized not as one genre, but as several. The purposes and features of dictionaries, for example, do differ in important ways from those of field guides, for example. Nonetheless, reference materials (and we use the term *materials* to signify the growing role that electronic reference sources are playing in education and elsewhere) do have some things in common. With regard to purpose, reference materials are written to provide specific pieces of information sought by the reader—the meaning of a word (in dictionaries), the location of a city (in atlases), the identity of an animal (in field guides), and so on. Featurally, reference materials are often highly organized, whether by category, alphabetically, or in some other way, and have devices such as tables of content, indexes, headings, and page guides to aid the reader in locating the information sought. Titles of and introductions to reference materials generally indicate what kind of information the reader might expect to find (and not to find) in the text. Illustrations are common either for explanatory or identifying purposes.

For young readers, reference materials pose a dual challenge. On the one hand, they must have the skills necessary to navigate through and locate the particular information they need. On the other hand, they must be able actually to decode and comprehend that information (encyclopedia entry, dictionary definition, etc.) once they get there. However, meeting these dual challenges may be uniquely empowering to young readers, who have read a very "grown-up" type book for the purpose of finding out just what they wanted or needed to know.

We do not know of any studies on how very young children learn to use reference materials specifically, although there are studies on how young children learn to search for information using these along with other nonfiction sources (e.g., Korkeamäki & Dreher, 2000; Korkeamäki, Tiainen, & Dreher, 1998). Taberski (1996) provided an image of young children at work with reference materials in a video about read-aloud and shared reading. In the video, Taberski talked about the importance of including nonfiction books in a primary classroom. In response to one nonfiction read-aloud, two of her students chose to write a glossary of river words that included such terms as *canal, estuary,* and *water.* Their glossary contained 15 words, arranged alphabetically, with illustrations and definitions. In sharing this reference material with her class, Taberski emphasized the purpose of a glossary, and she pointed out that the authors of this glossary had organized the entries alphabetically so that their readers could find the information they needed more easily. Taberski underscored what the children had modeled for their classmates—both a purpose and many key features of reference materials.

It is difficult to find reference materials that young readers can read on their own or even with assistance. Certainly some are more reader friendly than others—we are particularly impressed, for example, with the National Geographic Society's (2000) *Our World: A Child's First Picture Atlas* and Kingfisher's (1995) *The Kingfisher First Dictionary.* Many primary-grade students will need considerable support to locate the correct reference material to meet their specific information need, navigate the text in order to locate the needed information, and read the actual entry or entries with that information. Reference books for young readers should have many clues, such as the title and picture on the cover, as to the type of book it is and the type of information children might find within it. Devices to aid navigation should be prominent and easy to follow (e.g., with tabs for each alphabet letter). Entries should have supportive characteristics such as larger print, short, simple passages, and illustrations that help to convey meaning. Most importantly, the materials should be appealing to teacher and student alike, as a great deal of modeling and repeated use is necessary to help children develop competence with these texts.

CONCLUSION

We hope we have demonstrated that there is a rich trove of nonfiction texts for even young readers, including at least some that they are likely to be able to read themselves. And although the focus of this chapter has been on nonfiction *books,* when other formats are considered, such as magazines and electronic texts, the wealth of nonfiction texts only increases. We hope we have also demonstrated that, although more research is certainly needed, presently available research indicates that young children can interact successfully with nonfiction texts. Indeed, in our vision of a quality early literacy classroom, nonfiction texts are well represented (Duke & Bennett-Armistead, 2003). Books and other displayed materials include an ample supply of nonfiction as well as fictional materials. Children are inspired to select nonfiction, as well as fiction, titles for independent and take home reading. The teacher talks about and models her own reading of a variety of nonfiction texts, and children are encouraged to look for nonfiction texts in their homes and communities. Activities throughout the day, such as read-aloud and small group reading, include a variety of nonfiction as well as fiction selections.

In the nonfiction-rich classrooms we envision, children read nonfiction texts for the purposes for which they were intended (Purcell-Gates & Duke, 2001). For example, they read procedural texts for the purpose of actually carrying out a procedure; they search reference materials for particular pieces of information they are seeking. Children's learning throughout the school day is truly concept and content rich (Guthrie & McCann, 1997); children employ and enjoy many kinds of nonfiction as they learn about the world around them. Children make important reading–writing connections around nonfiction as well (Duthie, 1996; Stead, 2002). For example, they might write their own autobiographies using published autobiographies as models and inspiration, or they might draw on techniques found in Gail Gibbons' books when writing their own informational texts.

Finally, in our vision of quality early literacy classrooms children are not only exposed to nonfiction texts but taught *how* to read and write them (Duke & Bennett-Armistead, 2003). They are taught particular comprehension and composition strategies appropriate for nonfiction genres; they are made aware of particular features and characteristics of various kinds of nonfiction texts; they learn to evaluate and critique nonfiction texts for accuracy, representation, and style. Children's vision of what it means to read and write is not restricted to reading stories for pleasure but includes reading a variety of texts for a variety of purposes. Nonfiction becomes an important part of their literate lives.

REFERENCES

Bamford, R. A., & Kristo, J. V. (1998). *Making facts come alive: Choosing quality nonfiction literature K–8*. Norwood, MA: Christopher-Gordon.

Bamford, R. A., & Kristo, J. V. (2000). *Checking out nonfiction K–8: Good choices for best learning*. Norwood, MA: Christopher-Gordon.

Breen, K. (Ed.). (1988). *Index to collective biographies for young readers* (4th ed.). New York: R. R. Bowker.

Carr, J. (1982). *Beyond fact: Nonfiction for children and young people*. Chicago: American Library Association.

Caswell, L. J., & Duke, N. K. (1998). Non-narrative as a catalyst for literacy development. *Language Arts, 75*, 108–117.

Chall, J. S. (1983). *Stages of reading development*. New York: McGraw-Hill.

Derewianka, B. (1990). *Exploring how texts work*. Rozelle, N.S.W., Australia: Primary English Teaching Association.

Dowd, F. S., & Lyday, D. (1991). Integrating concept books for young children in the content areas. *Journal of Youth Services in Libraries, 5*(1), 67–75.

Dreher, M. J. (2000). Fostering reading for learning. In L. Baker, M. J. Dreher, & J. Guthrie (Eds.), *Engaging young readers: Promoting achievement and motivation* (pp. 94–118). New York: Guilford.

Dreher, M. J., & Dromsky, A. (2000, November). *Increasing the diversity of young children's independent reading.* Paper presented at the National Reading Conference, Scottsdale, AZ.

Duke, N. K. (2000). 3.6 minutes per day: The scarcity of informational texts in first grade. *Reading Research Quarterly, 35,* 202–224.

Duke, N. K. (2003). Reading to learn from the very beginning: Information books literacy in early childhood. *Young Children, 58*(2), 14–20.

Duke, N. K., & Bennett-Armistead, V. S., (with Auxley, A., Johnson, M., McLurkin, D., Roberts, E., Rosen, C., & Vogel, E. (2003). *Reading and writing informational text in the primary grades: Research-based practices.* New York: Scholastic.

Duke, N. K., Bennett-Armistead, S., & Roberts, E. (2003). Bridging the gap between learning to read and reading to learn. In D. M. Barone & L. M. Morrow (Eds.), *Literacy and young children: Research-based practices* (pp. 226–242). New York: Guilford Press.

Duke, N. K., Bennett-Armistead, S., & Roberts, E. (2002). Incorporating informational text in the primary grades. In C. Roller (Ed.), *Comprehensive reading instruction across the grade levels* (pp. 40–54). Newark, DE: International Reading Association.

Duke, N. K., & Kays, J. (1998). "Can I say 'once upon a time'?": Kindergarten children developing knowledge of information book language. *Early Childhood Research Quarterly, 13*(2), 295–318.

Duthie, C. (1996). *True stories: Nonfiction literacy in the primary classroom.* York, ME: Stenhouse.

Freeman, E. B., & Person, D. G. (Eds.). (1992). *Using nonfiction trade books in the elementary classroom from ants to zeppelins.* Urbana, IL: National Council of Teachers of English.

Guthrie, J. T., & McCann, A. D. (1997). Characteristics of classrooms that promote motivations and strategies for learning. In J. T. Guthrie & A. Wigfield (Eds.), *Reading engagement: Motivating readers through integrated instruction* (pp. 128–148). Newark, DE: International Reading Association.

Huck, C. S., Hepler, S., & Hickman, J. (1993). *Children's literature in the elementary school.* New York: Harcourt Brace College Publishers.

Kletzien, S. B. (1999, December). *Children's reading preferences and information books.* Paper presented at the National Reading Conference, Orlando, FL.

Kobrin, B. (1988). *Eyeopeners: How to choose and use children's books about real people, places, and things.* New York: Viking.

Kobrin, B. (1995). *Eyeopeners II: Children's books to answer children's questions about the world around them.* New York: Scholastic.

Korkeamäki, R., & Dreher, M. J. (2000). What happened when kindergarten children were reading and writing information text in teacher- and peer-led groups? *National Reading Conference Yearbook, 49,* 452–463.

Korkeamäki, R., Tiainen, O., & Dreher, M. J. (1998). Helping Finnish second graders make sense of their reading and writing in their science project. *National Reading Conference Yearbook, 47,* 334–344.

Lennox, S. (1995). Sharing books with children. *Australian Journal of Early Childhood, 20,* 12–16.

Longman. (1984). *Longman dictionary of the English language.* London: Author.

Miller, C. R. (1984). Genre as social action. *Quarterly journal of speech, 70,* 151–67.

Newkirk, T. (1989). *More than stories: The range of children's writing.* Portsmouth, NH: Heinemann.

Norton, D. E. (1995). *Through the eyes of a child: An introduction to children's literature.* Englewood Cliffs, NJ: Merrill.

Pappas, C. C. (1986, December). *Exploring the global structure of "information books."* Paper presented at the annual meeting of the National Reading Conference, Austin, TX. (ERIC Document Reproduction Service No. ED 278952)

Pappas, C. C. (1987, August). *Exploring the generic shape of "information books": Applying typicality notions to the process.* Paper presented at the World Conference of Applied Linguistics, Sydney, New South Wales, Australia. (ERIC Document Reproduction Service No. ED 299834)

Pappas, C. C. (1993). Is narrative "primary"? Some insights from kindergartners' pretend readings of stories and information books. *Journal of Reading Behavior, 25,* 97–129.

Pelligrini, A. D., Perlmutter, J. C., Galda, L., & Brody, G. H. (1990). Joint reading between Black Head Start children and their mothers. *Child Development, 61,* 443–453.

Purcell-Gates, V., & Duke, N. K. (2001, August). *Explicit explanation/teaching of informational text genres: A model for research.* Paper presented at Crossing Borders: Connecting Science and Literacy conference, a conference sponsored by the National Science Foundation, Baltimore, MD.

Read, S. (2001). "Kid mice hunt for their selfs": First and second graders writing research. *Language Arts, 78,* 333–342.

Smolkin, L. B., & Donovan, C. A. (2000). *The contexts of comprehension: Information book read alouds and comprehension acquisition.* Center for the Improvement of Early Reading Achievement Report #2-009. Ann Arbor, MI: University of Michigan.

Snow, C. E., Burns, M. S., & Griffin, P. (Eds.). (1998). *Preventing reading difficulties in young children.* Washington, DC: National Academy Press.

Stead, T. (2002). *Is that a fact? Teaching nonfiction writing K–3.* Portland, ME: Stenhouse.

Taberski, S. (1996). *A close-up look at teaching reading: Focusing on children and our goals. Video II: Read aloud and shared reading.* Portsmouth, NH: Heinemann.

Tower, C. (2002). "It's a snake you guys!": The power of text characteristics on children's responses to information books. *Research in the Teaching of English, 37,* 55–88.

Yopp, R. H., & Yopp, H. K. (2000). Sharing informational text with young children. *The Reading Teacher, 53,* 410–423.

Zarnowski, M., Kerper, R. M., & Jensen, J. M. (2001). *The best in children's nonfiction: Reading, writing and teaching Orbis Pictus Award books.* Urbana, IL: National Council of Teachers of English.

CHILDREN'S BOOKS CITED

Ardley, N. (1991). *The science book of things that grow.* New York: Gulliver Books.

Barton, B. (1989). *Dinosaurs, dinosaurs.* New York: HarperCollins

Berger, M. (2000). *Buzz! A book about insects.* New York: Scholastic.

Brown, D. (1998). *One giant leap: The story of Neil Armstrong.* Boston: Houghton Mifflin.

Dorling Kindersley. (2000). *Shapes galore.* New York: Dorling Kindersley.

Ehlert, L. (1989). *Eating the alphabet: Fruits and vegetables from A to Z.* San Diego, CA: Harcourt Brace Jovanovich.

Fowler, A. (1998). *Let's visit some islands.* Danbury, CT: Children's Press.

Freedman, R. (1987). *Lincoln: A photobiography.* New York: Clarion Books.

Fritz, J. (1981). *Traitor: The case of Benedict Arnold.* Illustrated by S. Marchesi. East Rutherford, NJ: Putnam.

Gofstein, M. B. (1989). *A little Schubert.* Illustrated by R. Woitach. New York: Trumpet.

Glaser, L. (1992). *Wonderful worms.* Illustrated by L. Krupinski. Brookfield, CT: The Millbrook Press.

Hewitt, S. (2000). *Nature for fun projects.* Brookfield, CT: Copper Beech Books.

Hoban, T. (1983). *I read signs.* New York: Mulberry.

Hurd, E. T. (1990, illustrations copyright 2000). *Starfish.* Illustrated by Robin Brickman. New York: HarperCollins.

Johnson, S. (1995). *Alphabet city.* New York: Puffin Books.

Katzen, M., & Henderson, A. (1994). *Pretend soup and other real recipes: A cookbook for preschoolers and up.* Berkeley, CA: Tricycle Press.

Kingfisher. (1995). *The Kingfisher First Dictionary.* New York: Kingfisher.

Kirk, D. (2000). *Miss Spider's ABC.* New York: Scholastic Press.

Krull, K. (1996). *Wilma unlimited: How Wilma Rudolph became the world's fastest woman.* Illustrated by D. Diaz. San Diego: Harcourt Brace.

Lorenz Books. (1996). *Let's look at shapes.* New York: Anness Publishing.

Lundell, M. (1995). *A girl named Helen Keller.* Illustrated by I. Trivas. New York: Scholastic.

Morris, A. (1990). *On the go.* New York: Mulberry Books.

National Geographic Society. (2000). *Our world: A child's first picture atlas.* Washington, D.C.: Author.

Pallotta, J. (1994). *The spice alphabet book: Herbs, spices, and other natural flavors.* Illustrated by L. Evans. Watertown, MA: Charlesbridge.

Parks, R., & Haskins, J. (1997). *I am Rosa Parks.* Illustrated by W. Clay. New York: Dial/Puffin.

Pinkney, A. D. (1998). *Duke Ellington.* Illustrated by B. Pinkney. New York: Scholastic.

Reid, M. E. (1996). *Let's find out about ice cream.* Photos by J. Williams. New York: Scholastic.

Royston, A. (1991). *Diggers and dump trucks.* Illustrated by J. Cradock-Watson & D. Hopkins, photography by T. Ridley. New York: Simon and Schuster.

Voss, G. (1993). *Museum numbers.* Boston: Museum of Fine Arts.

Walsh, M. (1997). *Do monkeys tweet?* Boston: Houghton Mifflin.

8

Local Texts: Reading and Writing "of the Classroom"

Beth Maloch
James V. Hoffman
Elizabeth U. Patterson
The University of Texas at Austin

To step through the front door of Hempshill Hall Primary School in Nottingham, England is to take a step inside of a book. You are surrounded, bombarded, and immersed in print. There is print on the walls, on the ceilings, on the doors, on the windows, and on the furniture. You seek to orient yourself by focusing on just a small space and quickly realize that the print is not random and plastered but thoughtfully designed. The wall you see as you enter the school is a model of space (three dimensional at that) with all kinds of information and detail on planets and the solar system. As you attend even more carefully, you note that this is not a commercially prepared or packaged display. The work of students is clearly evident in the writing and the crafting of the display elements. Having found a point of reference, you can turn your attention back to the larger context and you begin to suspect that there is a fundamental plan at work here in this school regarding learning and teaching and literacy.

As with the print, students and teachers are working everywhere in the school, individually, in pairs, and in small groups. And all are engaged with reading and writing. You not only sense, you *see* the connection between the texts they are directly engaged with and the print that surrounds them. They are the ones who have created it, who use it, who sustain it, and who keep it alive. You realize this is not a book you have walked into but a language creation that is constantly unfolding.

Romanticized? Not in the least. We visited this school on the recommendation of our good friend Colin Harrison at The University of Nottingham. We went on separate occasions and came away with exactly the same impression. Bruce Joyce visited this school several years earlier and described it in similar terms (Joyce, Calhoun, Puckey, & Hopkins, 1997). The school continues to score "off the scale" in terms of achievement in comparison to similar schools in the area. Privileged? No. Hempshill Hall is a fairly typical public school, in demographic terms, serving a working class community in north central England. Special? Yes. The fact that there has been practically zero turnover in teachers in the past 10 years tells you a lot about the leadership in the school and the ways teachers work collaboratively. Changes are guided by a shared vision for teaching and learning.

As educators, we have much to learn from this school. As literacy educators, we have much to learn regarding the pervasive uses of texts to support learning. For the purposes of this chapter, we are particularly interested in the dynamics of the texts "of the classroom" (i.e., those created within and by those who learn and teach). We argue that these kinds of texts, what we are calling *local texts*, and the conditions that surround their creation and use (the local literacies of the classroom) are vital to an effective reading and language arts program.

In this chapter, we discuss the construct of local texts and begin to explore the range of possible local texts in the classroom. We consider critical issues related to the use of and potential value of local texts and include practical recommendations for teachers.

LOCAL TEXTS: A CONCEPTUAL FRAMEWORK

Our use of the term *local texts* is situated within Barton and Hamilton's (1998) construct of literacy as a set of social practices.

> Literacy is a social practice … Literacy practices are the general cultural ways of utilizing written language, which people draw upon in their lives. In the simplest sense literacy practices are what people do with literacy. (p. 6)

Literacy practices are evident in all aspects of community life and in almost all cultures. Barton and Hamilton used the phrase *local literacies* to describe and discuss the various literacies found in homes and communities. They used the term to focus attention on the literacy activity that occurs in everyday community life. In this chapter, however, we borrow their term and consider the literacy practices found in the everyday life of classrooms. We suggest that teachers and students, as a learning community, take up, revise, and create a set of social practices within their classrooms. These social practices, though clearly and heavily influenced by institutional forces, are created and re-created daily in the actions of teachers and students.

Local texts, as we define them here, are the written texts created or constructed by classroom participants, and are both a part of and a reflection of those social practices. We use the word *local*, derived from the Latin word *locus*, meaning *of the place*, intentionally to highlight the situated nature of these texts and their uses in classrooms. Local texts are integrally related to the ongoing instructional events in the classroom and serve a number of functions within the classroom community, including the documentation of classroom life, the support of learning, and the affirmation of students and their work.

Furthermore, local texts are *authored*, not just produced, by the teacher and/or the students. An example makes this distinction more clear. If a teacher, for instance, copies by hand a poem written by an outside author onto a chart in the room for display or instructional purposes, this text would not be considered local as it has not been authored by the teacher and/or the students. Thus, local texts are authored by the classroom participants. In turn, classroom participants are the audience for these texts, with some texts geared toward an audience of one (e.g., personal journal), and others targeted to the entire class (e.g., class book, inquiry chart).

LOCAL TEXTS: CONNECTIONS TO RESEARCH AND THEORY

We are certainly not the first to talk about the importance of texts created within the classroom. Our views on local texts and their importance in the classroom have been influenced by many who puzzled over similar issues long before us. Here, we link our thoughts on the importance of local texts to research and theory in three areas: psychological, pedagogical, and social.

Psychologically, the notion of local texts fits quite nicely within a socioconstructivist paradigm, one that assumes that knowledge is constructed over time and across participants or members of a community. Vygotsky (1978) noted that "human learning presupposes a specific social nature and a process by which children grow into the intellectual life of those around them" (p. 88). Rather than learning through the transmission of information, skills and understandings are appropriated through guided participation in cultural activities (Bruner, 1990; Vygotsky, 1978; Wertsch, 1991). Local texts are both a part of and a reflection of the social interactions that occur within a classroom culture.

Pedagogically, local texts, though not labeled as such, have been recommended by educators working within a language experience approach (LEA) in which teachers guide students to discuss recent experiences and create stories in their own language. Perhaps the most highly recognized approach to the cocreation of texts by teachers and students is found in the work and writings of Sylvia Ashton-Warner. The "organic" vocabulary approach used by Ashton-Warner (1963) was particularly effective in using the local literacies of indigenous students, who lived outside the cultural mainstream, as a bridge into school literacy. Ashton-Warner and others noted that by building on students' oral language and experiences, the LEA helps students build bridges between oral and written language through an interactive writing experience.

In the area of literature response, researchers have discussed the benefits of valuing and organizing children's responses to literature through writing. Roser and Hoffman (1992), for example, considered how a teacher can use language charts to record children's ideas from stories, help them recall other stories, and notice similarities and differences among stories. In doing so, language charts offer a way of both facilitating and documenting children's changing responses to literature. Similarly, Alvermann (1991) recommended the use of "discussion webs" as a tool and strategy to promote text discussions. The discussion web strategy revolves around a graphic aid or organizer to guide children's thinking about the ideas they want to contribute to a discussion.

In contrast to these more public, local texts, the use of journals offers children more personalized opportunities for writing. From learning logs to dialogue journals, individual writing opportunities have been recommended across the curriculum as a way for students to write to learn and as a way to document and reflect on personal experience. Calkins (1994), for example, suggested that students, like all writers, can benefit from keeping a Writer's Notebook in which "bits of life" are recorded as a way of documenting personal experiences that may become more formal writing topics.

Finally, viewing local texts from a social perspective, the coconstructed nature of texts produced in the classroom can create spaces for students to introduce their own ways of knowing and their own prior experiences into the classroom. All of the educators mentioned earlier noted the instructional or pedagogical possibilities and implications of both the creation and use of locally constructed texts. A more socially situated theme that cuts across that discussion, however, is a drawing on and valuing of students' words and lives. Local texts can provide a bridge into academic literacies by building on and valuing home literacies. At the same time, texts constructed and coconstructed by students offer students more control and agency within the classroom. In *For a*

Better World: Reading and Writing for Social Action, for example, Bomer and Bomer (2001) defined stances that teachers might want to encourage in their students in order to foster critical literacy:

> Habits of listening and considering different sides; the ability to collaborate, deliberate, and differ; respect for others as civic equals; a commitment to avoid and resist repression and discrimination; the development of concerned social agendas; a deep understanding of the traditions and concepts that create and sustain democracy; and fluency in communicative and democratic processes. (p. 14)

Within this notion of "critical literacy," students are encouraged to read, respond, and write honestly about things that matter to them, ideas that seem important to create and maintain openness and acceptance in the classroom. "Whether students are reading or writing, they are participating in a social world right here in the classroom, and they need language as a tool for thinking about that world and negotiating their ways of being in it" (Bomer & Bomer, 2001, p. 18). Thus, local texts provide opportunities for students to bring their own lives and experiences into the classroom and learn ways to use these literacies to change their world. In the following section, we share a range of possibilities of local texts that serve these and other purposes.

LOCAL TEXTS: A RANGE OF POSSIBILITIES

In the opening pages of this chapter, we began with an impressionistic view of Hempshill Hall, focusing on the large, public texts on display. Though these texts were what first drew our attention, upon a closer look, we also found teachers and students using local texts in more personal formats. For example, at Hempshill Hall, all students have a "comment book" that stays with them from the first day they enter as preschoolers to the day they graduate from the school. Over these years, they faithfully keep their comment book with them, taking it home every night and bringing it back to school the next day. In the comment book are recorded the comments of teachers, the head-master, and parents about the students and their development. It is a living record of growth and accomplishment in literacy that promotes communication among all those invested in the success of the learner. Thus, Hempshill Hall provides an exemplary demonstration of the complementary, even dynamic uses of public and private local texts.

Clearly, other schools, other learning communities have local texts outside of Hempshill Hall, many of which we observed in our own studies of the classroom literacy environment. For the past 2 years, we have been involved in a study of reading teacher preparation sponsored by the International Reading Association (see Roller, 2001). We have followed more than 100 graduates from eight teacher preparation programs into their first 3 years of teaching and have documented the impact of these preparation programs on their teaching of reading. Our observations in these classrooms have been focused on the texts and the ways in which texts are being used instructionally with students (the instruments and procedures for conducting these observations are described in chap. 12 in this book).

In this section, we draw on these data to highlight the range of different kinds of local texts that are being used in elementary classrooms. Although we have tried to be as comprehensive as possible, we are certain that there are other types of local texts that are being created and recreated in classrooms even as we write this chapter. We divide the following descriptions of texts into two types: public (i.e., those to which other students have direct access); and private (i.e., those texts that are primarily under the control of the individual student).

Public Local Texts

Public local texts are texts to which both the teacher and the students have access. These texts are often found posted on the wall in the form of charts, but can just as easily be found in the form of books or notebooks that are made available to the classroom participants. The public local texts we have identified tend to function in a number of ways, including: (a) as a guide for the students in a process of how to do something independently, (b) as an instructional aid used by teachers to support the study of a particular topic, (c) as an aid to the class in organizing and managing their work, or (d) as a display of personal local texts that are being recognized and/or celebrated. A partial listing of the public texts that we have observed includes inquiry charts, class stories, language experience stories, and others that we explain next.

Inquiry Charts. Inquiry charts, charts that help track and compile information researched within the classroom, have taken a variety of formats ranging from a simple KWL (Know–Want to Know–Learned, Ogle, 1986) organizational pattern to more elaborate charts that reflect data sources and cross-checking of information (see Hoffman, 1986). In many cases, these charts serve as instructional aids that are used actively by the teacher and the students as they move through an inquiry project (e.g., the Civil War; the life cycle of a butterfly). Individual charts—particularly in the early primary grades—or group charts may be used to record information as it is gathered.

Innovations and Class Stories. Class work on text innovations (e.g, transforming *Brown Bear, Brown Bear, What Do You See?* (Martin, 1967) to *First Grader,*

First Grader, What Do You See?) is common in primary-grade classrooms that value local texts. These kinds of texts are used actively as a part of instruction.

Language Experience Stories.   Here again, and particularly in the primary grades, these experience stories, cocreated by the teacher and students, provide the basis for instruction in emergent and early reading skills.

Graphic Organizers.   We have seen quite a few graphic organizers used to support comprehension instruction. Typically, the teacher uses organizers/tools like Venn diagrams or story maps as an instructional aid in a lesson. The format may be used repeatedly with different stories or texts to encourage the independent application of the strategy being taught.

Language Charts.   Author studies, genre studies, and thematic studies of literature are charted using a matrix format to guide the analysis of literature being read. Character charts, plot lines, and book comparisons are often included in this kind of work.

Word Walls.   These come in a variety of formats, and the functions may vary from one classroom to the next (e.g., spelling, decoding, vocabulary development). Regardless, as local texts, they share the quality of changing and growing over time based on input from the students.

Process Charts.   These charts are local texts that direct students toward the application of particular strategies. Two examples we observed of process charts are those that remind students of strategies to use when they encounter a word they do not recognize or charts that remind students of strategies to use when picking a topic about which to write or a new book to read.

Organizational and Management Charts.   The variety is endless in these types of charts (e.g., classroom helpers). They change over time with input from the students, and they are functional in the sense that they guide activity in the classroom.

Books.   We found numerous examples in our research of books in classroom libraries written by the students from that classroom. Sometimes these are individually authored books, sometimes group authored, and sometimes class authored.

Rubrics.   Quite honestly, we were surprised in our research at the wide use of rubrics in elementary classrooms. The rubrics are used for the students and the teachers to negotiate the evaluation of student work. Most often we saw these in the area of student writing. They range from the simple (e.g., five-point holistic scales with descriptions for the qualities of each) to elaborate (e.g., separate scales for such factors as content, organization, fluency, etc.). Some appear directly influenced by state writing evaluation schemes, whereas others appear drawn out of and using the ideas of the students in the class. We also saw rubrics as part of "project" evaluations as in social studies or science research projects.

Work Displays.   Work displays are one of those important bridge points between personal and public texts. Teachers display the personal products of students publicly to feature the positive qualities of the work completed.

Personal Local Texts

Personal local texts are local texts that are under greater control of the individual student with more restricted access by other students. Smaller physical size of the texts is an obvious point of distinction, but not nearly as crucial as the issue of ownership and control. In classrooms that rely a great deal on local texts, we typically find analogues between public texts and personal texts. In other words, for most public local texts there is a personal local text that parallels its use—or at least there is a long-term plan for a personal local text that parallels its use (e.g., an inquiry chart is a scaffold toward a personal inquiry journal for the student; a literature study chart is a scaffold toward a personal literature response journal). The direction can go the other way as well (e.g., what starts as entries into a personal literature response journal can be added to to create a public display).

Journals.   As we saw when we visited Hempshill, the possibilities for journals are endless. The fact that they might be written in by others (e.g., a dialogue journal with a teacher) does not take away from their individual student focus.

Portfolios.   We were impressed in our observations in classrooms with the number of teachers who are using individual student portfolios as an active part of their work with students. Students exert a great deal of decision making in the development of these portfolios. They are directly involved in the evaluation process and in choosing artifacts that represent growth.

Computer Files.   Technology is changing the nature of literacy in the classroom, and our observations reveal that more and more students are having opportunities to engage with technology in the classroom. We see students using personal journal files, drafts for papers in process, portfolios, and even web pages. In some sense these are the same kinds of local texts as described earlier, just in a different medium, but we suspect that there is more than just a difference in the medium. New possibilities are emerging.

"Worksheets."   We discuss in a later section the notion that not all local texts are of equal value. Many teachers create worksheets that students then complete. Technically, these might be regarded as personal local texts. Our classroom investigations reveal that teachers who rely on local texts for teaching do not rely on "worksheet" formats often, or if they do, they tend toward the very open-ended formats.

As we come to the end of our list, we again want to emphasize its illustrative purpose. It is by no means exhaustive. Our goal with this description of local texts was to highlight the range and variation across classrooms. However, it is in the use of these texts that we are able to determine their value and effectiveness concerning teaching and learning. We focus on this question of usefulness in the next section.

LOCAL TEXTS: USEFULNESS
AND VALUE IN CLASSROOMS

Why is it that when we walk into a school like Hempshill that is filled with print, we immediately assume a productive and enjoyable learning environment? Are print-covered walls inherently valuable to a student's learning? One reason that we may immediately assume productivity is that print-covered walls are in some ways a reflection or a record of productive work that has occurred in the classroom. We have a better sense of this classroom community because of the print and artifacts that surround us.

In some sense, therefore, local texts are a record of what has occurred or is occurring in a classroom. The potential usefulness of local texts, however, does not stop at documentation. If they only serve to represent the "goings-on" of classrooms, local texts can become static artifacts of the classroom culture. If, however, local texts are used not only to document the events in the community, but to facilitate ongoing teaching and learning, they become a dynamic and critical part of the classroom community. Just as availability of books does not guarantee their usage and thus, their value, the presence of local texts in a classroom does not ensure their contribution to students' learning.

In this way, a critical component of the value of local texts concerns the purposefulness of its use. In other words, why are these texts being used by teachers and by students? Are students able to articulate their uses for such texts and if so, do these articulations relate to teachers' goals and purposes for the texts?

This purposefulness of use is taken up further in the conclusion. Before moving to the conclusion, we would like to discuss three caveats concerning local texts and their use in classrooms.

LOCAL TEXTS AND THE ENVISIONED CLASSROOM

It is hard to imagine an elementary classroom in which local texts are not in any way in use. At the same time, it is hard to imagine a classroom in which we could not be doing more. We have no specific formula for how to get there, but we can offer some suggestions on strategies to start this journey.

- *"Read" your room.* Read your own room for the variety and qualities of the local texts that are being used. Take pictures to document your journey. Take some of your students along and query them at the same time; it is remarkable the sense of perspective they can provide. Use this exercise as a way to get a sense of where you are and continue to use it as a means of judging the effectiveness of the changes you are making.
- *Read other rooms.* Follow the same procedures in other classrooms. Your efforts to expand effectiveness will be enhanced when you work collaboratively to learn with others.
- *Think locally.* Challenge yourself in all the teaching you do to have some kind of local text that is accessible to the students you are teaching.
- *Think relationally.* For every public local text with which you work, think about ways in which this kind of text can be a scaffold toward independent work with a personal local text for the student (e.g, a class rubric for writing moves to become a personal editing checklist). Similarly, for every personal local text, think of the possibilities for a public local text that builds on the personal (e.g, a personal literature response journal to a class chart).
- *Think across the curriculum.* Local texts can provide an important bridge point between the language arts curriculum and the other content areas. Local texts are a bridge that links the processes of literacy to the functions of literacy.
- *Think dynamically.* Classrooms do not begin the year immersed in local texts. Local texts build and change throughout the year as students and teachers act and interact within their classroom. Likewise, if texts remain on the wall throughout the year, without reference by the teacher or students, they can become like wallpaper, invisible to the participants. Plan for and expect dynamic and changing texts in your classroom.

- *Create space and design.* Fill your walls and classrooms with text, but do not clutter. This is a challenge for all of us as we manage texts in our workspace. Design is important.

Again, our envisioned classroom is not one that solely uses local texts. "Imported texts," texts published and/or authored by others outside the classroom, are of course valuable. There must be a balance of both. It is not a "from–to" journey that begins with language experience and "graduates" to imported text. It is a continued valuing of both in the classroom as they must be in our lives outside of school.

THREE CAVEATS

First, we do not suggest in this chapter that all local texts are equally useful or valuable. In other words, as mentioned earlier in the case of worksheets, not all local texts are created equal. The ways in which these texts come about and the ways they are used are important. Local texts should draw on students' lives and knowledge and should be used in purposeful and instructive ways.

Second, we are not arguing here for the exclusion of imported texts. Many imported texts, as already described in previous chapters of this book, are valuable and critical to classroom instruction. We suggest, instead, that although local texts are a critical component of building and maintaining instruction, learning, and community, the combination of local and imported texts, used in purposeful and strategic ways by the teacher and students, allows for a more diverse and comprehensive usage of texts.

Finally, although our emphasis in this chapter has been on *local* construction of texts, we want to reiterate that one critical benefit of the use of local texts in classrooms is the opportunity they provide to reach beyond the classroom walls. Local texts open spaces for children to bring their experiences and their words into the classroom. In many ways, the genesis of local texts is not in the classroom but in the lives of children. It is in the classroom where these outside lives and more formal, academic experiences merge in valued ways, often resulting in the construction of local texts.

CONCLUSION

The composing of written texts, like the composing of oral ones, is a distinctly sociocultural process that involves making decisions, conscious or otherwise, about how one figures into the social world at any one point in time (Dyson, 1993, p. 7)

In our research, we have interviewed students regarding the texts in their classrooms. We have "read the room" with them. Invariably, the local texts are the ones that spark the most talk, the most enthusiasm, and expose the greatest depth of understanding. As we puzzled over the patterns in the students' talk about local texts, four themes stood out to us that echo Dyson's comment regarding writing and the social context: (a) *community*—in talking about local texts students tend toward the "we" in describing their purposes and functions, (b) *identity*—students use these texts in terms of describing themselves as readers, writers, and learners, (c) *voice*—students talk about the local texts in their classrooms in the sense of "I/We have something to say that is important enough to be recorded, remembered and shared," and (d) *agency*—students talk about the local texts in ways that reveal a sense of control over the world in which they live and work. In essence, we believe that local texts form the roots of critical literacy. Just as Friere (1970) found literacy to be a tool for liberation among the oppressed, we believe that local texts nurture this stance among the young developing readers and writers in our classrooms. Local texts provide a way for students to take more control of their environment and to use literacy in ways that benefit their lives.

REFERENCES

Alvermann, D. E. (1991). The discussion web: A graphic aid for learning across the curriculum. *The Reading Teacher, 45,* 92–99.

Ashton-Warner, S. (1963). *Teacher.* New York: Simon & Schuster.

Barton, D., & Hamilton, M. (1998). *Local literacies: Reading and writing in one community.* London: Routledge.

Bomer, R., & Bomer, K. (2001). *For a better world: Reading and writing for social action.* Portsmouth, NH: Heinemann.

Bruner, J. S. (1990). *Acts of meaning.* Cambridge, MA: Harvard University Press.

Calkins, L. M. (1994). *The art of teaching writing* (2nd ed.). Portsmouth, N.H.: Heinemann Educational Books.

Dyson, A. H. (1993). *Social words of children learning to write in an urban primary school.* New York: Teachers College Press.

Freire, P. (1970). *Pedagogy of the oppressed.* New York: Herder and Herder.

Hoffman, J. V. (Ed.). (1986). *Effective teaching of reading: Research and practice.* Newark, DE: International Reading Association.

Joyce, B., Calhoun, E., Puckey, M., & Hopkins, D. (1997). From England: Inquiring and collaborating at an exemplary school. *Educational Leadership, 54,* 63–66.

Martin, B. (1967). *Brown bear, brown bear, what do you see?* New York: Holt & Company.

Ogle, D. M. (1986). K-W-L: A teaching model that develops active reading of expository text. *The Reading Teacher, 39,* 564–571.

Roller, C. M. (Ed.). (2001). *Learning to teach reading: Setting the research agenda.* Newark, DE: International Reading Association.

Roser, N. L., & Hoffman, J. V. (1992). Language charts: A record of story time talk. *Language Arts, 69,* 44–52.

Vygotsky, L. S. (1978). *Mind in society: The development of higher psychological processes.* Cambridge, MA: Harvard University Press.

Wertsch, J. V. (1991). *Voices of the mind: A sociocultural approach to mediated action.* Cambridge, MA: Harvard University Press.

9

Electronic Text in the Classroom

Michael L. Kamil
Helen S. Kim
Stanford University

Diane Lane
Hilliard City Schools, Hilliard, OH

The typical classroom contains a great deal of print, in books, magazines, newspapers, student work, and signs on the walls. It is not always obvious that we think of the computer sitting in the back of the classroom as containing print, but it does. When we think of a reading lesson in a typical classroom, we think of students sitting in groups with books. We do not think of them sitting at the computer, but we should. When we think of students writing, we think of pencil and paper, not keyboards and computers, but we should. When we think of students reading, we do not think of them sitting in front of a computer, but we should. When we complain about students not reading, what we mean, most often, is that students are not attending to a book, magazine, newspaper, or other source of conventional print. We forget that a great deal of student leisure time is spent in front of computers, surfing the web, sending instant messages or e-mail to friends, or doing other activities that require a great many literacy skills. Many of our concepts about print, reading, writing, and even instruction have not kept pace with the changing nature of print.

In this chapter, we examine the types of electronic texts that can and should be found in elementary classrooms. Because this is a relatively new form for reading materials, we begin by demonstrating the importance of these types of text, identifying the different types of electronic text, and describing what we know about each type. We then describe the relationship of multimedia information to electronic text. We also discuss the relationship between reading and writing electronic text. To illustrate the uses of electronic text in elementary classrooms, we describe an example of some current uses of electronic text incorporated in a school program. Finally, we speculate on what some of the future demands for reading electronic text will be.

WHAT IS ELECTRONIC TEXT?

Electronic texts can be classified in two major categories. The first is simply any text that is presented on a computer screen. This type of electronic text is the most common. It includes most of the text that we find in e-mail, help screens on computers, and instructions supplied on the screen for computer programs. The primary characteristic of this type of text is that it exists in a digital form, that is, it can be transmitted from one computer to another electronically or it can be simply copied and placed on a diskette for use in another program or computer. In addition, the appropriate computer program can change it to appear larger or smaller, in different fonts, and even in different colors. Until fairly recently, this was the only type of electronic text that existed.

The second category of electronic text is any electronic text that is augmented by either hyperlinks, hypertext, or multimedia additions to the text (hypermedia). A *hyperlink* is an electronic connection between some element (a word or phrase) of electronic text and some other text element. The most common use of *hypertext* is found on the Internet, where clicking on a hyperlinked word or phrase calls up additional text information related to the word or phrase. On the Internet, a link can also lead to a different web site, an elaboration of a word or phrase, or some multimedia presentation such as a video or an audio clip. These are referred to as *hypermedia*, because the contents go beyond text.

The two categories of electronic text require different strategies for reading when compared with conventional text. Electronic text from the first category—text that is simply the same as conventional text except for the fact that it is presented on a computer screen—although very similar to conventional text, does require some navigational strategies that are different, as for example, turning pages. A reader must learn how to "page" through the text a page at a time or scroll though it line by line.

Text from the multimedia category is very different from conventional text. Multimedia text can be connected to all sorts of other representations such as pictures, sound, video, or any combination, and accessed by the reader or automatically played at specific points during reading. The reader must make decisions about how to integrate the multimedia information with the text information. The closest a reader comes to doing this in conventional text is when the text is accompanied by pictures, charts, diagrams, or other graphics. Decisions must be made about when to depend on the text and when to depend on the multimedia information. As with simple electronic text, navigation strategies are also important.

Multimedia text can even be designed to help readers comprehend the information by linking to other sources, having the text translated to speech, or even providing definitions or illustrations of concepts. Reading multimedia text is more involved and requires additional skills from those required by conventional text. In the next sections, we examine what we know about the reading of electronic texts and multimedia information.

WHAT DO WE KNOW ABOUT READING ELECTRONIC TEXT?

For simple electronic text that is presented on the computer screen, there is a set of trade-offs that can be thought of in terms of the ability to read the text. A typical finding is that it is 15% to 20% less efficient to read from a computer screen than it is to read from traditional hard copy. (For a discussion of the research on reading from computer screens, see Kamil & Lane, 1998a.) More specifically, either it takes a reader 15% to 20% longer to read a passage, or comprehension is decreased by 15% to 20% if time is held constant. Some of this reduced efficiency is due to screen resolutions. That is, the computer screen is often not as clear as hard copy. In addition, computer screens can display less information at a time compared to printed pages. A typical screen display is often only capable of displaying 15 double-spaced lines, whereas a printed page has between 25 and 30, depending on the margins. Some of the reduced efficiency is due to navigation—the ability to get new pages on the computer screen in a quick and easy manner. Because so little text is on the screen at one time, the reader must wait while new pages are displayed. Whatever the cause, this is a serious disadvantage in electronic text. Probably because reading at the computer is more difficult, most individuals—children and adults—report a preference for reading conventional text over electronic text (see, for example, Kim & Kamil, 2000).

However, a major advantage of electronic text is that it is searchable. It has a dramatic advantage in that the computer can locate a word or a phrase in a large amount of text far faster than a human can. The computer can find repeated instances of whatever is being searched very rapidly, whereas a reader of conventional text must turn each page and scan it to find a word or phrase. Thus, for many search tasks, electronic text is far superior to conventional text. One exception is that the computer often cannot "tell" what the reader meant. For example, if the reader wants to search for the word *reading* and misspells it *reeding*, the computer is unable to understand what almost every reader does: that the reader wanted to search for *reading*. In this case, the computer search fails.

Another advantage of electronic text is that, depending on the software in which it appears, it can be resized, or even changed to a different font. It might even be formatted so that lines of text are longer or shorter, double-spaced instead of single-spaced, or that the color of the print and the background are different from the original. This characteristic is useful for changing the text into more readable formats, for different purposes. Electronic text can be easily revised for content, and individualized for the reader or learner.

Finally, electronic text can be transported in very compact form or electronically. A common CD-ROM disk can hold hundreds of books in electronic form, allowing a whole library of books to be carried on a single disk. Electronic text can be sent from any computer to any other computer anywhere in the world in short order, so long as both computers are connected to the Internet or some other computer network. Conventionally printed text can be faxed, but it is received only as copies of the original, not as electronic text that can be manipulated.

HOW MUCH ELECTRONIC TEXT IS THERE?

Electronic text has become extremely popular, but why should we worry about it? One reason is that the amount of electronic text may soon approach or even exceed the amount of conventional text in the world. Lawrence and Giles (1999) reported that since 1997, the Internet had grown from 320 million web pages to 800 million web pages by February, 1999. This estimate may be much too small. A visit to the Google (www.google.com) search engine on December 24, 2003 showed that it had indexed 3,307,998,701 web pages. This number represents only those web pages that can be searched by automated computer programs. Many sites prevent search engines from examining them, making this estimate conservative. Furthermore, this estimate of electronic text, large as it seems, does not include all of the electronic text stored on individual computers, on CD-Rom disks, in e-mail correspondence, and the like. The important point is that there is a very large amount of electronic text and more of it is being created every day.

By contrast, the number of different books in the world seems to be approximately 6.5 billion (Howell & Berthon, 2000). This range represents different titles, not number of copies. There are still clearly far more books than web pages, but the fact that there is so much electronic text available means that our pedagogy has to take it into account.

Finally, Woodruff, Aoki, Brewer, Gauthier, and Rowe (1996) found that over 72% of all web pages contained GIFs (a graphic picture format), JPEGs (another graphic format), or video clips. Thus, the great majority of web pages clearly contain multimedia information, not just text.

These numbers are important because they suggest that it is essential that teachers prepare their students to read and understand electronic text as well as conventional text. In the future, no student (or adult) will be able to avoid electronic text or multimedia information. Students need to be taught to read electronic texts in addition to the conventional texts they already learn to read. The amount of electronic and multimedia text is expanding exponentially, and our students need to be able to deal with it if they are to be literate in the modern world. Both types of electronic text should be present and be used in instruction in classrooms of today to prepare our students for tomorrow.

WHAT ARE THE CHARACTERISTICS OF ELECTRONIC TEXT?

A common assumption is that text in electronic form is the same as conventional text, except for the medium (computer vs. paper). Based on limited evidence, we conclude that electronic text *can* be the same as conventional text, but that it often is *very different*. Two characteristics are worth mentioning.

Genre of Electronic Text

In other chapters in this volume, there is a discussion of the various genres of text and their relationship to reading and reading instruction. A basic distinction is between story genres and expository, or information, genres (see Duke & Tower, chap. 7, this volume) An important question is whether electronic text follows the same pattern of genres as conventional text. The answer is a bit complicated. There is no reason that electronic text should be limited in genre. It is possible to write electronic text in any genre. More importantly, there are examples of all sorts of genres of electronic text. However, the important question is whether the genres of text are the same in electronic and conventional formats.

Because the Internet is so dominant when it comes to electronic text, one way to determine what different genres of text exist in electronic format is to examine text on web pages. The answer is somewhat surprising. Predominantly, text on the Internet is informative prose, either expository or procedural. Although there is some story text, there is evidence that the vast majority of electronic text is information. Kamil and Lane (1998b) found that, in random samples of Internet web pages, 95% were information text. Although web pages with story text are becoming more common, they remain a very small portion of the total.

Readability of Electronic Text

Kamil and Lane (1997, 1998b) also found that text on the Internet was written at a very difficult level. For random samples of Internet pages, Kamil and Lane (1998b) found the average readability was about 10th grade level. One objection to this finding is that any generalization about 2.1 billion web pages may be inappropriate. However, Kamil and Lane did repeated samples and always found similar results. Similar findings were also reported in a study by Kim and Kamil (2000) using different criteria for selecting pages.

When Kamil and Lane looked at pages specifically designed by teachers for students, they found that the overall readability of text on these pages were at an average grade level of 9.3, an estimate similar to the difficulty of web pages, in general. This meant that the pages averaged three to five grade levels *above* the grade levels of the students for whom they were recommended.

On many of these pages, there were recommendations of pages for further study. These were links to other pages that students were expected to read for follow-up activities, independent reading, and other, similar activities. For the pages to which students were referred, the difficulty was 4 to 6.6 grade levels above the students' placement. Thus, the pages to which students were referred for further reading were even more difficult than the pages designed by the teachers. In addition, the sites were examined for genre. Only two sites contained text that could be classified as anything other than exposition or procedural.

What does this mean for classrooms? We elaborate on this later, but for now, there are two clear generalizations. First, electronic text is very important and it should be part of what is read in all classrooms. Second, instruction should include ways to read and comprehend electronic text. Heeding these generalizations will prepare students for reading in the future.

WHAT ARE THE CHARACTERISTICS OF MULTIMEDIA TEXTS AND DOCUMENTS?

Multimedia texts are electronic texts that include information in more than one modality. That is, in addition to text, they may include pictures, graphs, audio, video animations, or hypermedia links. Some multimedia text is simply conventional text with pictures or diagrams. When electronic text is combined with multimedia information, the combinations are often described as *multimedia documents*. Because so much electronic text contains multimedia information, there are important opportunities and challenges for reading and learning to read in primary-grade classrooms.

One important feature of many electronic multimedia documents is that they have the potential to support comprehension by providing information (context, definition, examples, and even pronunciations of words) that cannot be contained in conventional text. That is, such documents can offer alternative types of instructional support to students as they read. Surprisingly, although multimedia information is becoming widely available, there is little empirical guidance for the selection or use of these types of materials. Despite the limited amount of research, there is some agreement on the effects of using multimedia information. In the following sections, we offer a set of guidelines for the evaluation of multimedia texts for use in the classroom and some suggestions for the instruction that should accompany their use.

What Makes Multimedia Documents Effective?

Based on our review of the limited amount of research on multimedia texts, we offer the following five guidelines for effective multimedia documents:

Multimedia Documents Should Contain Appropriate Visual Representations.   Carefully selected *visual representations* can support text comprehension. Many studies have found that adding visual supports such as illustrations and diagrams to text can yield higher levels of long-term recall than text without illustrations.

Learners are apt to pay more attention to pictures when they accompany descriptions that are complex or difficult to visualize (Peeck, 1993). Superfluous visual information that accompanies texts is most likely ignored by students. When such information is ignored, it fails to help students comprehend and remember the text information. Levin, Anglin, and Carney (1987) concluded that decorational pictures, or pictures that are irrelevant to the text and primarily used to make a text more visually appealing, were not conducive to learning.

These studies suggest that effective multimedia documents should have visual supplements that are well elaborated, clearly identified, and specifically linked with the text information. Multimedia documents that are especially helpful for retaining information should have visual aids that are well integrated with the text so that students can make connections between the visuals and text information. These visuals should not be presented in isolation. Instead, they should be clearly labeled with elaborated definitions, when necessary, to help students actively select, interpret, and contextualize important information.

Dynamic Visual Images May Facilitate Comprehension.   In effective multimedia documents, the visuals should be appropriate to the content of the text. When documents contain a large amount of spatial and visual information, the dynamic presentation of visual images may help children to imagine complex information. Dynamic images, in particular, may help children to visualize changes in spatial relationships and remember salient information. As an example, children who were shown dynamic video images had higher scores on story comprehension than those who were shown static images (Sharp et al., 1995).

Verbal and Visual Information Should Be Presented Together.   Information that is processed both verbally and visually may be more memorable because there are two ways to remember it instead of one. In a study by Mayer and Moreno (1998), participants who received simultaneously presented verbal and visual information outperformed those who received only visual or only audio information on tasks of recall and problem solving.

Several studies have shown the benefit of coordinating the presentation of verbal and visual information to maximize learning. In particular, multimedia documents can augment the learning of visual and verbal information by presenting the information together. For example, visual information, such as pictures, video, and diagrams should have the verbal descriptions integrated with the visual and presented simultaneously. However, presenting two sources of information may place high demands on the learner. To overcome potential problems, learners should be given control over the presentation speed and the opportunity to review the information. The verbal information should be integrated effectively with visual, or picture based and graphical information. Multimedia documents that provide non-coordinated verbal and visual information, such as presenting an audio description immediately preceding or following the picture presentation, are not as effective as coordinated presentations.

One special type of verbal information is important to note. There is evidence that adding speech to reading at the computer assists students in learning to read (National Reading Panel, 2000). Software that allows readers to have the text read to them is widely available and would certainly help students learn to read and practice what they have learned without constant teacher supervision.

Prior Knowledge Should Determine the Selection of Multimedia Documents. The effect of prior knowledge on learning with multimedia information has significant implications for children. Although much research on this topic was conducted with older students, it does seem that students with low prior knowledge can benefit from hypermedia. However, it is also clear that students who do not have relevant domain knowledge can have difficulties with hypertext comprehension (Lawless & Kulikowich, 1996).

The interaction of prior knowledge and reading or learning from hypertext appears to be mediated by learner and task variables. In a study with 2nd grade children, Shin, Schallert, and Savenye (1994) found a significant interaction with learner control and the amount of prior knowledge. This suggests that students with low prior knowledge would be more successful within a more limited learner control environment. In effect, these students perform better when they have fewer choices about what they should read and how to read it. This study also suggested that children who have low subject matter expertise should have multimedia text with fewer user-controlled options for hypertext navigation and browsing.

Developmental Factors Affect the Way Children Process Multimedia Documents. When introducing multimedia information in the primary grades, there are some special developmental considerations. In multimedia documents where pictures, diagrams, graphs, and charts give supplementary information, proficient readers integrate the verbal and visual information in a cohesive way. However, recent research suggests that younger children may not be proficient at such integration. Moore and Scevak (1997) studied students in Grades 5, 7, and 9 reading science texts with multimedia components. The older students displayed a greater ability to link text and visual aid information explicitly than younger students did. The authors concluded that the explicit linking of text and diagrams and the ability to make referential connections is not commonly found among the younger children, especially when reading science texts. Small, Lovett, and Scher (1993) noted that many adults do not attend to information in visuals unless explicitly instructed to do so, and cited research finding that children often need directions to pay attention to visuals.

CLASSROOM IMPLICATIONS OF RESEARCH ON MULTIMEDIA DOCUMENTS

Collectively, the research on multimedia text and documents offers several implications for what the ideal multimedia text in a primary classroom might look like. Multimedia texts can help children understand text by offering carefully selected representations of difficult or hard to visualize concepts in the text. Furthermore, the use of dynamic visuals to illustrate spatial relationships and information may help children to get a richer model of the information than the presentation of static images. Effective visual representations are those that are elaborated with clear definitions and coherently referenced and linked with the text information. When appropriate for the learning task, the verbal and visual information should be coordinated for a deeper processing of the information. Children should be given the opportunity to control the speed of the multimedia presentation, as well as several opportunities to review the information.

Finally, the interaction of prior knowledge and development with learner and task variables is a critical variable in the selection and evaluation of multimedia texts. Although the data are tentative, preliminary research with young children suggests that children who have low prior knowledge may perform better in more limited user control hypertext environments. Above all, however, it is important that multimedia documents and electronic text become part of classroom reading material. In the next section we consider some of the instructional implications of including electronic text in the classroom.

Instruction for Reading Multimedia Texts

Research suggests that the ability to form connections between visual elements and text is developmental, and that even older students and adults often have difficulty in effectively processing visuals within conventional texts. However, because multimedia documents also require the integration of several other unique components such as sound, dynamic visuals, animations, videos, and hypertext, these difficulties may be heightened. Explicit strategies for synthesizing verbal and visual information are skills that appear to be developed and refined over time and experience. Consequently, guidance and instruction may be necessary when introducing multimedia texts in the classrooms. The research underscores the notion that merely presenting the texts and visual aids together may not be sufficient for children, especially younger ones, to process efficiently. Teachers need to be explicit in highlighting the connections.

In particular, additional instruction and strategies for evaluating and attending to visually and verbally presented information and referencing it with the text may be necessary for young children to comprehend and utilize the multimedia supplements. Kirby (1993) observed that students might need to be taught strategies and methods for complex and deep processing of visuals. Teaching strategies in the primary grades to review and integrate information critically in visuals and text may reduce the chance that children will skim or ignore the aids. In addition, children should be clearly instructed to attend to the specific goals and purpose for the use of the multimedia information so that they can look for and attend to relevant information.

Reading Multimedia Texts With Hyperlinks

For multimedia texts that include hyperlinks, greater contextual support for the hyperlinks within the documents may be one way to help children predict the content and relevance of links. With respect to the special case of reading texts with hyperlinks, additional strategies may be necessary for proficient reading and navigation. Hypertexts, or electronic texts that include links to additional information or content, demand special skills for monitoring comprehension, the timing and navigation of links to prevent problems such as disorientation or distraction. In addition, children who are accustomed to reading linear documents may become confused or distracted by following links incorporated within the text of documents. Preliminary research found that the use of specific strategies, such as being able to identify important text nodes and read them longer, can help students read these materials better.

In an experiment with graduate students highly experienced in reading online documents, Kim and Kamil (1999) identified several strategies that were used to predict the content and relevance of hyperlinks, allowing readers to monitor the timing and access of links. Some example strategies include interpreting the URL's of hyperlinks to predict the relevance of the link before leaving the document, and constant metacognitive monitoring of comprehension. Young readers or children who have not had much experience with reading online documents are not likely to have a developed repertoire of sophisticated strategies. With respect to introducing multimedia documents with hyperlinks to primary grade children, explicit teaching of a diverse array of strategies for basic navigation and reading may be critical to successful reading outcomes.

SUMMARY OF CLASSROOM IMPLICATIONS
OF USING ELECTRONIC TEXT

When implementing multimedia texts in primary-grade classrooms, the research suggests that there are developmental differences in the ability to synthesize the combined presentation of verbal and visual information. Merely presenting multimedia information does not appear to be sufficient for children to utilize the verbal and visual information proficiently. Children may need additional instruction in reading multimedia texts, such as the learning of specific strategies for referencing visuals with text, attending to salient information in visually presented data, or interpreting graphs. Children should have clear learning goals and understanding of the task before viewing the multimedia material, and be aware of what kinds of information they should be attending to in the materials. Given the special demands of reading multimedia texts with hyperlinks, specific instruction and strategies for navigating, monitoring comprehension, and interpreting links may be necessary for children to interact and learn with hypertext.

Our current knowledge on the effective design and implementation of multimedia texts for children is rudimentary. As we learn more, our use of electronic text and multimedia information will be refined. Because we believe that it is important to teach children to read and understand these types of text, we look to practice for additional guidance.

IMPLEMENTING ELECTRONIC TEXTS IN CLASSROOMS: AN EXAMPLE

Implementation of computer technology in schools has been slow compared to other realms. Equipment, software, and training are expensive for school districts. However, the district from which this example is drawn has had the benefit of state money and local bond levies to support technology. In the last 5 years, there has been a major change in the training, hardware, and software provided for students' advancement in the world of technology.

The starting point was one computer, with a limited amount of software, in each classroom. Each teacher was expected to know the software and the operations of the computer without any instruction. Time played a huge factor in dealing with this new animal in the classroom. Computers and software were used mainly for reinforcement of skills. Many of the software programs were formatted in the same manner as workbooks with fill-in-the-blank items, sequences of pictures and text, reading a passage and finding the main idea, comprehension questions, and so on. The students enjoyed this new format, but it was an expensive tool for the simple reinforcement of skills.

The state and district became aware that computers alone would not help students become technology-literate. When computer education for teachers was funded, each teacher was given 2 days of intensive professional development (in a 2-year period) and offered additional workshops to become more knowledgeable in the basic aspects of computers. This included the use of the hardware and the new software purchased. In addition, a support system was established. Each school had a teacher assigned as a technology person who worked as a trouble-shooter. This person was a classroom teacher who received a stipend for the extra responsibilities. Eventually the district formed a Technology Department and hired extra full-time technology specialists, or as they were fondly called, "the Techies." Their responsibilities included working with teachers and students. They informed and directed teachers in the use of computer software and answered the many questions asked. A Techie and a teacher would collaborate on integrating technology and curriculum into a classroom activity. The Techie would play an important role in this inclusion activity by modeling, instructing, and working with individual students.

As of this writing, each classroom in Grades K–5 has four to five computers with a printer. Each classroom is also equipped with a television and VCR. Other equipment (scanner, digital camera, and six laptops on a cart for use in classrooms) is shared by the entire school.

Once the technology was in place, a new question needed to be answered: How should technology in an elementary school setting serve instruction in literacy? The answer was a set of written benchmarks for the grade levels written by the members of the Technology Department. The perspective on technology developed by the team is that computers should be used purposefully to accomplish tasks or to create products rather than only as devices to deliver supplementary instruction. This is an important paradigm in thinking in the district. The students are being taught to use many resources to develop a product that they have authored and constructed on their own. It is a process that begins in kindergarten and is emphasized throughout the grades.

Kindergarten in any school is a challenge in itself. In this school, the kindergarten class is made up of some students who have been in day care since infancy as well as students who have never seen a piece of print in their homes. When exposed to the computer, all of the students, regardless of their background, seem to enjoy the experience.

In kindergarten, students have their first exposure to simple software at the computer, some instructional help in reading, and the opportunity to begin creating multimedia documents. The students usually receive their first introduction from a parent during center time. They are taught and become independent in the use of simple software programs designed for kindergarten students. As the year progresses and the class is working on a theme, teachers schedule time for the technology specialist to come and help in the classroom with the students and computers. The teacher collaborates with the media specialist to organize software and resources related to the content topics being discussed in class.

At the beginning of a unit or theme, the teacher reads the information to the students and opens a class discussion. A common theme that is used is connected to the habitat the students are studying in science. The topic is discussed with the group and ideas are generated and written on chart paper. The students then write and draw what they have learned about the topic on a piece of paper. The teacher and the technology specialists instruct the children on using KID PIX, a child's version of Hyperstudio. The students copy their writing and drawing on the computer. The entire class contributes work that becomes a slide show on the computer. A hardcopy of the text is made into a book for the class to share. This is usually done in the spring of a half-day kindergarten. These activities allow students to be introduced to computer activities, combine reading and writing, and show that both reading and writing are goal-directed.

In first grade, the development continues, adding both technical and cognitive sophistication. An example of this occurred in one first-grade class. After reading Eric Carle's book *Have You Seen My Cat?*, the students walked around the school asking if anyone had seen their principal. They took a digital camera with them, taking pictures of everyone they had asked about the location of the principal. Using KID PIX, they wrote a new story called *Have You Seen My Principal?* The students enjoyed their story because it had a common background to which they could relate. Other multimedia projects in first grade focus on science topics or individual slide shows of only a few pages. The students are gaining the knowledge and independence to work on their own or class-assigned topics.

By midyear of second grade, the students have continued to work with the computer, but the teacher is expecting that the students find their own material through research. The teacher and media specialist gather material on a topic and bring it to the classroom or the students may go to the library for resources. The resources include books, CDs, tapes, and movies. The students conduct research using the books and CDs, writing about the topic based on what they have learned. Again, although the teachers have modeled all this since kindergarten, the additions are in the sophistication of both the technical skills and the literacy skills.

One example of this modeling occurred as students in a second-grade class were studying Europe. The students were asked to create a list of things that they would want to know about a different country. The teacher charted these items during shared writing. These topics included, for example, school, food, clothes, transportation, sports, what children did for fun, what the flag looked like. The teacher made sure that these topics could be found in the table of contents or index of the different countries' books. The students knew how to use these information tools. After picking their country, they could also bring in resources from home. Some brought in books from home or the library, or some parents helped the child to do research on the Internet. After gathering the information, the students assembled their data on a simple graphic organizer made of a large piece of construction paper. They then transferred it from their rough draft to KID PIX to create a slide show. This project became a slide show of the European countries. A hardcopy of the slide show was printed for each child to take home and share with parents.

Another use of the computer in second grade is publishing material written by the students. (This may also be done in kindergarten and first grade, but the child dictates and an adult or older student does the writing on the computer.) Starting in second grade, students can write a story, poem, or letter. After it has been proofread, the student then writes it on the computer using a child's word processing program.

The intermediate grades continue to foster and support the learning process. The third-grade teachers bookmark pages on the Internet for the students to use in research. Students begin to use CD-Rom encyclopedias and resource discs independently for genre studies, social studies, and science. Using specific software, graphs, tables, and charts can be created for the topics studied. These are then incorporated in compositions and presentations.

Fourth- and fifth-grade students are given the full use of the Internet, with teacher or volunteer supervision, for research projects. They use the library media support for their studies. In addition to personal projects, the fifth-grade class, using specific web-creating software, has developed a web page for the school that they update regularly. This year, a fifth-grade group started a school newspaper using the software template for the organization of the paper.

Electronic texts are used in the gifted and special education programs as tools for fitting each student's needs. The gifted program begins to use the Internet at an earlier age because of the students' higher reading and comprehension ability. This can be an advantage to the classroom because the gifted students can tutor their peers.

The Internet can be a great asset for finding information, but the teachers or parent helpers usually do the actual work on the Internet for the students in the primary grades. They gather information for the students by using bookmarks or making hard copies as it is usually too difficult for young children to use the Internet without a good reader, older student, or an adult helping.

Incorporating electronic texts in the classroom can only be accomplished when classroom teachers are confident in their abilities to use the appropriate technology. Teachers need time to learn and absorb these new tools. In the school we are describing, change is happening slowly, but it is occurring. Teachers in the entire school have learned, and now use, technology and electronic text more constructively each year. Five years ago, the only use of computers was software games and books. Now with a broader knowledge base, teachers are integrating electronic text into the curriculum. Students are using computers for research everyday. In the library students gather information from electronic encyclopedias, information books, topic CDs, and the Internet. They are using standard computers as well as laptops. Their thirst for knowledge and understanding on their topic has increased with the addition of electronic texts. Because they have access to so much more information, from so many different sources, students, with the teachers' guidance, are learning to evaluate texts and compare information. They are discriminating more between fact and opinion that contributes to their understanding of a topic, a process that enhances their reading and learning about the topic. In essence, electronic texts in these schools are helping the students and teachers become more enriched learners.

WHAT DOES THE FUTURE HOLD?

We will continue to see increasing reliance on computers and electronic text of all sorts. What we need to guarantee is that efforts to incorporate these new materials in classrooms have several types of support. First, teachers need appropriate support for hardware and software. Second, there has to be appropriate thought given to curriculum that makes use of these new computer technologies. Finally, we have to insure that students are offered appropriate instruction to be able to use electronic texts effectively and efficiently.

These are not optional. In the future, literacy will include the ability to read all forms of text, not just conventional print. We must prepare students for that future.

REFERENCES

Howell, A., & Berthon, H. (2000). *Preserving access to digital information (PADI): An opportunity for global cooperation activities.* Available: http://www.ifla.org/VI/4/conf/howell.pdf

Kamil, M., & Lane, D. (1997, December). *Using information text for first grade reading instruction: Theory and practice.* Paper presented at the National Reading Conference, Scottsdale, AZ.

Kamil, M., & Lane, D. (1998a). Researching the relationship between technology and literacy: An agenda for the 21st century. In D. Reinking, M. McKenna, L. Labbo, & R. Kieffer (Eds.), *Handbook of literacy and technology: Transformations in a post-typographic world* (pp. 323–341). Mahwah, NJ: Lawrence Erlbaum Associates.

Kamil, M. L., & Lane, D. (1998b, December). *Information text, task demands for students, and readability of text on the Internet.* Paper presented at the National Reading Conference, Austin, TX.

Kim, H., & Kamil, M. L. (1999, December). *Exploring hypertext reading and strategy use for structured vs. unstructured texts.* Paper presented at the National Reading Conference, Orlando, FL.

Kim, H., & Kamil, M. L. (2000, December). *Children's preferences, motivation, and learning in electronic and multimedia texts*. Paper presented at the National Reading Conference, Scottsdale, AZ.

Kirby, J. R. (1993). Collaborative and competitive effects of verbal and spatial processes. *Learning and Instruction, 3*, 201–214.

Lawless, K., & Kulikowich, J. (1996). Understanding hypertext navigation through cluster analysis. *Journal of Educational Computing Research, 14*, 385–399.

Lawrence, S., & Giles C. (1999). Accessibility of information on the web. *Nature, 400* (6740), 107–109.

Levin, J. R., Anglin, G. J., & Carney, R. N. (1987). On empirically validating functions of pictures in prose. In D. M. Willows & H. A. Houghton (Eds.), *The Psychology of Illustration: Vol. 1. Basic Research* (pp. 51–86). New York: Springer-Verlag.

Mayer, R. E., & Moreno, R. (1998). A split-attention effect in multimedia learning: Evidence for dual processing systems in working memory. *Journal of Educational Psychology, 90*, 312–320.

Moore, P. J., & Scevak, J. J. (1997). Learning from texts and visual aids: A developmental perspective. *Journal of Research in Reading, 20*, 205–223.

National Reading Panel. (2000). *Report of the National Reading Panel: Teaching children to read*. Bethesda, MD: National Institute of Child Health and Human Development.

Peeck, J. (1993) Increasing picture effects in learning. *Learning and Instruction, 3*, 227–238.

Sharp, D., Bransford, J., Goldman, S. R., Risko, V. J., Kinzer, C. K, & Vye, N. (1995). Dynamic visual support for story comprehension and mental model building by young, at-risk children. *Educational Technology Research and Development, 43*, 25–42.

Shin, C., Schallert, D., & Savenye, W. (1994) Effects of learner control, advisement, and prior knowledge on young students' learning in a hypertext environment. *Educational Technology Research & Development, 42*, 33–46.

Small, M., Lovett, S., & Scher, M. (1993). Pictures facilitate children's recall of unillustrated expository prose. *Journal of Educational Psychology, 85*, 520–528.

Woodruff, A., Aoki, P., Brewer, E., Gauthier, P., & Rowe, L. (1996, May). *An investigation of documents from the World Wide Web*. Paper presented at the Fifth International World Wide Web Conference, Paris, France. Available: http://www5conf.inria.fr/fich_html/papers/P7/Overview.html

III

Some Issues
Surrounding Text Selection

10

The Selection
and Use of English Texts
With Young English
Language Learners

Georgia Earnest García
Eurydice Bouchereau Bauer
University of Illinois at Urbana-Champaign

María is 6 years old. She is Mexican-American, and she and her parents speak Spanish. María knows some English from watching television and listening to English-speaking adults and children in the larger community at the store, gas station, and park. Her parents want her to learn English, but they also want her to continue to develop her Spanish. Spanish represents the family's culture and is a key part of her family's identity and heritage. María has many relatives who speak Spanish, and the family periodically travels to Mexico for special events and holidays. Her parents have enrolled her in a bilingual first-grade classroom, where she will receive literacy and content area instruction in Spanish, along with beginning English-as-a-second-language (ESL) instruction.

Tuan also is 6 years old. He is Vietnamese and speaks Vietnamese with his grandparents and parents but speaks English with his older brother and sister. Tuan's parents are worried that he is rapidly losing his Vietnamese. Because they speak very little English, they are concerned that they will not be able to communicate with their own son. There are few relatives who live nearby who speak Vietnamese. They do not plan to visit Vietnam anytime soon. Because Tuan's school district does not offer an English/Vietnamese bilingual education program, his parents have enrolled him in a sheltered English program. In this program, his ESL trained teacher will use special ESL techniques to help him acquire English and other academic subjects as he learns to read and write in English.

Wen-Hsien is from Taiwan. Like María and Tuan, she also is 6 years old. At home, Wen-Hsien speaks Mandarin to her parents and grandparents. However, there are only five other English Language Learners, and two other Mandarin speakers, enrolled at Wen-Hsien's school, not enough students to warrant a sheltered English program or bilingual education program. Accordingly, Wen-Hsien will be placed in an all-English classroom that predominantly serves native English speakers. The classroom teacher, who only speaks English and who has no ESL training, will teach her literacy and content area topics in English. She also will receive an hour of daily ESL instruction from an ESL specialist hired by the district. Because her parents do not want her to lose her Mandarin, she also attends Chinese school for 5 hours every Sunday.

María, Tuan, and Wen-Hsien represent some of the experiences of English Language Learners, that is, second-language learners of English, currently entering U.S. schools. Demographic reports indicate that at least 22% of the school-age population in the United States live in homes in which a language other than English is spoken (Anstrom, 1996; Crawford, 1997). Although it is not unusual for some English Language Learners, such as Tuan and Wen-Hsien, to receive school instruction only in English, we need to remember that these children also use another language at home. Therefore, even though they may not receive school instruction in their native (home) language, they are bilingual learners who are thinking and constructing knowledge across two languages and cultures.

Classroom teachers, school administrators, and policymakers often ask how they can best meet the literacy needs of English Language Learners. This chapter provides guidance in the selection and use of English text with English Language Learners in a variety of school settings: bilingual, ESL, and all-English. From the outset, we need to state that we know considerably more about the reading processes, instruction, and selection of text for young monolingual (one language) children and native-English-speaking children than we do for bilingual (two language) children or English Language Learners (García, 2000). In an attempt to guide educators, curriculum developers, and policymakers in an area that is not well researched, we summarize briefly what has been written about the reading development and instruction of young English Language Learners and bilingual children. Under the heading of reading instruction, we then discuss what has been written about the selection of English text for these populations. Then, drawing from this review, we conclude the chapter with several recommendations for the selection and use of English text with English Language Learners.

THE READING DEVELOPMENT OF YOUNG ENGLISH LANGUAGE LEARNERS

English Language Learners and native-English speakers appear to employ some of the same general reading processes while reading in English (García, 2001; Gregory, 1996). For example, phonological awareness and word recognition strategies are key features of beginning reading for both groups of children. English Language Learners and native-English speakers also make use of graphophonic (sound–symbol), lexical (vocabulary), semantic (meaning), and syntactic (language structure) knowledge to decode and comprehend text. They rely on experiential knowledge and knowledge of text (topic, genre, author) to make hypotheses and inferences to guide their reading.

In addition, due to their exposure to two languages, English Language Learners may develop enhanced metalinguistic awareness (knowledge about language) that may aid them in their English reading (see Bauer, 2000). Their use of reading processes and their responses to English text also may differ from those of monolingual native-English speakers (García, 2001). Factors that may differentially affect their reading development in English and use of reading processes include their exposure to two languages, literacy development in the native language, structure of the native language, their oral proficiency in English, and their previous experiences with literacy artifacts (e.g., reading of the Qur'an) and literacy events (e.g., storybook reading). English Language Learners also may develop cognitive strategies (e.g., translating) that are unique to their bilingual status, strategies that may help them in their English reading. We organized the discussion that follows so that we briefly review each of these factors and delineate each factor's possible effect on English Language Learners' reading development and/or use of reading processes.

Exposure to Two Languages

A number of researchers have reported that bilingual children younger than 6, who have been exposed to two languages, demonstrate enhanced metalinguistic awareness, the ability to talk about, analyze, and play with language, compared to monolingual children (Bialystok, 1997; Bruck & Genesee, 1995; Galambos & Goldin-Meadow, 1990; Göncz & Kodzopeljic, 1991). By the age of 3, most bilingual children are able to separate their languages (Pérez & Torres-Guzmán, 2002). In a case study of a young German/English bilingual,

Bauer (2000) extended the discussion on metalinguistic awareness by showing that her 2-year-old daughter generally responded to the reading of texts in German and English according to the language in which the book was read.

Bruck and Genesee (1995) proposed that young bilingual children develop a heightened awareness of language because they intuitively analyze the similarities and differences in the languages. Based on Bauer's work with her German/English bilingual daughter, Bauer and Montero (2001) suggested that young bilingual children who are immersed in print-rich environments in two languages may develop a keen understanding of the concept of text. As Bauer and Montero explained, they are aware of "which aspect of text is tied to the language and which is not" (p. 124). Several researchers have reported that 5- and 6-year-old bilingual children outperform monolingual children on referential tasks such as demonstrating that they know that the length of a word does not correspond to the size of the referent (e.g., mosquito vs. ox; Bialystok, 1997; Göncz & Kodzopeljic, 1991). Bilingual children also outperform monolingual children on grammaticality judgment tasks, in which they show that they are more aware of the type of grammar or sentence structure that is acceptable in a particular language (Galambos & Goldin-Meadow, 1990). Gregory (1996) reported that even when major exposure to English occurs in school, 5- and 6-year old English Language Learners tend to have good memories for words and the ability to develop excellent sight vocabulary. We suspect that their memory for words is triggered by their exposure to print in two languages and to increased metalinguistic awareness.

Native-Language Literacy Development

Gregory (1996) noted that it is not unusual for English Language Learners who have had some literacy instruction in their native language to develop good sound–symbol correspondence knowledge that they can readily apply to English decoding. Other researchers have reported that children who have developed phonological awareness in their native languages (e.g., French, Punjabi, Spanish) typically can transfer this knowledge to reading in a second language (e.g., English, French) without formal instruction (Chiappe & Siegel, 1999; Comeau, Cormier, Grandmaison, & Lacroix, 1999; Durgunoğlu, Nagy, & Hancin-Bhatt, 1993). According to Gregory (1996), even children who are learning to write in languages that are less phonologically oriented, such as Mandarin, can transfer their knowledge of symbol–meaning correspondence and their attention to detailed differences in character construction to their English reading.

Several researchers have reported that English Language Learners who have been read to in their native language can transfer their knowledge of reading, texts, genres, and story lines to their English reading (Goldman, Reyes, & Varnhagen, 1984; Gregory, 1996; Jiménez, García, & Pearson, 1995, 1996). For example, Goldman and her colleagues reported that Spanish/English bilingual children were able to transfer their knowledge of fables from their Spanish reading to their English reading when they were allowed to use their Spanish for the English retelling. According to Gregory (1996), when English Language Learners are exposed to reading in English that is similar to what they have heard in their native language, then positive cross-linguistic transfer occurs and the children are able to make more accurate predictions and inferences.

Researchers who studied older English Language Learners (8–13 year olds) have reported that these students often use similar comprehension strategies while reading in English and their native languages, indicating cross-linguistic transfer (García, 2001; Jiménez et al., 1995, 1996). Although cross-linguistic transfer is not automatic with all bilingual readers, it does seem to characterize those students who are strong readers (García, 1998; Jiménez et al., 1995, 1996). In a study with Spanish/English bilingual sixth- and seventh-graders, Jiménez and his colleagues (1996) concluded that the strong English readers had a unitary view of reading across the two languages, a view that focused on meaning and that enabled them to make use of cross-linguistic transfer. However, the poor English readers focused on how the words were decoded and/or pronounced in each of the languages and thought that reading was different in each of the languages. Jiménez et al. (1996) speculated that the bottom-up view of reading held by the poor English readers may have accounted for their lack of use of cross-linguistic strategies and limited use of comprehension strategies.

Language Structure of the Native Language

Researchers who investigated the cross-linguistic transfer of phonological awareness have pointed out that students who already have well-developed phonological awareness in their native language should be able to use this awareness to decode in their second language (Durgunoğlu et al., 1993; Verhoeven, 1994). These findings imply that bilingual children may not need much instruction on sound–symbol correspondences in the second language if the correspondences are consistent with what they already know in their native language. On the other hand, these same researchers warn that it is very likely that the children will need instruction on sound–symbol correspondences that do not occur in their native languages.

Differences in the structure of English and the native language also may mean that English Language Learners will make some mistakes in English pro-

nunciation while orally reading or may not be able to differentiate among certain phonemes during a listening task (García, 1994; Gregory, 1996). There is
some evidence that when Asian children read English orally, they may skip unfamiliar grammatical structures that do not exist in their native language (such
as she/he, plurals, or verb endings). However, García and Gregory both warned
that these behaviors rarely reflect receptive or comprehension difficulties and
should be evaluated in terms of their impact on students' actual text comprehension and not their accurate oral reading of a text.

Oral English Proficiency

Although young bilingual children's literacy development in the native language is a better predictor of their English literacy development than their
English oral proficiency (García, 2001), English oral proficiency does play a
role in their literacy development. For example, due to their limited English
oral proficiency, English Language Learners will not recognize all of the words
that they can decode in English. García (1991) and Saville-Troike (1984)
both noted that unknown English vocabulary usually is one of the most difficult linguistic factors that English Language Learners face. Gregory (1996)
also observed that English Language Learners are not as adept as native-English speakers at using semantic cues, such as meaningful combination of words
(e.g., bread and butter), and syntactic cues (grammar) to figure out the meanings of words that they can decode.

Previous Experiences With Literacy Artifacts and Events

The background knowledge and literacy experiences that English Language
Learners bring to English reading also may differ considerably from their native-English-speaking peers (García, 1991; Jiménez et al., 1996). Gregory
(1996) pointed out that how children have been exposed to print in the native
language may affect how they respond to beginning reading instruction in English. For example, Gregory (1996) reported that parents of Mandarin-speaking
children from the People's Republic of China or Hong Kong may not appreciate
their children's early attempts to write their names in English when the names
are not written correctly because learning to produce beautiful script in Mandarin is highly valued and requires practice and hard work. In addition to attending school in English, these children often attend Chinese school on the
weekends, where they practice writing Chinese characters in exercise books. If
the parents believe that their children first must learn to read and write words
correctly before they can participate in book reading and writing activities, then

they and their children may not be comfortable with pretend reading, invented spelling, and/or parent–child book reading. Gregory (1996) explained that in this situation "a love of books ... comes after reading is learned and not as a necessary prerequisite to it" (pp. 32–33).

Similarly, children who come from Arabic backgrounds and who are learning to read the Qur'an often learn to decode and recite text without necessarily knowing what it means (Farah, 1998; Gregory, 1996). Gregory suggested that because these children rely on religious leaders to interpret the Qur'an, they may be hesitant to question the author's intent.

Bilingual Strategies

Sometimes, English Language Learners use strategies unique to their bilingual status to demonstrate or aid their comprehension of English text. For example, Bauer and Montero (2001) reported that while reading books, Bauer's young German/English-speaking daughter often code-switched (i.e., used German words in her English responses to texts or vice versa as well as alternated using statements in German and English). Researchers who have studied Spanish/English bilingual children between the ages of 8 and 13 found that these children often use code-switching and paraphrased translating (putting what they have read in English into their own words in Spanish) to make sense out of English text (García, 1998; Jiménez et al., 1996). A number of researchers have reported that Spanish/English bilingual children demonstrate enhanced comprehension of English text when they are allowed to use Spanish to retell or explain what they have read in English (García, 1991, 1998; Goldman et al., 1984; Jiménez et al, 1996).

THE READING INSTRUCTION OF YOUNG ENGLISH LANGUAGE LEARNERS

In the previous section, we discussed what we knew about the reading development of English Language Learners. Although the topics that we covered have important instructional implications, very few researchers have investigated how instruction can improve the English reading development of English Language Learners in Grades K–3 (García, 2000). In the next section, we review what we do know about the type of literacy instruction that English Language Learners often receive and how several early literacy activities in English can be adapted to meet the cultural and linguistic needs of English Language Learners. We also discuss several researchers' findings and recommendations related to how English Language Learners respond to English text.

Instructional Practices

Unfortunately, we do not know very much about the optimal literacy instruction for English Language Learners either in their native language or in English (García, 2000). Several researchers who investigated the type of literacy instruction provided to English Language Learners reported that these students typically receive instruction that is teacher-directed, whole-class, and passive, regardless of the language of instruction (Moss & Puma, 1995; Padrón, 1994; Ramirez, Yuen, & Ramey, 1991). In a study that evaluated the type of reading instruction provided to first- and third-grade English Language Learners who were receiving Title 1 services, Moss and Puma (1995) reported that the students' performance was adversely affected by low teacher expectations and unqualified teachers. Forty percent of the students' first-grade teachers and 33% of the third-grade teachers did not think that the students had the background experience needed to do school work. Sadly, the type of instruction that the students received did not match many of the instructional features that have been reported as being effective with English Language Learners (August & Hakuta, 1997; Tikunoff et al., 1991). Among others, these include high teacher and student expectations; high student engagement; active teaching strategies with clear communication, appropriate explanations, and clarification; use of both the native language and English to mediate instruction; incorporation of the home culture; and integration of ESL instruction with content area instruction.

We suspect that teachers of English Language Learners who are informed about bilingualism and second-language acquisition issues, and who use this information in their instructional decision making and assessment practices, are able to adapt many of the same high quality literacy practices that are touted for monolingual native-English-speaking students. However, how well English Language Learners respond to or benefit from English literacy instruction probably depends on a range of factors. Among others, these include the students' literacy development in the native language; their oral English proficiency; the teacher's use of ESL techniques to "shelter" (support) beginning English Language Learners' literacy instruction (e.g., visuals, props, gestures, hands-on activities, and slowed and carefully delivered speech); the provision of native language instruction or support; and the teacher's identification and incorporation of students' linguistic and cultural experiences into literacy instruction.

For example, a major and expected feature of early literacy instruction in the United States is adult–child storybook reading. When English Language Learners are exposed to adult–child storybook reading in their native language and have developed enough oral English proficiency to understand the oral reading of English texts, then they usually are attentive to storybook reading in English. They also are attentive to other types of early reading practices that typically accompany adult–child book reading, such as shared reading and pretend reading. Bauer (2000) reported that her young German/English bilingual daughter responded positively to shared reading and pretend reading in both languages. Her daughter had been raised in a "one language, one parent rule" household, had been exposed to adult–child book reading in both languages, and was developing emergent literacy and oral fluency in both languages simultaneously.

Other researchers have reported that if young students are not very proficient in English and/or not used to adult–child book reading, then they sometimes are not engaged in pretend reading or teacher read-alouds of English books (Carger, 1993; Gregory, 1996; Tsai & García, 2000). When teachers use the native language and/or ESL techniques to shelter students' understanding of the English books being read, then their participation usually improves (Battle, 1993; Carger, 1993; Peregoy & Boyle, 2001). Carger (1993) described how kindergarten English Language Learners of Mexican descent became engaged in pretend reading after hearing a storybook with culturally familiar features read three times. After the initial reading of the story in English, the children had difficulty doing the pretend reading even though Carger allowed them to use Spanish and English. Carger credited their improved pretend reading in English to the provision of felt figures and a felt board during the second pretend reading of the book and to the reading of the book in Spanish before the third pretend reading. Carger explained that the felt figures and felt board and the use of Spanish helped to scaffold the children's pretend reading in English. Battle (1993) also found that Mexican-American kindergartners in a bilingual classroom actively became engaged in English storybook reading when the teacher used Spanish to explain or translate unclear parts and accepted and built on students' spontaneous and authentic responses in Spanish and English.

According to Battle (1993), the students' participation in English storybook reading also was enhanced by the teacher's choice of storybooks that included topics or situations that the children found engaging and the teacher's collaborative book reading style that initiated and built on student talk. Other researchers have noted the importance of encouraging students to relate personally to the text. Thornburg (1993) found that teachers in a family literacy program were not able to get English Language Learners to respond to storybook reading in English when they asked story grammar or prediction questions. However, when they asked the children to relate the story to their own lives, then their participation increased.

Several researchers conducted ethnographies that examined the literacy participation and development of English Language Learners in all English classrooms (Fitzgerald & Noblit, 2000; Schmidt, 1993). Schmidt documented the literacy participation of a Southeastern Asian child and a child from India in an all-English kindergarten setting that emphasized reading, writing, listening, and speaking through social interaction instruction with thematic units, minilessons, and centers. She reported that the children often seemed lost and confused about the purposes of formal literacy instruction and were not able to participate effectively in small group literacy activities. She concluded that, compared to their native-English-speaking peers, the two children had problems with "oral directions, sequence relationships, vocabulary knowledge, and idiomatic expressions" (p. 192). Schmidt's data remind us of Tabors and Snow's (2001) warning that English Language Learners in the all-English classroom face the double risk of not becoming fully literate in English and of losing proficiency and literacy development in their native language.

Fitzgerald and Noblit (2000) compared the use of a balanced literacy approach in English with 8 Latina/o English Language Learners who were enrolled in a first-grade, all-English-speaking classroom with 12 other native-English-speaking students enrolled in the same classroom. The balanced literacy approach that was implemented included daily word study activities, literature responses, writing, and guided and unguided reading. Fitzgerald, who was the classroom teacher, explained that she wanted the students to understand and develop both *local knowledge* (e.g., sound–symbol correspondence, sight words, word meanings) and *global knowledge* (e.g., how to use various meaning-getting strategies and interest in reading; p. 7).

According to Fitzgerald and Noblit (2000), a purpose of their study was to see if balanced literacy instruction designed for native-English speakers, without cultural or linguistic adaptations, would be just as effective with English Language Learners. They argued that the balanced literacy approach was effective because by the end of the school year, all of the English Language Learners had made some progress and had demonstrated the same type of variation in their literacy development as the native-English speakers, except in one area: receptive vocabulary. In this domain, all of the English Language Learners performed considerably lower than their native-English-speaking classmates. Tabors and Snow (2001) warned that findings like Fitzgerald and Noblit's "suggest that the early accomplishments of the children seem almost language free—centered around recognizing sight words and decoding regular words but not focused on integrating comprehension into early reading processes" (p. 173). Given that one of the major comprehension problems that English Language Learners face is unfamiliar English vocabulary, the Latina/o students' poor performance in this area is particularly problematic. Anderson and Roit (1996) reported that comprehension of English text, not decoding, appears to be the major problem for English Language Learners and, therefore, should be a major aim of their literacy instruction.

Close examination of the Fitzgerald and Noblit (2000) study from a second-language perspective raises several other issues. First, even though the authors claimed that no instructional adaptations were made, several of the techniques that the teacher reported using to make her instruction comprehensible are recognized features of sheltered ESL instruction (e.g., her slow enunciation of English words and use of facial expressions and gestures). Second, we suspect that some of the variation in the literacy progress of the English Language Learners might have been due to varied levels of native-language literacy development, variations that were not taken into account. For example, about half of the English Language Learners, although making some progress, still continued to perform poorly on the various literacy measures. The one English Language Learner who repeatedly was cited as being successful scored 100% on an English sentence dictation task (in which the sound represented was counted but not the correct spelling) as early as December, even though he did not know English at the beginning of the school year. This child had arrived in the United States from his home country one month prior to entering the classroom. Given what we know about the transfer of phonological awareness in bilingual children, it is very likely that he already knew sound–symbol correspondences in Spanish and was able to transfer this expertise to English. Because the researchers did not explore the English Language Learners' literacy development in Spanish or use Spanish to explore how the children were making sense out of English literacy instruction, several key questions about the students' literacy performance and understanding of English literacy instruction were left unanswered.

Other researchers who investigated the type of literacy instruction provided to English Language Learners have warned that it is important to adapt instruction so that it meets the students' linguistic and cultural needs (Anderson & Roit, 1996; García, 1998; Reyes, 1991). As Reyes explained:

> What is often ignored in program implementation is the fact that students who do not belong to the "culture of power" may not always understand the rules of classroom discourse. The high regard that Hispanics hold for teachers as authority figures in the classroom, for example, suggests that they rely upon, and expect direct instructional intervention from the teacher. They look for it. (p. 310)

In a study of a sixth-grade, process-oriented, bilingual classroom, Reyes observed that the Latina/o students needed more explicit help with standard language conventions in English and the selection of English texts for independent reading than was generally provided by a process approach. Others have noted that because vocabulary is such an important issue for English Language Learners, teachers need to give this domain considerably more attention than they normally would in an all-English setting (Anderson & Roit, 1996; Gersten & Jiménez, 1994). Finally, numerous researchers have noted the importance of allowing English Language Learners to use their native language to respond to and discuss English text, even when the language of instruction or assessment is English (Battle, 1993; Carger, 1993; García, 1991; Goldman et al., 1984; Reyes, 1991; Saville-Troike, 1984).

Text Issues

Few researchers have focused on the content and language of texts and the effects that specific types of texts may have on English Language Learners' reading. Bauer (2000) provided an alternative perspective on the role of text in understanding bilingual students' participation in early literacy activities. She observed that the format of the text differentially affected her young German-English daughter's responses to text during shared and pretend reading. For example, when predictable/rhythmic texts were read and her daughter participated in shared or pretend reading, she very rarely code-switched (i.e., used German with an English reader, or vice versa). Instead, she appeared to concentrate on repeating the predictable/rhythmic refrains and read the text in the language in which it had been read. Bauer concluded that the repetitive and predictable structure of texts such as *Brown Bear, Brown Bear, What do you see?* (Martin, 1967) provided her daughter with the scaffolding that she needed to remember the text as it had been read to her, enhancing her shared reading/pretend reading in the respective language.

On the other hand, texts that were not predictable/patterned and that focused on life experiences to which Bauer's daughter could relate resulted in more code-switching as she used the language that responded to the event or person being depicted in the text to discuss the text. The reading of realistic fiction that related to her life, such as *Black, White, Just Right* (Davol, 1993) resulted in more adult–child discussion as her daughter interrupted the reading to make comments and made it easier for the adult to scaffold higher order questions and responses.

Gregory (1996) reviewed the experiences of young English Language Learners in Britain who were exposed to storybook reading in English texts along with their English-speaking classmates. In an analysis of two texts, she explained why the English Language Learners were attentive during the oral readings of one of the texts (*The Clay Flute*; Rehnman, 1989) but not as attentive during the second one

(*Don't Blame Me*; Rogers, 1990). Although she acknowledged the "difficult" language in the *The Clay Flute*, she pointed out that the English Language Learners seemed to be attracted to the text because it emphasizes "universal values," has language "rich in imagery and uses many words" that they will want to remember (e.g, witch, horrible, scream; p. 120). In addition, she observed that the book has a clear purpose and is clearly organized, with engaging illustrations. By contrast, *Don't Blame Me* is "culture-specific" to England, has colloquial language, and includes very few words that English Language Learners would want to remember. The book does not have a clear plot, relies on nuanced humor, and the illustrations are not easy to see from a distance.

Carger (1993) noted the importance of selecting culturally familiar text when teachers attempt to get young English Language Learners with limited English proficiency involved in early reading events in English such as pretend reading and teacher–child read-alouds. She pointed out that books that include characters, events, and environments with which the children can identify help the children to "link their own schemata for background experiences" and "may make comprehension easier and school less threatening" (p. 543).

CONCLUSION

In closing, we present several recommendations that we think are helpful for the selection and use of English text with English Language Learners in a variety of settings, whether bilingual, ESL, or all English. At the end of each recommendation, we also have listed one or two references for further reading:

- English Language Learners should be given the opportunity to interact with a variety of texts (narrative and informational) in English and the native language. Several researchers have pointed out that beginning English Language Learners often use English texts to shape their working hypotheses about English and to further their knowledge of English sound–symbol correspondence, vocabulary, and syntax (Franklin, 1999; Gregory, 1996). English texts also can introduce English Language Learners to rhetorical styles and to American culture. For further information on the use of narrative and informational text with English Language Learners, see Peregoy and Boyle (2001). These authors explained how English Language Learners benefit from thematic instruction that incorporates both narrative and informational text. They also recommended titles of English books for English Language Learners.
- Reading a text in the native language that later will be read in English helps to scaffold the students' comprehension of the English text by

providing them with key knowledge about the topic, genre, story structure or text structure, and vocabulary. If the teacher does not know the native language, then she may ask other native speakers, such as an aide, tutor, parent, or older student, to read the text in the native language. Peregoy and Boyle (2001) explained how native language support may be given in all-English or ESL settings. Pérez and Torres-Guzmán (2002) provided guidelines for the reading of books in Spanish. They also presented titles of Spanish books that they recommend for young Spanish-speaking readers.

- For teacher read-alouds, we recommend books in English that have universal values, memorable language, and clear plots or organization. Gregory (1996) pointed out that "If a story is memorable and contains important messages to children, they will understand the overall meaning and gradually be able to memorise chunks of the language it uses to communicate" (p. 119). Gregory (1996) included titles of English books that she considers "memorable" for young English Language Learners.

- Predictable books with illustrations that match the text particularly are helpful for read-alouds, shared reading, choral reading, and pretend reading because both the repetitive nature of the books and the illustrations help to scaffold the student's comprehension and participation. According to Urzua (1999), it is "much easier for children learning ESL to make the connections between the symbols on the page and the language connected to the symbols when they are well acquainted with the rhythm, vocabulary, and syntax of the predictable texts" (p. 32). Peregoy and Boyle (2001) and Pérez and Torres-Guzmán (2002) identified predictable books for English Language Learners and/or Spanish speakers.

- Texts (narrative and informational) that include characters, events, and/or settings with which the students can personally identify, along with questions that tap into students' personal experiences, may result in enhanced student discussion. Bauer (2000) emphasized the importance of presenting English Language Learners with opportunities to participate in book reading with realistic fiction as well as predictable texts. See Bauer (2000) and Bauer and Montero (2001) for more information on how English Language Learners respond to different types of texts.

- Providing a listening center in which students may listen to audiotapes of texts in their native language and in English on similar themes or plots (e.g., different versions of Cinderella) or to translated or dual-language versions of texts can help students create bridges between the two languages. Listening to a parallel or similar version of the text in the native language also helps to scaffold the student's comprehension of the English text. Gregory (1996) discussed the benefits of building on students' knowledge of texts in two languages.

- When a parallel or similar text is not available in the native language, then providing native-language support or asking a native speaker to provide this type of support is helpful. Summarizing the text in the native language prior to reading the text and allowing students to use their native language to respond to English text or to ask questions increase the students' opportunity to understand the text and to participate in the book reading. Battle (1993) illustrated how native-language support can help enhance English Language Learners' comprehension of English text.

- Providing props (physical objects, felt figures, illustrations or photos), using gestures, and acting out what is being read can all help to shelter English Language Learners' comprehension of English text. Careful enunciation of the words in the text and a slower reading of the text also may be helpful for beginning English Language Learners. Peregoy and Boyle (2001) explained how teachers can shelter English reading instruction for English Language Learners.

- In selecting text for independent, guided, or formal reading instruction, the focus needs to be on decoding *and* meaning. Because English Language Learners are not fluent English speakers, they will not automatically recognize all of the meanings of English words as they decode them. Therefore, it is important to select text for English Language Learners that allows them to practice decoding on concepts that they already know in their native language and for which they know the meanings in English or are being taught the meanings in English. Gregory (1996), in particular, illustrated the importance of combining decoding instruction with meaning.

- In selecting text for reading instruction, it is important to choose text that includes meaningful vocabulary useful to students in their everyday lives. Gregory (1996) pointed out that English Language Learners often use English reading as an opportunity to acquire more English vocabulary. Peregoy and Boyle (2001) provided information on how reading instruction and vocabulary instruction can be combined for English Language Learners.

- Finally, because comprehension rather than decoding appears to be a major problem for many English Language Learners, several researchers recommend that beginning reading instruction for English Language Learners should emphasize an interactive approach, in which students are taught and encouraged to use both bottom-up and top-down strategies (Anderson & Roit, 1996; Gregory, 1996). Anderson and Roit explained the interactive approach and provided guidelines for the English reading instruction of English Language Learners.

REFERENCES

Anderson, V., & Roit, M. (1996). Linking reading comprehension instruction to language development for language minority students. *The Elementary School Journal, 96,* 295–309.

Anstrom, K. (1996). *Defining the limited-English-proficient population: Directions in language and education.* Washington, DC: National Clearinghouse for Bilingual Education.

August, D., & Hakuta, K. (1997). *Improving schooling for language-minority children: A research agenda.* Washington, DC: National Academy Press.

Battle, J. (1993). Mexican-American bilingual kindergarteners' collaborations in meaning making. In D. J. Leu, C. K. Kinzer, L. M. Ayre, J. A. Peter, & S. Bennett (Eds.), *Examining central issues in literacy research, theory and practice: 42nd Yearbook of the National Reading Conference* (pp. 163–169). Chicago, IL: The National Reading Conference.

Bauer, E. B. (2000). Code-switching during shared and independent reading: Lessons learned from a preschooler. *Research in the Teaching of English, 35,* 101–131.

Bauer, E. B., & Montero, K. (2001). Reading versus translating: A preschool bilingual's interpretation of text. *National Reading Conference Yearbook, 50,* 115–126.

Bialystok, E. (1997). Effects of bilingualism and biliteracy on children's emerging concepts of print. *Developmental Psychology, 33,* 429–440.

Bruck, M., & Genesee, F. (1995). Phonological awareness in young second language learners. *Child Language, 22,* 307–324.

Carger, C. L. (1993). Louie comes to life: Pretend reading with second language emergent readers. *Language Arts, 70,* 542–547.

Chiappe, P., & Siegel, L. S. (1999). Phonological awareness and reading acquisition in English and Punjabi-speaking Canadian children. *Journal of Educational Psychology, 91,* 20–28.

Comeau, L., Cormier, P., Grandmaison, E., & Lacroix, D. (1999). A longitudinal study of phonological processing skills in children learning to read in a second language. *Journal of Educational Psychology, 91,* 29–43.

Crawford, J. (1997). *Best evidence: Research foundations of the Bilingual Education Act.* Washington, DC: National Clearinghouse for Bilingual Education.

Davol, M. (1993). *Black, white, just right.* Morton Grove, IL: Albert Whitman.

Durgunoğlu, A., Nagy, W. E., & Hancin-Bhatt, B. J. (1993). Cross-language transfer of phonological awareness. *Journal of Educational Psychology, 85,* 453–465.

Farah, I. (1998). Sabaq: Context of learning literacy for girls in rural Pakistan. In A. Durgunoğlu & L. T. Verhoeven (Eds.), *Literacy development in a multilingual context: Cross-cultural perspectives* (pp. 249–265). Mahwah, NJ: Lawrence Erlbaum Associates.

Fitzgerald, J., & Noblit, G. (2000). Balance in the making: Learning to read in an ethnically diverse first-grade classroom. *Journal of Educational Psychology, 92,* 3–22.

Franklin, E. (1999). The fiction writing of two Dakota boys. In E. Franklin (Ed.), *Reading and writing in more than one language: Lessons for teachers* (pp. 95–113). Alexandria, VA: Teachers of English to Speakers of Other Languages.

Galambos, S. J., & Goldin-Meadow, S. (1990). The effects of learning two languages on levels of metalinguistic awareness. *Cognition, 34,* 1–56.

García, G. E. (1991). Factors influencing the English reading test performance of Spanish-speaking Hispanic children. *Reading Research Quarterly, 26,* 371–392.

García, G. E. (1994). The literacy assessment of second-language learners: A focus on authentic assessment. In K. Spangenberg-Urbschat & R. Pritchard (Eds.), *Kids come in all languages: Reading instruction for second-language learners* (pp. 183–208). Newark, DE: International Reading Association.

García, G. E. (1998). Mexican-American bilingual students' metacognitive reading strategies: What's transferred, unique, problematic? *National Reading Conference Yearbook, 47,* 253–263.

García, G. E. (2000). Bilingual children's reading. In M. L. Kamil, P. B. Mosenthal, P. D. Pearson, & R. Barr (Eds.), *Handbook of reading research* (Vol. 3, pp. 813–834). Mahwah, NJ: Lawrence Erlbaum Associates.

García, G. E. (2001). A theoretical discussion of young bilingual children's reading (Preschool–Grade 3). *National Reading Conference Yearbook, 50,* 228–237.

Gersten, R., & Jiménez, R. T. (1994). A delicate balance: Enhancing literature instruction for students of English as a second language. *The Reading Teacher, 47,* 438–449.

Goldman, S. R., Reyes, M., & Varnhagen, C. K. (1984). Understanding fables in first and second languages. *National Association for Bilingual Education Journal, 8,* 835–866.

Göncz, L., & Kodzopeljic, J. (1991). Exposure to two languages in the preschool period: Metalinguistic development and the acquisition of reading. *Journal of Multilingual and Multicultural Development, 12,* 137–163.

Gregory, E. (1996). *Making sense of a new world.* London: Paul Chapman Publishing LTD.

Jiménez, R. T., García, G. E., & Pearson, P. D. (1995). Three children, two languages, and strategic reading: Case studies in bilingual/monolingual reading. *American Educational Research Journal, 32,* 31–61.

Jiménez, R. T., García, G. E., & Pearson, P. D. (1996). The reading strategies of bilingual Latina/o students who are successful English readers: Opportunities and obstacles. *Reading Research Quarterly, 31,* 90–112.

Martin, B. (1967). *Brown bear, brown bear, what do you see?* New York: Henry Holt and Co.

Moss, M., & Puma, M. (1995). *Prospects: The Congressionally mandated study of educational growth and opportunity: First year report on Language Minority and limited English proficient students.* Washington, DC: U.S. Department of Education.

Padrón, Y. (1994). Comparing reading instruction in Hispanic/limited English-proficient schools and other inner-city schools. *Bilingual Research Journal, 18,* 49–66.

Peregoy, S. F., & Boyle, O. F. (2001). *Reading, writing, and learning in ESL: A resource book for K–12 teachers.* New York: Longman.

Pérez, B., & Torres-Guzmán, M. E. (2002). *Learning in two worlds: An integrated Spanish/English biliteracy approach* (3rd ed.). Boston: Allyn & Bacon.

Ramirez, J. D., Yuen, S. D., & Ramey, D. R. (1991). *Longitudinal study of structured English immersion strategy, early-exit and late-exit bilingual education programs for language-minority children. Final report to the U.S. Department of Education* (Executive Summary and Vols. I and II). San Mateo, CA: Aguirre International.

Rehnman, M. (1989). *The clay flute.* Stockholm: R & S Books.

Reyes, M. (1991). A process approach to literacy using dialogue journals and literature logs with second language learners. *Research in the Teaching of English, 25,* 291–313.

Rogers, P. (1990). *Don't blame me.* London: The Bodley Head.

Saville-Troike, M. (1984). What really matters in second-language learning for academic achievement? *TESOL Quarterly, 18,* 199–219.

Schmidt, P. R. (1993). Literacy development of two bilingual, ethnic-minority children in a kindergarten program. In D. J. Leu, C. K. Kinzer, L. M. Ayre, J. A. Peter, & S. Bennett

(Eds.), *Examining central issues in literacy research, theory and practice: 42th Yearbook of the National Reading Conference* (pp. 189–196). Chicago, IL: The National Reading Conference.

Tabors, P. O., & Snow, C. E. (2001). Young bilingual children and early literacy development. In B. Newman & D. K. Dickinson (Eds.), *Handbook of early literacy research* (pp. 159–178). New York: Guilford.

Thornburg, D. (1993). Intergenerational literacy learning with bilingual families: A context for the analysis of social mediation of thought. *Journal of Reading Behavior, 25,* 321–352.

Tikunoff, W. J., Ward, B. A., van Broekhuizen, L. D., Romero, M., Castañeda, L. V., Lucas, T., & Katz, A. (1991). *A descriptive study of significant features of exemplary special alternative instructional programs. Final report and Vol. 2: Report for practitioners.* Los Alamitos, CA: The Southwest Regional Educational Laboratory.

Tsai, M. L., & García, G. E. (2000). Who's the boss: How communicative competence is defined in a multilingual preschool classroom. *Anthropology and Education Quarterly, 31,* 230–252.

Urzua, C. (1999). The everyday surprise: Nourishing literacy in classroom environments. In E. Franklin (Ed.), *Reading and writing in more than one language: Lessons for teachers* (pp. 29–47). Alexandria, VA: Teachers of English to Speakers of Other Languages.

Verhoeven, L. T. (1994). Transfer in bilingual development: The linguistic interdependence hypothesis revisited. *Language Learning, 44,* 381–415.

11

Heavy (and Heavy-Handed) Issues Surrounding Book Selection

Nancy Roser
University of Texas at Austin

Not so long ago, a list of the issues that surrounded the selection of texts for elementary classrooms would not have been be a very long one. First, until approximately the mid-1980s, the majority of books occupying classroom space were selected by someone other than the teacher and children—whether by a superintendent, a state board of education, a local school board, a textbook selection committee, or some combination of these (Farr, Tulley, & Powell, 1987). And although that decision-making process itself could be somewhat rancorous, once the texts were installed in classrooms, they tended to enjoy a peaceful (if not bland) term of adoption.

A second reason for the lack of stir surrounding book selection was that the classroom book collection was just too slim to be much of an issue. In fact, other than the adopted texts for each curricular area, there were few "other books" available on classroom shelves. And, in particular, there were few books children might actually choose to read (Martinez, Roser, Worthy, Strecker, & Gough, 1997; Worthy, 1996; Worthy, Moorman, & Turner, 1999).

The third, and perhaps most important, reason for the dearth of controversy surrounding books in classrooms was that children's trade books were not the ready commodity in yesterday's instructional programs they are becoming today (Galda, Ash, & Cullinan, 2000). Huck, Hepler, Hickman, and Kiefer (2001) reported that 5,000 to 6,000 children's books are published each year, an increase that parallels the instructional emphasis on literature in classroom literacy programs. The increase in available titles has meant the potential for more books (of varying quality), more choices, more genre, more representation, and the hope that more teachers and children are selecting and bringing books to classrooms.

Given a proliferation of trade books, it seems logical that teachers and children would be having more say over what books occupy their classrooms. For example, teachers direct more discretionary funds toward trade book purchases, and often make their own choices for classroom literature study and for read-alouds. Children may own more books because of the increased number of available paperbacks, their propensity to collect and trade popular series books (e.g., *Goosebumps* by R. L. Stine [Scholastic] and *Animorphs* by K. A. Applegate [Scholastic]), and the book club flyers that enable them to order reduced-cost books. Yet, at the same time that the real-life inhabitants of classrooms may be playing a more active role in determining the nature and kinds of print that appear in the classroom collection, there has been little guidance and fewer external checks on the burgeoning collections. More "unadopted" literature has crept or swept into classrooms, whether peripherals of the textbook programs, text sets for literature circles, donations to the classroom library, or titles selected and paid for with teachers' personal funds. And, as the book supplies swell, more folks seem to have became suspicious of the books taught, recommended, or made available to children (O'Neal, 1990).

This chapter considers the external and internal influences on classroom book selection, including influences on the textbook adoption process, the external pressures on classroom trade book collections, and the self- and stealth-censorship imposed from "within." The final section reviews factors that probably should influence the selection of books in the classroom.

TEXTBOOK ADOPTION: "I BELIEVE THAT THE INCLUSION OF CANDY IN THIS ILLUSTRATION MAY NEGATIVELY INFLUENCE CHILDREN'S DENTAL HYGIENE."

In the course of looking out for the best interests of public school children, and serving *in loco parentis*, well-intentioned (and perhaps less well-intentioned) committees pore over textbooks being considered for an approved adoption list. A great many voices and interest groups in board rooms and state houses speak passionately on the subject of "what the children should (and should not) read" (see for example, Delfattore, 1992). Needless to say, some groups and individuals are more vocal than others, making their charges as detailed, passionate, and eloquent as they can. Textbook adoption in Texas, in particular, has a reputation for being something of a sideshow; in one textbook hearings session I sat through in the late 1970s, objections were raised to the number of times boys were depicted holding cats versus girls holding dogs. Vocal opponents of book characters speaking in dialects had their say. People rose to argue against any story with a witch for a character, any depiction of unhealthy snacks (including a birthday cake or candy), characters that seemed too independent or too questioning of authority, and general unpleasantness (there went *Hansel and Gretel*, and just about any other folktale you can think of). In debate over one textbook, a "regular" rose to object to the inclusion of a photograph of Martin Luther King, Jr. because, as the testifier exhorted, King had once been photographed with a known Communist. At times, it seemed, the ridiculousness prevailed even when the voices were not raised, as text publishers and decision makers appeared eager to duck criticisms by anticipating what particular groups would find objectionable, and then moving preemptively to ensure that adopted texts did not contain those features or traits.

Katherine Paterson (1989) described an editor's written request to use a section of *Bridge to Terabithia* (Paterson, 1978) in a reading textbook:

> Enclosed was the section all scrubbed up and shiny, ready for inclusion in the textbook.... As I read it, I realized that something very peculiar had happened. I can't remember every painful detail, but I know that in the original, Mrs. Myers, the country schoolteacher, says that Leslie's scuba diving is an unusual hobby—for a girl. In the expurgated version the words "for a girl" were excised, lest Mrs. Myers be deemed sexist (which of course she was). Jesse was not permitted to say, "Lord, Leslie," and the children were not to fill Pepsi bottles with water to put in their stronghold in the woods. It seemed to me—and I readily admit that I was reading with no objectivity whatsoever—it seemed to me that any detail that delineated character or made a definite statement had been removed. All the color and flavor of the story had been blanded out. There was nothing left that could have offended any right-minded adult—or indeed, any left-minded adult. (p. 135)

During the past two decades, concerns about the contents of textbooks have not lessened, and perhaps have become more widespread. In the mid-1990s, as I worked with a state committee of teachers, administrators, and community representatives to produce state standards for reading and language arts (from which textbooks would be built), one appointee to the writing committee continuously objected to both the committee's process and the successive drafts of the standards. During a break, I asked the objector directly, "What are you most afraid will happen here?" She answered just as directly, "I am afraid of promoting a homosexual agenda in the state." There had been no talk of sexual preference in the committee, nor even any suggestion of a book title that might be recommended within the state standards. In fact, all decisions about specific titles were to be left open for districts and teachers. Nevertheless, this concerned (and sometimes obstreperous) delegate had heard of a children's book entitled *Heather Has Two Mommies* (Newman, 1989/2000) and another called *Daddy's Roommate* (Willhoite, 1990/2000), and she intended to stay on guard in case such inappropriateness migrated into adopted texts. Had there been such a state-generated list of recommended books, these two titles of concern probably would not have earned placement as exemplars of the best of children's literature. But what if there had been such a list, and what if these two books had qualified? Who, then, should make the decision about when, if, and with whom, texts with sensitive topics should be shared?

Judy Blume (2001), one of the most frequently censored writers for children and a passionate spokesperson for the National Coalition against Censorship, made a distinction when decisions are being made for all children and for individuals:

> I gave a friend's child one of my favorite picture books, James Marshall's *The Stupids Step Out*, and was amazed when she said, "I'm sorry, but we can't accept that book. My children are not permitted to use that word. Ever." ... I may not agree, but I have to respect this woman's right to keep that book from her child as long as she isn't trying to keep it from other people's children. (p. 11)

Because a state spends tax dollars on behalf of "all children," the divergent wishes of the citizenry are heard and considered. Hence, textbooks, paid for by public funds, will likely continue to reflect the concerns of the most vocal, the most organized, and (yes) the biggest buyers (Texas, California, and Florida). Teachers and their associations have sometimes (but not often) been among the most vocal. And although some banished books have been reinstated, and some narrow views have been overturned, it will take a more informed understanding to represent and defend challenged literature.

In a newsletter produced for the conservative Eagle Forum, spokesperson Phyllis Schlafly (1995) offered some suggestions for selecting books for children that included selecting few award winners and choosing only books published before 1970 (i.e., before books began to reflect realism and a diverse populace). Other interest groups have different but equally strongly held notions. The Council for Interracial Books for Children, for example, speaks up against biased or unfair depictions of cultures, races, or genders in both textbooks and trade books. Thus, there is a vigilant watch over texts at the macro level. However, what (or who) safeguards the collection that makes its way into the elementary school classroom?

OUTSIDE PRESSURE ON TRADE BOOK SELECTIONS IN THE ELEMENTARY CLASSROOM: IT DIDN'T START WITH HARRY POTTER

Traditionally, it has been middle school, junior high, or secondary classrooms and libraries that have been the targets of external book challenges (whether from parents, organized interest groups, or other concerned citizens). Typically, any list of books that has been challenged, restricted, or banned contains titles predominantly for older children or adults (Karolides, Bald, & Sova, 1999). Historically, it has been young adult literature for which the National Council of Teachers of English /SLATE (Support for the Learning and Teaching of English) has prepared defenses (e.g., Rationales for Challenged Books CD, NCTE/IRA, 1998). Furthermore, materials written to advise teachers how to deal with challenged books have explained that it is "the English teacher" who should be considered the expert in recommending appropriate books for the program.

Where does that leave the elementary teacher? Little wonder that a mild-mannered boy with glasses, a scar, and a talent for quidditch, caught elementary schools a bit off guard. Harry Potter (Rowling, 1998) books received the most challenges of any title or series of books in the United States in both 1999 and 2000 (American Library Association, 2001). A challenge means that a formal written complaint was filed with a library or school concerning a book's appropriateness. The American Library Association website described the nature of the concerns about Harry as inclusion of "occult/Satanism," and "anti-family themes." The State Board of Education in South Carolina almost sent Harry packing. A superintendent in Michigan was successful (for a time) in removing the books from library shelves and restricting access (Simmons & Dresang, 2001). Surely, more elementary teachers are becoming aware that the autonomy of book selection they thought they enjoyed was a fantasy.

But it did not start with Harry Potter. Individuals and groups have challenged In The Night Kitchen (Sendak, 1995) for its nude child, The Bridge to Terabithia (Paterson, 1978) for its "bad words" and "depressing theme," Nappy Hair (Herron, 1997) for its joyous portrayal of ... nappy hair, The Lorax (Seuss, 1971) for its "politically correct" environmental messages, as well as dozens of other titles elementary students enjoy and gravitate to. Authors such as Judy Blume, Roald Dahl, Walter Dean Myers, Katherine Paterson, Lois Lowry, and Robert Cormier appear on the same "Most Challenged" lists, as do Mark Twain, Maya Angelou, John Steinbeck, and J. D. Salinger. The American Library Association reported challenges to children's books on the rise during the first half of the last decade (Scales, 1995), although Suhor (1999), in an NCTE/SLATE newsletter, reported there was some evidence for a reduction in cases. (The reduction, however, may also signal internalization of censorship issues by teachers and media specialists, or "self-censorship," a topic addressed in the next section of this chapter.)

It was initially the parents of Ruth Sherman's Brooklyn, New York, third graders who objected to *Nappy Hair*, a picture book written in the rhythmic "call-and-response" style of traditional African-American churches (Martin, 1999). Ms. Sherman wanted her children to meet characters in picture books who reflected their own ethnicities, and the children loved the book's spirit, celebration, and messages of self-love: At the book's end, the Lord, looking with pride on His creation, "this cute little brown baby girl," thinks, "Well done," and tells the multitudes: "And she's got the nappiest hair in the world." To which the relatives respond in unison, "Ain't it the truth." Even in light of the book's spill-over joy, triumphant faces, and musical language, some parents based their objections on the argument that the images of African-Americans were derogatory in the story. Furthermore, they thought it inappropriate to share this historically negative image of nappy hair in a racially mixed group. After the fuss and fury, Ms. Sherman learned that many of the protestors had not read the entire book, and in the end, only one of the 50 parents who eventually levied complaints had a child in Ms. Sherman's class. But the damage was done, and the teacher left her classroom and the district, "so shaken by the confrontations with the hostile parents" (Martin, 1999, p. 285) that she did not say good-bye to her children.

The strongest reactions from political, religious, and parent groups are often in response to the presence of one of the five "S's" in texts: satanism, sexuality, swear words, suicide, and stereotypes. (I do not know where violence and religious viewpoint fit in this list, but they, too, are causes for challenging books.) Seemingly, attempts to proscribe ideas and materials are not the exclusive province of any one region, socioeconomic level, or background. Districts that have been the most successful in countering pressures and blocks have put into place specific procedures for challenges. For example, the NCTE/IRA Joint Task Force on Intellectual Freedom includes the following recommendations for steps at the local level (see also Simmons & Dresang, 2001):

- Make certain there are selection policies and procedures on file in your school and district, as well as complaint procedures and forms. (If these policies and forms are not in place, participate in developing them).
- Locate, collect, or develop written rationales for the use of particular texts. (NCTE/IRA [1998] provides the following features in their written rationale for texts: the book's intended grade level and audi-

ence, a plot summary, theoretical support and redeeming values of the text, its literary qualities and summaries of reviews, suggested teaching plans, possible objections, a specific treatise on why the book should not be banned, and a list of "alternate books.")

- Stay in touch with supervisors with regard to the development of class texts, reading lists, and nonprint media and materials.
- Find alternative choices for students who opt out of a particular reading.
- Engage students, colleagues, parents, professional organizations, and the larger community in discussions related to intellectual freedom. (see http://www.ncte.org/positions/common_ground.shtml, retrieved July 24, 2003.)

There is a decided difference between censorship from outside sources and the kinds of informed book selection decisions teachers make when they call on their own professional and personal knowledge. Teachers claim to make text decisions based on knowing children—their interests, backgrounds, skills, development, and needs. Even so, there are indications teachers may need more help with developing written rationales in preparation for book challenges, as well as with their school districts' policies for handling book complaints. Without such support, whether through fear and/or weariness, teachers in charged environments may begin to second-guess their own knowledge base and impose self-censorship (Cerra, 1994).

TEACHER SELF-CENSORSHIP AND STEALTH CENSORSHIP

With books in more abundant supply in the instructional program, and with increased understanding that books in baskets, books in crates, books on turn racks, and books on shelves promote children's reading and literary meaning making, it seems logical that teachers step up to assume more "local control" of selection decisions. Huck et al. (2001) stressed the very important distinction between *book selection* and *book censorship*. Selection, they explain, is an inclusive term, an attempt to include a book in a collection based on its literary qualities. Censorship, by contrast, is an excluding term, an attempt to impose one's beliefs on others by proscribing access to a book based on objectionable content. Jenkinson (cited in Cerra, 1994) called censorship the "suppression, alteration, restriction of access, or removal of books because of the ideas contained within them" (p. 44). Examples of distinctions between censorship and selection appear in Table 11.1.

Even so, with limited resources, selection implies "deselection," making it critically important that teachers operate with a set of selection guidelines.

TABLE 11.1
Censorship as Distinguished From Selection From the National
Council of Teachers of English Board of Directors (1982)

Examples of Censorship	Examples of Selection Guidelines
Exclude specific materials or methods.	Include specific materials or methods.
Example: Eliminate books with unhappy endings.	Example: Include some books with unhappy endings to give a varied view of life.
Make excluding decisions.	Make including decisions.
Example: Review your classroom library and eliminate books that include stereotypes.	Example: Review your classroom library. If necessary add books that portray groups in nonstereotypic ways.
Seek to limit access to ideas and information.	Seek to increase access to ideas and information.
Example: Eliminate all books that portray drug abuse because drug abuse is a menace to students.	Example: Include at appropriate grade levels books that help students understand the personal and social consequences of drug abuse.
Make decisions on parts of a work in isolation.	Make decisions based on seeing the relationship of parts to each other and to the work as a whole.
Example: Remove this book because here is an example of profanity.	Example: Determine whether the profanity is integral to the portrayal of character and development of theme.

When books are "deselected," it should not be for reasons other than the book's fit, literary quality, accessibility to children, and potential for serving instruction broadly. Freedman and Johnson (2000/2001) described self-censorship as teachers choosing "not to use certain books for fear that these texts will create controversies leading to confrontations with parents, the members of the wider community, or school administrators" (p. 357). Suhor (1999) presented a viewpoint from experts that suggests the number of cases of challenged books has decreased because teachers and librarians are capitulating to perceived pressures by choosing not to use the books that cause a stir. Cerra (1994) maintained that the further from a network of support a teacher or librarian is, the more likely the book selection will be influenced by the anticipation of varied groups' displeasure. One teacher I know quietly slid Harry Potter into her desk drawer and did not finish it as a read-aloud (to the children's dismay) when her principal explained ever so gently that reading the book was likely to cause him grief within community groups. "*Harry,*" another teacher told me without remorse, "can't be read aloud in this school, but children can bring it from home to read on their own." A website for defenders of *Harry Potter,* originally calling itself *Muggles for Harry Potter* (and now called *KidSpeak: Where Kids Speak Out for Free Speech*) has currently posted a similar story of children who must bring letters from home before they are allowed to check out *Harry* from the library. That particular *KidSpeak* website (of spirit and support) could inspire the creation of additional websites for defenders of valuable literature, such as *Freedom Marchers for Cassie Logan, Families for Gilly Hopkins,* or *Disturbers of the Universe* for Jerry Renault.

Self-censorship means action may as likely come from a school staff member as from some watchdog organization. In her study of teachers' reasons for avoiding specific pieces of literature, Wollman-Bonilla (1998) charged cowardice:

> As teachers carry out the work of selecting texts for classroom use, many seem to lack the courage to present non-mainstream perspectives and experiences, and they lack faith in children's ability to recognize and handle difficult issues. (p. 287)

Wollman-Bonilla contended that teachers' desire to avoid sensitive issues such as discrimination and racism by avoiding books that contain those issues is becoming more prevalent. Other issues teachers may be avoiding through self-censorship are those that focus on women, on racial and ethnic groups other than white Europeans, and on the poor (Jipson & Paley, 1991).

Similarly, in her study of elementary teachers' self-censorship, Cerra (1994) found that 70% of her survey subjects reported they would alter an award-winning text when reading it aloud if that text contained offensive language; 16% reported they would choose another book; only 14% indicated they would read the book as written. Of the 375 respondents to the survey (all teachers of Grades 1 to 6), 53% indicated they would reject a book for inclusion in the school library on the basis of whether it contained sexual subject matter. Rates of rejection ranged from 12% for political subject matter to 62% rejection on the basis of racism as subject matter. Of the respondents, 74% agreed with the current practice of textbook publishers altering a text to reduce its reading difficulty. Cerra contended that, even though 76% of the teachers strongly agreed that elementary students should have First Amendment rights, the teachers' beliefs contrasted with their preferred actions.

Even with all the rich possibilities for genuine questions, grand conversations, self-dialogue, and reflection that occur in the presence of the best of books (Eeds & Wells, 1989), some teachers seem to "opt for safer titles" and more secure routes (Freedman & Johnson, 2000/2001, p. 358). One reason may be the difficulty in developing clear goals and justifications for the books that are selected and shared in the classroom; another may be the challenge of explaining clearly and convincingly the relevance of controversial book choices to parents. As a result, teachers may consciously be selecting less provocative texts, and (some would argue) as a result, engaging students in less meaningful thought and talk.

Ultimately and frighteningly, authors themselves may move to self-censor, as Mildred Taylor described, writing in the 25th anniversary edition of *Roll of Thunder, Hear My Cry* (Taylor, 1976/2001):

> In recent years, because of my concern about our "politically correct" society, I have found myself hesitating about using words that would have been spoken during the period my books are set. But just as I have had to be honest with myself in the telling of all my stories, I realized I must be true to the feelings of the people about whom I write. (Foreword).

Self-censorship is deplorable when it takes the easy road solely to avoid the tougher, when students are not given opportunity to ponder, weigh, and discuss tough issues, and when students are not trusted with the best examples of children's literature. Ultimately, to dodge and duck is not the answer. Books on "safe" lists today (*Swiss Family Robinson* or *National Velvet*) may not stay safe bets. As Harris (1995) wrote, "Few classics would pass the 'purity' tests" (p. 277).

But teachers must also be alert for another threat to access: stealth censorship. *Stealth censorship* is the term some experts use when they refer to a set of selection (or deselection) principles on which teachers may operate, sometimes without even being aware. These are the unexamined biases and tastes, foibles and idiosyncrasies—the result of background and ideological stances—that can affect the book selections in classrooms or libraries. Some researchers contend that teachers are typically unaware of their biases, and may not even be aware of the unstated values and beliefs particular texts convey (Jipson & Paley, 1991). The result may be as simple as a second-grade teacher avoiding *Days with Frog and Toad* (Lobel, 1976) because in the unexamined recesses of his life, he really does not like talking animals. Or it may mean a teacher's failure to become knowledgeable (because of personal tastes) with some of the best science fiction, high fantasy, or sports adventures that could enlist particular young readers. As a result, the classroom collection may take on the preferences and personality of the one who fills its shelves and racks.

However, stealth censorship could be even more insidious than unexamined preferences and missing genre, such that it results in a book collection that misrepresents or underrepresents particular peoples, ideas, and lives. Beverley Naidoo (1995), author of *Journey to Jo'burg* (1986), a book blocked by immigration authorities from entering South Africa because of its wrenching portrayal of apartheid, reminded us: "Adults act as gatekeepers to children's knowledge ..." (p. 32). Suzanne Fisher Staples (1996), author of *Shabanu: Daughter of the Wind* (1989), explained that "because of the nature of stealth censorship, it is difficult to document and impossible to quantify" (p. 1). Wollman-Bonilla's (1998) research indicated that teachers may avoid texts with frightening themes, those that fail to represent dominant social values, and those that identify racism and sexism as social problems. It follows that if teachers choose to exercise primary responsibility for book selection, they must clearly understand the aims of their classroom collection, their goals for the use of particular texts, their children as literate and social beings, and themselves as challengers, guides, and arbiters of multiple perspectives.

HOW TEACHERS SHOULD SELECT TRADEBOOKS FOR THE CLASSROOM

Some authorities have recommended that a classroom contain at least five to six books per child (Fractor, Woodruff, Martinez, & Teale, 1993). Huck et al. (2001) referred to classroom collections of 500 or more books. With tens of thousands of children's books in print, selecting 500 may feel like an overwhelming task. Harris (1995) charged that her "interactions with teachers across the country indicate that many are unaware of trends, issues, authors, and books.... Further, many lack knowledge about sources that provide this type of information" (p. 278).

Given the date of her writing, I cannot help but think things may be changing. My own experiences with teacher knowledge of children's books are quite different. Teachers I know spend their "butter and egg" money on children's books. Sessions at professional conferences that feature children's authors spill eager attendees out the doors. Authors signing books patiently put up with long (and equally patient) lines. My undergraduates studying to be teachers pounce on a new "Polacco," "Pinkney," or "Mora." Talk in the teachers' room includes ideas for read-alouds. Special educators are introducing book circles into their groups. One teacher I know despaired of her addiction to buying books online. Websites with teacher reviews proliferate. Even so, the questions persist: How to make the best choices? How to keep current? How to provide access? How to evaluate fairly (taking judgment beyond personal preferences and response)? The following list of considerations is intended as "ponderables" when book selections are being made for the classroom:

1. *Quality.* So little time, so much to read. The quality of literature should be a prime consideration for the classroom collection. Because literature is an art

form, it is not unusual to find the characteristics of fine art used to judge it. But, teachers *use* the art; it does not just hang there. Whether characterizing it by qualities of fine writing style, broad appeal, originality, freshness, or harmony of art and words, we think we know it when we see it.

2.*Interest*. However, when turned-off readers are part of the mix, then *high interest* zooms to the top of the stack, too. Sometimes young readers are "nudged" to quality through passion for favorites. Consider, for example, what Alvin Schwartz and R. L. Stine may be doing for literacy.

3. *Diversity*. Here, diversity applies to the authors and illustrators whose works are included in the classroom collection, as well as topics and characters, represented in culturally accurate ways. It means selections that mirror the experiences of those beyond one's own family.

4. *Representativeness*. The ideal book collection would include information books, traditional literature (myths, legends, folktales), poetry, rhymes and songs, picture storybooks, biography, realistic and historical fiction, fantasy, easy readers, and more. It would also include technology and all the issues that collide when children conduct research in a cyber library.

5. *Familiarity*. Children gravitate to the familiar (as do we). If a topic, genre, or author is already a favorite, by sliding in another choice there is likelihood of a crowd pleaser. Even though authors and illustrators with a body of works attract our attention, just because you and your class love Eric Carle is no reason not to scrutinize carefully a later book (*"Slowly, Slowly, Slowly," said the Sloth,* 2002) making sure that the selection adds to the collection.

6. *Recognition, reviews, and trusted recommendations*. Although the subjects in Cerra's (1994) study reported little teacher attention to published reviews, Cerra did not ask about websites, teacher chatrooms, and plain old teacher lounge exchanges. The reviews in *The Horn Book* are exquisitely crafted, but the kids on Amazon.com unload some real skinny on the books they read. Jalongo (1988) contended that the typical child reads 600 children's books in his or her entire childhood. How many authors and illustrators and titles that leaves out!

7. *Access*. Accessibility can be defined not just as books physically within reach, but also achievable in terms of level and challenge. In a study with my colleagues of second-grade classroom libraries (Martinez et al., 1997), we learned that children chose to read what they could manage. When a majority of the classroom collection is beyond children's levels, there are fewer opportunities to read (and achieve).

8. *Dust free*. Teachers should not be afraid to purge the classroom collection. Some contain far too many dated, worn, and unappealing books. A regular purging saves valuable classroom shelf space for the best titles that can be provided. A book, after all, should contribute more than its volume to the classroom space.

9. *Price.* In the reality of the $1.5 billion dollar book industry, teachers ante up their share. But we wait for the paperbacks, for the reissues, for the donations, for the used book stores to be restocked, and for public monies to be redirected. Other options include writing small grants, begging, and becoming best friends with teachers near retirement.

CONCLUSION

To comply with the First Amendment, to be sensitive to elementary readers, and to be attentive to parents' and others' concerns, perhaps teachers who make book selection decisions could take a principled stance for their "local control" by borrowing three improbable factors from the mathematics curriculum: distance, rate, and time. Teachers could then argue that these three factors should influence book selection and deselection in the following ways: *Distance* could argue that the closer the book selector is to the child, the better the "selector" knows the "selectee," the better the book selection and recommendation are likely to be. It follows that the closer and more knowledgeable the decision maker is to the texts themselves, the more likely the selections will be appropriate. This would mean that teachers, with a shorter *distance* between themselves and learners, would likely make more knowing decisions about appropriate book choices than would principals, supervisors, or school boards. It would also mean that teachers, particularly of young children, would need to call on the knowledge and understanding that parents have as books are selected. Parents' distance from the learner is even shorter, so parents must become critically important advisers as books are chosen and shared with children.

The second variable of the mathematical borrowing is *rate.* Surely the pace, or rate, at which challenging books are introduced and tackled makes a difference, too. If themes are sensitive, topics are tough, and ideas need pondering, the book can be approached slowly with thought and talk interleafing its pages. Think of the richness of talk from classrooms when texts worth talking about are shared (Eeds & Wells, 1989). For example, in-depth talks nearly always surround the tough and uncomfortable issues in *Shiloh* (Naylor, 1991) in which young Marty defies a parent's wishes for what he judges the greater ethical good of preventing harm to an animal. The text has suffered challenges because of its tough moral and ethical dilemmas. But by taking the book on together (as a read-aloud), and by stopping to talk (slowing the *rate*), even second graders (perhaps not the real audience for this book) consider the issues deeply, hear one another, and wrestle with shades of an issue:

Child 1:   Judd turned nicer. [Judd is the abusive owner of Shiloh, a dog that continually runs away, and that Marty secretly shields.]

Teacher: What makes you think he turned nicer?
Child 1: By giving him water.
Teacher: At the beginning he wouldn't do that?
Child 1: What he ... well, what made him nicer was at the beginning when Judd gave Marty water he didn't, um, put ice in it.
Child 2: But then at the end he put ice in it because Judd started to feel sorry.
Teacher: Are people nice to Judd?
Children: [Various voices]
Child 3: Not everybody.
Child 4: Marty was mean.
Teacher: What do you mean, Sarah?
Child 4: Because he would ... he kept on telling lies. And big lies to him because about the dog.
Child 5: That's not mean.
Teacher: Is it mean or not truthful?
Child 6: Not truthful because ...

In the gray area between selection and censorship, there is also the option that teachers (and parents) refer to as postponement or delay, the *time* factor. It is not that you will *never* allow your child a particular movie or lyric, but the time is not right (the child is too young or inexperienced). The work itself is not being censored or censured, but rather, purposefully postponed. Adults are not saying "never," but rather "not now." It is not censoring Garden's *The Year They Burned the Books* (1999) or Hentoff's *The Day They Came to Arrest the Book* (1983) by not including them in a fifth-grade collection. It is timing their introduction. When my children were very young, I knew they would love the antics of Peter, Turtle, and Tootsie in *Superfudge* (Blume, 1980). The book is sidesplittingly funny, but in chapter 10, readers learn that Santa Claus has an identity. My children were not yet ready for that revelation. Even so, they were too savvy for me to skip pages, so I "censored." Out of their sight, I carefully removed the chapter with a razorblade, right next to the spine. It is the only time I ever did that, but I did it. (But *why* did it have to be Judy Blume? Hasn't she had enough?) Years later, when I heard Judy Blume read from *Places I Never Meant to Be* (2001), I felt chastised by her passion. Even so, did I actually join the would-be censors of Judy Blume? Or, did I use the factors of distance (I know these children and their childhood world today), rate (no amount of "slowing to talk" would make this chapter the right way for me to broach this topic with my kids), and timing (our new copy has a chapter 10). It makes sense to me: Selection responsibility should be based on distance (the closer you are, the better you understand the readers for whom you choose), rate (slowing the pace for treatment of sensitive but worthwhile topics), and time (being willing to say "not yet" to valuable selections).

That leaves us with heavy-duty responsibility.

REFERENCES

American Library Association. (2001, January). *Harry Potter again tops list of most challenged books*. Retrieved from http://www.ala.org/pio/presskits/midwinterawards2001/challenged.html

Blume, J. (Ed). (2001). *Places I never meant to be*. New York: Aladdin Paperbacks.

Cerra, K. K. (1994). Self-censorship and the elementary school teacher. In J. E. Brown (Ed.), *Preserving intellectual freedom: Fighting censorship in our schools* (pp. 36–50). Urbana, IL: National Council of Teachers of English.

Delfattore, J. (1992). *What Johnny shouldn't read: Textbook censorship in America*. New Haven: Yale University Press.

Eeds, M., & Wells, D. (1989). Grand conversations: An exploration of meaning construction in literature study groups. *Research in the Teaching of English, 23*, 4–29.

Farr, R., Tulley, M., & Powell, D. (1987). The evaluation and selection of basal readers. *The Elementary School Journal, 87*, 267–281.

Fractor, J. S., Woodruff, M., Martinez, M., & Teale, W. H. (1993). Let's not miss opportunities to promote voluntary reading: Classroom libraries in the elementary school. *The Reading Teacher, 46*, 476–484.

Freedman, L., & Johnson, H. (2000/2001). Who's protecting whom? I Hadn't Mean to Tell You This, a case in point in confronting self-censorship in the choice of young adult literature. *Journal of Adolescent & Adult Literacy, 44*, 356–369.

Galda, L., Ash, G., & Cullinan, B. (2000). Children's literature. In M. Kamil, P. Mosenthal, P. D. Pearson, & R. Barr (Eds.), *Handbook of Reading Research, Vol. III* (pp. 361–379). Mahwah, NJ: Lawrence Erlbaum Associates.

Harris, V. J. (1995). "May I read this book?" Controversies, dilemmas, and delights in children's literature. In S. Lehr (Ed.), *Battling dragons: Issues and controversy in children's literature* (pp. 275–283). Portsmouth, NH: Heinemann.

Huck, C., Hepler, S., Hickman, J., & Kiefer, B. (2001). *Children's literature in the elementary school* (7th ed). New York: McGraw-Hill.

Jalongo, M. R. (1988). *Young children and picture books: Literature from infancy to six*. Washington, DC: National Association for the Education of Young Children.

Jipson, J., & Paley, N. (1991). The selective tradition in children's literature: Does it exist in the elementary classroom? *English Education, 23*, 148–159.

Karolides, N., Bald, M., & Sova, D. (1999). *100 banned books: Censorship histories of world literature*. New York: Checkmark Books.

Martin, M. (1999). Never too nappy. *The Horn Book, 75*, 283–288.

Martinez, M., Roser, N., Worthy, J., Strecker, S., & Gough, P. (1997). Classroom libraries and children's book selection: Redefining "access" in self-selected reading. In C. K. Kinzer, K. A. Hinchman, & D. J. Leu (Eds.), *Inquiries in literacy theory and practice: Forty-sixth yearbook of The National Reading Conference* (pp. 265–272). Chicago: National Reading Conference.

Naidoo, B. (1995). Undesirable publication: A journey to Jo'burg. In S. Lehr (Ed.), *Battling dragons: Issues and controversy in children's literature* (pp. 31–38). Portsmouth, NH: Heinemann.

National Council of Teachers of English/International Reading Association (1998). *Rationale for challenged books*, CD-ROM. Urbana, IL: Author

National Council of Teachers of English/International Reading Association. (nd) *Common ground: Speak with one voice on intellectual freedom and the defense of it.* Urbana, IL: NCTE. Retrieved from http://www.ncte.org/positions/common_ground.shtml

O'Neal, S. (1990). Leadership in the language arts: Controversial books in the classroom. *Language Arts, 67,* 771–775.

Paterson, K. (1989). *The spying heart: More thoughts on reading and writing books for children.* New York: E. P. Dutton.

Scales, P. (1995). Studying the first amendment. *Book Links, 5,* 20–24.

Schlafly, P. (1995). A child's reading list. *Education reporter,* The Eagle Forum. Retrieved from http://www.eagleforum.org/educate/1995/sept95/ersept6.html

Simmons, J. S., & Dresang, E. T. (2001). *School censorship in the 21st century: A guide for teachers and school library media specialists.* Newark, DE: International Reading Association.

Staples, S. F. (1996). What Johnny can't read: Censorship in American libraries. *Digital Library and Archives.* Retrieved from http://scholar.lib.vt.edu/ejournals/ALAN/winter96/pubCONN.html

Suhor, C. (1999, May). Censorship cases down, various organizations report. *SLATE Newsletter, 24*(2), 1.

Wollman-Bonilla, J. (1998). Outrageous viewpoints: Teachers' criteria for rejecting works of children's literature. *Language Arts, 75,* 287–295.

Worthy, J. (1996). Removing barriers to voluntary reading for reluctant readers: The role of school and classroom libraries. *Language Arts, 73,* 483–492.

Worthy, J., Moorman, M., & Turner, M. (1999). What Johnny likes to read is hard to find in school. *Reading Research Quarterly, 34,* 12–27.

LITERARY WORKS CITED

Blume, J. (1980). *Superfudge.* New York: Dell.

Carle, E. (2002). *"Slowly, slowly, slowly," said the Sloth.* New York: Philomel.

Garden, N. (1999). *The year they burned the books.* New York: Farrar Straus Giroux.

Hentoff, N. (1983). *The day they came to arrest the book.* New York: Dell.

Herron, C. (1997). *Nappy hair.* Illustrated by J. Cepeda. New York: Alfred A. Knopf.

Lobel, A. (1976). *Days with Frog and Toad.* New York: Harper & Row.

Naidoo, B. (1986). *Journey to Jo'burg.* Illustrated by E. Valasquez. New York: Lippincott.

Naylor, P. (1991). *Shiloh.* New York: Atheneum.

Newman, L. (2000). *Heather has two mommies.* Illustrated by D. Souza. Los Angeles: Alyson Wonderland. (Original work published 1989)

Paterson, K. (1978). *Bridge to Terabithia.* New York: HarperCollins.

Rowling, J. K. (1998). *Harry Potter and the sorcerer's stone.* New York: Scholastic.

Sendak, M. (1995). *In the night kitchen.* New York: HarperCollins.

Seuss, Dr. (1971). *The Lorax.* New York: Random House.

Staples, S. F. (1989). *Shabanu: Daughter of the wind.* New York: Knopf.

Taylor, M. (2001). *Roll of thunder, hear my cry.* New York: Phyllis Fogelman Books. (Original work published 1976)

Willhoite, M. (2000). *Daddy's roommate.* Los Angeles: Alyson Wonderland. (Original work published 1990)

IV

Assessing
the Text Environment

12

Studying the Literacy Environment and Literacy Practices as the Basis for Critical Reflection and Change

James V. Hoffman
The University of Texas at Austin

Misty Sailors
The University of Texas at San Antonio

> Questioning everything in the environment, from the bottom up, is an important task for teachers. We cannot necessarily change it all but we can certainly become aware of the messages, the hidden as well as the obvious, the commonplace as well as the gaudy. We can peel the cover back a bit, peek underground, disclose the undisclosed—at least for ourselves. And in telling what is untold, we can become stronger in shaping our own environments, until they become places that more fully reflect what we know and value.
>
> —Ayers, 2001, p. 51

The research on texts and teaching reading, summarized in this volume, provides a rich perspective for educators to examine effective teaching practices. In this chapter, we present a tool and a process for educators to use in the study of the classroom literacy environment. The tool, the TEX-IN3 (TEXt Inventory, TEXts In-use, & TEXt Interviews), is designed to capture the qualities, uses, and understandings of the literacy environment of a classroom. The process is one that encourages individual, collegial, and critical reflections on current literacy instruction practices. We begin by offering a theoretical framework for the study of the classroom literacy environment as a basis for critical reflection and change. Next, we present a detailed description of the components of the TEX-IN3. Finally, we offer specific recommendations on procedures for the use of the instrument to assess the classroom literacy environment.

A THEORETICAL FRAMEWORK FOR TEXTS AND THE LITERACY ENVIRONMENT

We do not regard the literacy environment as a static set of physical objects that passively surround the learner and teacher but rather as an integral part of a dynamic social context that both influences and is influenced by those who work within it. Barton wrote extensively regarding literacy and its social context. Framed as part of the "new literacy studies " movement (Barton, 1994; Gee, 1996; Street, 1995) and working in collaboration with the Literacy Research group at the University of Lancaster, Barton argued for the construct of literacy as a set of social practices, that is, as the ways in which a particular society uses and values literacy. From this perspective, all literacy acts (reading and writing), are situated in particular times and places. The intentions, uses, and values of the literacy practices of the members of a society are indicative of the role literacy plays in the lives of those members (Barton & Hamilton, 1998; Barton, Hamilton, & Ivanic, 2000; Langer, 1987). We are guided by Barton and Hamilton's (2000) definition of literacy:

> Literacy is a social practice.... Literacy practices are the general cultural ways of utilizing written language, which people draw upon in their lives. In the simplest sense literacy practices are what people do with literacy. (p. 7)

Literacy practices are inclusive of values, attitudes, feelings, and social relationships. They include:

> ... people's awareness of literacy, constructions of literacy, the discourses of literacy, and how people talk about and make sense of literacy. These are processes internal to the individual; at the same time, these practices are the social processes which connect people to one another (Barton & Hamilton, 2000, p. 9)

Within this broad view, literacy practices are not always observable. How people think about literacy, their awareness of it, their constructions of it, how they talk about it, and how they make sense of it, are internal processes. One way to examine literacy practices overtly is through the observation of those literacy events that take place in particular social contexts. We think of these literacy events as observable episodes "which arise from practices and are shaped by them" (Barton & Hamilton, 2000, p. 8) According to Barton and Hamilton, "texts are a crucial part of literacy events and the study of literacy is partly a study of texts and how they are produced and used" (p. 8).

We can think, as Bruner (1990) suggested, of a child's participation in the literacy events in any literate community as "plays in action." Those around the child are the actors in the ongoing play and serve as the coconstructors of the child's lived reality, especially his literate reality. Watching and interacting with individuals, tools, and artifacts in his environment, the child is being constructed, and in turn is constructing, the literacy practices of the community around him. All members of this community are in a constant state of becoming literate, and are surrounded by various types of literacy practices in various contexts and for various purposes. They acquire literacy, and the values placed on it, as a by-product of its use (Edelsky, 1994).

Barton and Hamilton (2000) suggested that one of the best ways for students and others to increase their understanding of literacy is for them to reflect on their own literacy practices. We argue that teachers might also benefit from such a reflection on the literacy practices around them as one of the members of this community. The plan we offer for reflection and professional development is grounded in these theoretical principles that are part of the new literacy studies framework.

STUDYING THE LITERACY ENVIRONMENT WITH THE TEX-IN3(M)

The instrument and procedures described in this section draw on both quantitative (observable) and qualitative (interpretive) traditions in classroom research (Shulman, 1986). The tool we present and the procedures to be followed can be used by an individual teacher working alone. However, it is highly recommended that a more collaborative and collegial model be followed. This can take the form of a buddy system, study group, a school-inservice plan, or a university course of study.

The TEX-IN3(M) is designed as a tool for studying the literacy environment for reading and language arts instruction in the elementary and middle school grades (Hoffman, 2001). The TEX-IN3(M) builds on the research of others who have investigated the relationship between the literacy environment, literacy teaching, and student learning (e.g., Duke, 1999, 2000; Henk, Moore, Marinak, & Tomaseiit, 2000; Loughlin & Martin, 1987; McGill-Franzen & Allington, 1999). The TEX-IN3(M) includes procedures for: (a) inspecting, capturing, and rating the range and qualities of texts in the classroom; (b) observing students and teachers as they engage with these texts in the flow of instruction; and (c) interviewing students and teachers regarding the forms, functions, and uses of the texts in the classroom. The version of the TEX-IN3(M) described in this chapter is a simplified version designed for use in professional development. It is a derivative of a more comprehensive instrument (TEX-IN3) designed specifically for use in research (Hoffman, 2001). Procedures for the training of observers (Sailors, 2001) and information on the reliability of the instrument and training (Duffy & Sailors, 2001) are available for the full version of TEX-IN3.

The TEX-IN3(M) is not a "value-free" examination of the literate environment of classrooms. Research suggests that teaching and learning are enhanced when the classroom environment offers an abundant supply of a variety of texts. Furthermore, the texts should be accessible to all the students in the class; the texts should be engaging in their content, language, and design; the students must be given choice, time, and supportive contexts to engage with these texts; and the teacher must provide the students with instruction in the use of these texts for a variety of purposes. All of these principles are applied in making judgments regarding the quality of the literacy environment.

The TEX-IN3(M) is designed to provide data that (a) captures and represents the range and qualities of texts in the classroom environment; (b) describes teachers and children as they engage with these texts during instruction; and (c) reveals the understandings of the forms, functions, uses, and valuing of theses texts by teachers and students.

The TEX-IN3(M) is divided into three major sections: (a) the Text Inventory, (b) the Texts In-Use Observation, and (c) the Text Interviews. In describing the use of the TEX-IN3(M), we assume a teacher and a partner or a teacher and a group of teachers are working collaboratively to study and reflect on their classroom literacy environments.

TEX-IN3(M): The TEXt Inventory

The Text Inventory requires a careful inspection of all of the texts in the classroom environment. This can be a time-consuming process, but we have found the investment of time and attention to detail are crucial in achieving the goal of critical reflection. Careful notes should be taken in consideration of both the quantitative and qualitative features of the texts that are available. However, we must preface this discussion about the texts in the classroom environment with one statement: The Text Inventory is not limited to a counting of books in the classroom. It involves much more than counting and it involves much more than just books. To facilitate the inventory process, we created a set of 17 categories of texts. The categories are conceived of more as functional than theoretical. Al-

TABLE 12.1
TEX-IN3 (M): Text Types

Computers/Electronic Texts: This category includes all texts that are accessed and used through an electronic medium.
Examples: messaging systems (e-mail), Internet access (for research), software programs (reading and authoring programs), tests or test preparation, text files that are saved and accessed by students, books-on-tape (e.g., listening centers), and news or information shows.

Extended Text Process Charts: These are multisentence, connected texts that are procedural and guide students toward the use of a particular process or strategy. Some of them may be ongoing.
Examples: KWL charts, Language Charts, Inquiry Charts, Writing Process Charts, math strategies or algorithms, rubrics.

Games/Puzzles/Manipulatives: These are instructional materials designed for student use (often as independent or small group work). To be considered in this category, they must feature text prominently.
Examples: Bingo, Clue, Word Sorts, Magnetic Poetry.

Instructional Aids: Often these charts are used as a visual aid to support direct instruction or minilessons. They may remain displayed in the classroom after a lesson and be used as an artifact for that lesson or as a reference point for students (e.g., a color chart). Instructional Aid Charts focus on content whereas Process Charts focus on process.
Examples: poems for reading together, morning message, labels, vocabulary lists, Daily Oral Language (DOL) charts

Journals: The use of journals has become so widespread in classrooms over the past decade that their definition continues to expand. This rapid growth has led to some confusion about what counts as a journal. For example, some things referred to as workbooks in commercial programs are referred to as journals. In this text inventory, journals are defined from a fairly specific framework. Journals must be local texts created by the students (individuals or groups working together) based primarily on their work and writing.
Examples: Personal journals, literature response logs, content inquiry logs (math, science, and social studies), draft writing.

Leveled Books: These texts are created explicitly for instruction in reading and are leveled for difficulty and accessibility. Basal readers tend to be collections of short selections bound together and include carefully controlled vocabulary (either literature-based anthologies or skills-driven selections). "Little books" tend to be bound single selections that are carefully leveled (and even numbered) in terms of accessibility.
Examples: Basal anthologies (current adoptions), basal readers (out of adoption), "little book," decodable books

(continued on next page)

TABLE 12.1 *(continued)*

Limited Text Process Charts: This category includes letter/word-level texts that are procedural and guide the students in the use of a particular strategy or set of strategies. These are similar to the Extended Text Charts in purpose and design; however, they tend to focus at the letter or word level.
Examples: Word walls, alphabet charts, spelling "demon" charts.

Organizational/Management Charts: These displays are used to manage or organize the social, academic, or curricular work within the classroom.
Examples: Student-helpers chart, workboards, class rules, local or state curricular objectives, a chart for multiplication facts mastered by students, a skill mastery chart, a record of number of books read.

Portfolios: Student portfolios are locations for and an organizer for the work completed by students. Consider, when looking at portfolios, the range of texts collected; the processes of collecting texts; the access and use of these texts; and issues of control over these texts (e.g., what gets in, how, when).

Reference Materials: These are materials that are used as resources for finding information (e.g., word spellings; locations; how to do something).
Examples: Atlas, dictionary, encyclopedia, English grammar handbook, thesaurus, globe, maps.

Serials: This text type includes a variety of local and imported materials. Consideration of these texts should focus on qualities of topical relevance, accessibility for the students, quality of the publication, and the number of copies available (Is there one for every student? Is it promoted as a reference or on display?).
Examples: Ranger Rick, Highlights, Scholastic newspapers, classroom newspapers, school and community newsletters.

Social/Personal/Inspirational Text Displays: These might include inspirational posters about reading, student of the week displays, current events bulletin boards, etc.
Examples: "Star of the Week" posters, "Read, Read, Read" posters.

Student/Teacher Published Work: This category consists of locally authored (by a student, a teacher, or a combination of the two) books or publications and are on display for students to use. These texts tend to be more permanent than Work Product Displays.
Examples: Text innovations with big books, individual-student-authored books, reports/inquiry projects.

Textbooks: These are student texts that are typically identified with a subject/content area. Textbooks in this category have a clear instructional design for the teacher to use and the students to follow in learning new concepts and skills. Basal readers are not included in this category.
Examples: mathematics textbook, science textbook, English grammar book.

Tradebooks: These books do not have an obvious instructional design; they are often called "library books" or "children's literature."
Examples: Picture books (narrative, expository, procedural) and chapter books (same).

Work Product Displays: These are displays of teacher or student work that is being "celebrated" and set forward for others to read and enjoy.
Examples: model writing samples.

---

though the plan for categorization may not be exhaustive of all the possibilities, we have found the list encompasses most of the major text types found in elementary classrooms. We offer descriptions of these categories to assist in the inventory process in Table 12.1. This listing of text categories can serve as the basis for a worksheet for documenting the inventory. Figure 12.1 depicts an example of an actual documentation of the tradebooks found in one second-grade classroom. The observer listed the books in the classroom in the same way the teacher had them organized: by author, genre, and accessibility level as well as by physical placement in the classroom. This is just one way of documenting the text environment, with each text type described on a different page.

Once the inventory is complete, the next step is to rate the quality of the texts in the classroom environment. In the full TEX-IN3 instrument, a numeric rating for the quality of the texts in a classroom is assigned for each of the text categories using a five-point rubric scale. The rubrics are elaborate and draw on available research for each text type. For this modified version of the TEX-IN3(M), we recommend that the physical inventory be conducted for each text type but that overall rating be made using a holistic scale for all of the text types combined. The quality of the texts should:

1. vary in genre (narrative, procedural, and informational) and format (chapter and storybook);

2. be engaging—including texts that support the interests of the children in the class as well as curricular requirements (content), texts that are written in

15. Tradebooks

In Library Area:

11 Eric Carle books standing open on top of library bookcase at child eye level. Three bins labeled "Easy" with 100 books each. Four bins labeled "Medium" with about 75 books in each bin. Three bins labeled "Advanced" with about 80-100 books in each.

Three bins labeled "Animals" with about 30 books in each.
Further bins labeled: 50 Science, 30 Insects, 45 Plants and Gardens, 50 Places, 20 Holidays, 25 Alphabets, 50 Science, 30 Seasons, 30 Spanish.
Five more Eric Carle books displayed at child eye level.
5 Clifford books.
Bookcase filed with 11 titles with 25-30 copies of each (text sets), i.e., "The Good Bad Cat," "Down by the Bay," "Rain," "I Went Walking."
Two more bins both labeled "Folk Tales" with about 150 books in each. Wide shelves near the floor hold 150 books easily accessible by children sitting on the floor. Adjacent shelf holds 75 more.
Another shelf with 20 library books.
Another shelf with 100 trade books (very thin about 8 pages each). Commercially made yellow suitcase book containing 40 poetry books and 4 tapes and one big book entitled "Happy Poetry-ing." This is called "World of Poetry" by Lee Bennett Hopkins.
Two more bins "unlabeled" of trade books about 100 books in each.
Bin of 20 more labeled "Books on Families."
Books displayed at Science Earth Center Table: "Ants Go Marching, My Five Senses, and Earth." Also, display of 40 science books "Take another Look at Me."
One bin labeled "Plants and Gardening" with 25 books. Another bin of 20.
A metal display case by Troll containing 100 science oriented books with titles, e.g., Listen, Look, etc.
In the Math Center two bins of 100 books each. "The Baseball Counting Book" is prominently displayed. "The Shape Book" is a large format book also displayed. The "Big Book of How Things Work."
Two bins of 20 "Math Advantage-On My Own Practice."
On groups of children's desks in classroom are scattered approximately 5 bins of trade books 25-30 books in each.
Near science center, there is a wooden display case of 30 books, "Inch by Inch," "It's Mine," "A Color of His Own," etc. by Leo Leoni.
Glass and wood locked case (built into wall) containing a variety of trade and/or teachers guides etc.
Under this are three shelves displaying special authors and their books (20 each) Kevin Henkes, Pat Hutchins, Tomie DePaola. These are at children's height.
Along chalk tray at front of room 20 books are displayed i.e. Eric Carle.
40 commercially made trade books displayed at the Listening Center at the front of the room. (Includes cassettes).
In Social Studies area one bin of 20 books labeled "Families."
On Science Table area: large format book "Earth."

FIG. 12.1   Documentation of tradebooks.

language that is rich, literary, or imaginative, and texts with design features that extend, enrich, or support the text;

3. be accessible—including the physical accessibility of the texts for the children—as well as be physically inviting and displayed usefully;

4. offer a variety of challenge and support levels, including multiple levels of texts that support the many levels of learners found in typical classrooms;

5. represent and reflect the cultural and linguistic diversity that exists in the classroom;

6. include a combination of public texts (visible and accessible to most students most of the time) and personal texts (accessible and used mainly by individual students);

7. include a combination of local texts (created or authored by either the students or the teacher) and imported texts (published or produced elsewhere and brought into the class);

8. include a combination of extended texts (contain a significant amount of text beyond the word level such as phrases, sentences, and more) and limited texts (that operate primarily at the letter or word level);

9. include a combination of process texts that guide students toward a process to be used (e.g., how to figure out a word, how to inquire about a topic) and product texts (e.g., displays of student work).

A rubric for rating the overall quality of the text environment is presented in Table 12.2. A second rubric is presented in Table 12.3 that is for the "local texts" in the classroom. The local text rubric was added based on our research in classrooms that suggests the importance of these texts as key to an effective literacy program (see Maloch, Hoffman, & Patterson, chap. 8, this volume). For the purposes of personal reflection and change, the numerical rating of the classroom on these scales is not nearly as important as the inventory process itself.

TEX-IN3(M): Texts In-Use

It is through observing teachers and students as they engage and interact with the texts in the classroom that we begin to understand how the use of texts reveals the literacy practices of the classroom. The second component of the TEX-IN3(M), the Texts In-Use phase, helps focus on practices as they are imbedded in literacy events. In this phase, it is useful to work with a colleague or a group of colleagues who can share observation responsibilities. With the full TEX-IN3 Text In-Use observation plan, the entire class and three individual students in the class (one reading instructionally above grade level; one reading instructionally on grade level; and one reading instructionally below grade

TABLE 12.2
Holistic Ratings for Text Environment

5. Extremely Rich
Extremely rich text environment—large quantity and variety (rich range);
Diverse range of texts that meet the needs and interest of children;
Large, diverse range of cultural and linguistic texts;
Texts link across curriculum;
Local texts are plentiful in the classroom at both the personal and the public levels. The texts reflect uses of literacy that are functional to the daily life in the classroom;
Text environment is a combination of student and teacher input.

4. Rich
Rich resource for majority of students;
Diverse range of texts is more than adequate for the needs of class;
Diverse range of cultural and linguistic texts;
Some text types are represented exceptionally, others are adequate;
Local texts are clearly valued; imported texts are of high quality and support instruction;
Student input into classroom is apparent.

3. Functional
Functional resource for most of students;
Supply of texts is adequate; range may be limited (e.g., dominance of narrative tradebooks);
Little evidence of cultural or linguistic diversity;
Dominance of imported texts;
Some evidence of student involvement in creation of text environment.

2. Limited
Limited text environment;
Mediocre quality; directed toward the on-grade level reader;
Imported texts dominate; little or no local texts
Little attention to the organization of texts;
Student input into environment limited to Work Product Displays.

1. Inadequate
Severely limited text environment (not a meaningful resource for the vast majority of the children);
Few, if any local texts or poor quality (not accessible or functional);
Imported texts of low quality;
Restrictive worksheets and workbooks characterize the personal texts available for student use;
There is little evidence of student input into the text environment.

TABLE 12.3
Holistic Ratings for Local Texts in the Environment

Local texts are defined as texts ("of the place") and authored by the teacher, students, or children in the classroom (see Maloch, Hoffman, and Patterson, chap. 8, this volume)

5. Extremely Rich
Local texts visible everywhere in the classroom;
Texts used actively in support of learning;
There is evidence of local texts crossing areas of the curriculum;
Used procedurally (e.g., in management and classroom routines) as well as in support of content learning;
Appear in various stages of development in the classroom; may not all have a "published" look about them;
A number of the local texts are dynamic (added to) and change over time;Both public and private local texts.

4. Rich
Local texts more limited but it is clear that those present are valued and used regularly;
Both extended and limited local texts are in use;
Some of the local texts are dynamic;
Evidence of both public and private texts;
There is clear evidence in these classrooms that the students engage actively and regularly with these texts.

3. Functional
Some local texts are featured in the classroom;
Public local texts are primarily teacher controlled and show limited student input and ownership;
Changes in local text tend to be proceduralized (i.e., weather added to a calendar);
Local texts may cross curriculum areas but tend to be mainly tied to the reading/language arts curriculum and they tend to be tied to fairly routine activities.

2. Limited
Local texts are limited in number and variety and tend toward the functional and the display variety;
Little evidence of their dynamic use;
Private local texts are structured or used infrequently;
Show little evidence of enthusiasm or creative input of the children.

1. Inadequate
There are no local texts featured in the classroom in prominent ways;
Some routine charts and graphs may be present but these are largely functional in nature and teacher controlled.

level) are observed over three different time periods. The TEX-IN3 relies on direct observation and coding of behaviors. In the TEX-IN3(M) we offer the option of a direct coding of behaviors or a running narrative description. Both strategies yield valuable data on the texts used in a classroom.

We suggest that when using the TEX-IN3(M) system, the teacher (or colleague) focus, initially, on the teacher and one student only. We have found in using the instrument, however, that a richer picture of the classroom as a whole emerges when the focus is on three children (one from each of the groups previously listed). The observation procedures can be extended to include more students if there is interest in this question.

We suggest at least three observation periods (lasting about 20 minutes each), representing instruction not just during the reading/language arts periods but across the curriculum (e.g., science, math, social studies). Each 20-minute observation period begins with a *snapshot*. Between each snapshot, the observation turns to the focus student (or students) and the teacher for the observational *sweep*. During a sweep period, the observer shifts focus back and forth from the focus student to the teacher. Another snapshot concludes each observation period once again to illustrate the larger context of the classroom community.

The snapshots and sweeps are intended to capture the engagement of children with text and the context under which this engagement occurs. *Engaged,* for the purposes of this observation, indicates that the students are attending to text in some observable way—for example, following along as a teacher works with an instructional chart, reading independently from a tradebook, writing on a worksheet, or listening to a teacher reading aloud from a chapter book. The last example illustrates the fact that engagement does not require that the student be actually looking at the words on the page. The operating principle is that written text is a significant focus for the attention of the participants and is present during the interaction. A discussion of a story, for example, without the physical text present, would not be recorded as engaged with text. In addition, for the purposes of this instrument, there can be engagement with only one text type at any given moment.

For each snapshot, the observer focuses on all of the students in the classroom at a point in time, recording the number of students engaged with texts, under what context these engagements occur, and with which types of texts the children are engaged (see Table 12.4). There is room on the instrument for more qualitative data to be recorded in the "Comments" section. We have found these narrative comments add an additional dimension to the description of the ways in which the students are engaging (or not) with texts.

TABLE 12.4
TEX-IN3 (M): Texts In-Use: Snapshot

Number of students in room at time of snapshot:	With teacher	Without teacher	
1. Computers/Electronics			
2. Extended Text Process Charts			
3. Games/Puzzles/Manipulatives			
4. Instructional Aids			
5. Journals			
6. Leveled Texts			
7. Limited Text Process Charts			
8. Organizational/Management Charts			
9. Portfolios			
10. Reference Materials			
11. Serials			
12. Social/Personal/Inspirational			
13. Student/Teacher Published Work			
14. Textbooks			
15. Tradebooks			
16. Work Product Displays			Comments:
17. Writing on Paper			
Totals by working Context			

Number of Students Not Engaged with Text ___

Once the opening snapshot is completed, the observer shifts attention to the focus student and the teacher. The heart of the In-Use observation is called the *classroom sweep* (see Table 12.5). During the 20 one-minute intervals, the attention of the observer shifts cyclically from the focus student to the teacher. The first 10 seconds of the interval is spent observing the student to determine whether or not the child is engaged with text. If it is determined that he or she is engaged, then a decision is made regarding the context under which the engagement is occurring. If the child is *not* engaged with text, this is recorded as "not engaged." We use the numbers at the bottom of the record sheet as places to indicate engagement: a slash ("/") can be used to indicate engagement and a circle around the number indicates nonengagement. These numbers also serve as placeholders for keeping track of the time intervals.

The observer then turns the attention to the context under which the engagement occurred, whether the child is working with or without the teacher, and the text type with which the child (or teacher) is engaged. The observer then spends approximately 20 seconds recording this information. Turning the attention to the teacher, the same information is collected in the same manner: the first 10-second interval is used to make a decision regarding the engagement of the teacher with text, the context under which the engagement occurs, and the type of text the teacher is using at that moment. The second 20-second interval is spent recording this information. Following the sweep, a second snapshot is taken to give a broader picture of what is occurring in the classroom at that moment in time.

TABLE 12.5
TEX-IN3 (M): Texts In-Use: Sweep

Student	With Teacher	Without Teacher	
1. Computer/Electronics			
2. Extended Text Process Charts			
3. Games/Puzzles/Manipulatives			
4. Instructional Aids			
5. Journals			
6. Leveled Texts			
7. Limited Text Process Charts			
8. Organizational/Management			
9. Portfolios			
10. Reference Materials			
11. Serials			
12. Social/Personal/Inspirational			
13. Student/Tchr Published Work			
14. Textbooks			
15. Tradebooks			Comments:
16. Work Product Displays			
17. Writing on Paper			

Time Intervals 1 2 3 4 5 6 7 8 9 10 11 12 13 14 15 16 17 18 19 20

TABLE 12.5 (continued)

Teacher with	Individual	Small group	Whole class	
1. Computer/Electronics				
2. Extended Text Process Charts				
3. Games/Puzzles/Manipulatives				
4. Instructional Aids				
5. Journals				
6. Leveled Texts				
7. Limited Text Process Charts				
8. Organizational/Management				
9. Portfolios				
10. Reference Materials				
11. Serials				
12. Social/Personal/Inspirational				
13. Student/Teacher Published Work				
14. Textbooks				
15. Tradebooks				
16. Work Product Displays				Comments:
17. Writing on Paper				
Teacher's Guide				

Time Intervals 1 2 3 4 5 6 7 8 9 10 11 12 13 14 15 16 17 18 19 20

In addition to capturing the physical engagement with text, the TEX-IN3(M) offers a way to capture and record the oral texts generated by teachers and children during discussions of text (see Table 12.6). The intent is to capture the engagement with text ideas supported by the teacher that may not involve direct engagement with the physical text in the classroom. These ratings are designed to rate holistically both the quantity and quality of discussion that surrounds text during the In-Use component. The first rating, based on the quantity of oral discussion of text, focuses on the amount of time the teacher spends engaged in discussion surrounding the text. The more qualitative rating (based also on a scale of 1 to 5) focuses on the nature of the student-led and teacher-led participation and engagement during the discussion

TABLE 12.6
Holistic Ratings for Text Discussion

Quantity (Circle One Rating)

---

5. Pervasive. Guiding text discussion characterized most of the teacher activity during this period (roughly 75% or more of the observation points).

4. Extensive. Guiding text discussion characterized the majority of teacher activity during this period (roughly between 50% and 75% of the observation points).

3. Substantial. Guiding text discussion was a significant part of the teacher activity during this period (roughly between 25% and 50% of the observation points).

2. Limited. Guiding text discussion occurred but on a very limited basis during the period (roughly between 5% and 25% of the observation points).

1. None. Guiding text discussion did not occur during this observation (roughly, less than 5% of the observation points).

Quality (Circle One Rating)

---

5. Extremely Rich. High levels of student participation and engagement. The discussion operated at a high inferential and critical level with respect to the text. The discussion appeared almost spontaneous as in a naturally occurring conversation. The teacher was part of and not controlling of the discussion.

4. Very High. Participation in the discussion was broad. The teacher worked to include as many of the students as possible. The teacher was successful in moving the conversation at certain points to fairly high inferential and critical levels.

3. Functional. The discussion tended to follow an IRE (Teacher Initiation, Student Response, Teacher Evaluation Comment) sequence. Participation was limited. The teacher was clearly in control of the discussion and most of the discussion focused on literal details.

2. Limited. The discussion was limited to short questions by the teachers and answers by the students. The discussion was focused almost entirely on literal/factual recall of text.

1. None. There was no discussion or the limited discussion that took place was in the form of short questions by the teacher and even shorter answers by the students.

---

period. We found these ratings to add a unique dimension to the overall picture presented with regard to the engagement of teachers and children with text.

To illustrate what the Text-In-Use observation might look like, we turn to Ms. Smith's third grade classroom. In Figs. 12.2 through 12.5, we offer an example of a completed cycle for her class. During this observation period, the teacher and the children were engaged in learning how to use an Inquiry Chart. The teacher had just guided the children through the process with one on the board. The children were working in small groups and each group had a copy in their area. The students were also surrounded by various tradebooks and reference materials. Beginning with the snapshot in Fig. 12.2, this record indicates that there were a total of 21 students present in the classroom at the time of this snapshot. Ten students were working on the first section of their charts without the teacher (noted in Fig. 12.2 as working "without the teacher" with "Extended Text Process Charts"). Five students were engaged with their tradebooks (noted in Fig. 12.2 as working "without the teacher" with "Tradebooks"). Four other students were engaged with an encyclopedia (noted in Fig. 12.2 as working "without the teacher" with "Reference Materials"). One student was working with Ms. Smith as she was helping him fill out the first column of his Inquiry Chart (noted in Fig. 12.2 as "working with the teacher" with an "Extended Text Process Chart"). Finally, one student was not engaged with text during the time period of the snapshot; that information is reflected as "Not Engaged."

Figures 12.3 and 12.4 illustrate the next component of the In-Use observation, the *observation sweep*. This component has 20 time intervals. During the first interval, the observer documented the focus student's engagement with a tradebook as she was listening to another student read aloud (recorded as #1 in Fig. 12.3 as "working without the teacher" with "tradebook"). Turning attention to the teacher, the observer noted she was engaged with another group, demonstrating how to use the guide words in an encyclopedia (recorded in Fig. 12.4 as #1, working with a "small group" with a "reference material"). The attention then turned back to the student, noting that she was still engaged with the tradebook (recorded as #2 in Fig. 12.3), again, without the teacher. The observer then noted the teacher was still engaged with the same group and the same type of text (recorded as #2 in Fig. 12.4). On the third interval of this observation period, the observer documented the focus child as being engaged at this moment individually with the teacher at the computer (recorded as #3 in Fig. 12.3). The teacher is noted (as #3 in Fig. 12.4) as working under the same context and with the same text type. This observation continued for the remaining intervals with similar engagements with text (see "Comments," Figs. 12.3 and 12.4 for remaining explanation). It should be pointed out that during Intervals 10, 11, 12, and 19 (Fig. 12.3), the student was not engaged with text; we note this at the bottom of the chart as "not engaged." Notice, also, that this observer marked through the numbers as each time interval was completed.

We see from Fig. 12.3 that our focus child was engaged with text 80% of the time during the observation, under various contexts, and with a variety of text types. Similarly, we see from Fig. 12.4 that the teacher was also highly engaged

Number of students in room at time of snapshot: 21	With teacher	Without teacher	
1. Computers/ Electronics			
2. Extended Text Process Charts	1	10	
3. Games/ Puzzles/ Manipulatives			
4. Instructional Aids			
5. Journals			
6. Leveled Texts			
7. Limited Text Process Charts			
8. Organizational/ Management Charts			
9. Portfolios			
10. Reference Materials		4	
11. Serials			
12. Social/Personal/ Inspirational			
13. Student/ Teacher Published Work			
14. Textbooks			
15. Tradebooks		5	
16. Work Product Displays			
17. Writing on Paper			
Totals by working Context			

Comments: Sts working on Inquiry Charts— teacher constructed chart on board, students in small groups w/ ref. materials + tradebooks—each group has a chart. Students working in groups

Number of Students Not Engaged with Text __1__

FIG. 12.2   Classroom Snapshot #1 Subject Area: Science

Sara	With Teacher	Without Teacher
1. Computer/ Electronics	3, 4	5, 6
2. Extended Text Process Charts	9, 13	7, 8, 14, 18, 20
3. Games/ Puzzles/ Manipulatives		
4. Instructional Aids		
5. Journals		
6. Leveled Texts		
7. Limited Text Process Charts		
8. Organizational/ Management		
9. Portfolios		
10. Reference Materials		
11. Serials		
12. Social/ Personal/ Inspirational		
13. Student/ Teacher Published Work		
14. Textbooks		
15. Tradebooks		1, 2, 15, 16, 17
16. Work Product Displays		
17. Writing on Paper		

Comments: Sara is listening to another std. read from a tradebook. She moves to computer asking tchr. for help. Using website to gather data. Back to group can't find pencil; focuses alternatively on chart & tradebook.

Time Intervals 1 2 3 4 5 6 7 8 9 (10) (11) (12) 13 14 15 16 17 18 (19) 20

FIG. 12.3   Student # 1: Observation Sweep #1F

231

Teacher	With indivi	small group	Whole class	
1. Computer/ Electronics	3, 4			
2. Extended Text Process Charts	7, 8, 12, 13	5, 6, 10, 11, 14, 15, 16, 17	9	
3. Games/ Puzzles/ Manipulatives				
4. Instructional Aids				
5. Journals				
6. Leveled Texts				
7. Limited Text Process Charts				
8. Organizational/ Management				
9. Portfolios				
10. Reference Materials		1, 2		
11. Serials				
12. Social/ Personal/ Inspirational				
13. Student/ Teacher Published Work				
14. Textbooks				
15. Tradebooks	20	18, 19		
16. Work Product Displays				
17. Writing on Paper				
Teacher's Guide				

Comments: Teacher explains "guide words" to small group. Helps individuals w/ charts (uses example on board) - monitors / helps groups (i.e. unknown words + management)

Time Intervals 1 2 3 4 5 6 7 8 9 10 11 12 13 14 15 16 17 18 19 20

FIG. 12.4   Teacher Sweep

232

with text (100%), under various contexts and with a variety of text types. The observer turns one last time during this period to a general picture of the engagement with text throughout the classroom. An example of the second snapshot appears in Fig. 12.5. The observer also noted during this time period that text discussion characterized most of the teacher activity during this period (roughly 80%). In addition, the observer also noted that the quality of the discussion surrounding these texts was of a functional nature (a "3" on the holistic rubric). The discussion tended to follow an IRE (Initiation, Response, Evaluation) model during many of the interactions with the text (Cazden, 1988). The second snapshot concludes the observation of the first period.

In our example we focus on only one student and the teacher. However, we found that the richest descriptions of the use of text in classrooms come from observing more than just one student. The contrasts in how different students are engaged over the same period can be very revealing of text use. The goal is to create a database that reflects the frequency of engagements with the variety of texts in the classroom and the contexts under which those engagements occur. The data can be manipulated statistically to examine percentages and distributions (e.g., with respect to skill level of the students and the frequency of engagements with text). This kind of analysis is most useful when there are a large number of observations of students.

We found that some teachers are uncomfortable with the mechanical coding system used in the Text In-Use observation. An alternative approach is to use a narrative plan for initial data recording. Following the narrative plan, the observer records rich descriptions of the student and teachers in a journal over several 20-minute time periods. The observer using this model shifts attention back and forth between the teacher and the student(s). The descriptions should focus on the engagement, the context for the engagement, and the qualities of the texts and the tasks observed.

These narrative data can be interpreted using the following questions:

- Were the child and teacher engaged with high quality texts throughout the observation period?
- In what ways were the texts used to support learning or literacy development?
- Were texts created (oral or written) during the observation period?

TEX-IN3(M): Text Interviews

It is through the text interviews that the more covert or personal sense-making of literacy practices are revealed. These interviews reveal the discourse that sur-

Number of students in room at time of snapshot: $\underline{21}$	With teacher	Without teacher	
1. Computers/ Electronics			
2. Extended Text Process Charts		7	
3. Games/ Puzzles/ Manipulatives			
4. Instructional Aids			
5. Journals			
6. Leveled Texts			
7. Limited Text Process Charts			
8. Organizational/ Management Charts			
9. Portfolios			
10. Reference Materials		5	
11. Serials			
12. Social/Personal/ Inspirational			
13. Student/ Teacher Published Work			
14. Textbooks			
15. Tradebooks	5	2	
16. Work Product Displays			
17. Writing on Paper			
Totals by working Context			

Handwritten comments (right margin): Children working on Inquiry Charts. Teacher showing a group how to transfer words from tradebook to chart. 2 sts. getting markers; children highly engaged and excited...

Number of Students Not Engaged with Text $\underline{2}$

FIG. 12.5   Classroom Snapshot #2: Subject Area: Science

rounds the literate environment. Through the talk that surrounds the text in the classroom, insight is gained into the understandings, interpretations, values, and beliefs that are part of the literacy events that have been observed. In addition, the interviews give insight into the decisions the teacher has made as to what types of literacy events to engage the children in and what her purposes for those decisions were. As with the observations, the interview phase works best with collaboration among colleagues.

The student interviews are conducted with the same student(s) who was(were) the "focus" student(s) in the text In-Use observation phase. The interviewer asks the student to guide them on a tour around the classroom, "reading the room" and talking about the various forms of print and writing that are present. The goal of the student interview is to get at the deep understanding, uses, and valuing of the texts that the children encounter in their classrooms. We offer a set of probes that may be used to get at these notions; the observer and teacher may decide to change these questions to make them more conversational.

- *Form*: Tell me about this text or about a time that you used this text. What do you call this? How does it work?
- *Function*: What is this text for? Why would someone use it? What would you learn with this text?
- *Use*: Who uses this text? When do they use it? Do you use it? When?
- *Valuing*: Is this text important in your classroom? To whom? Is it important to you? Why?
- *Critical Stance*: What's the quality of this text? Why? Is it interesting? Attractive?

The same procedures should be followed with each of the focus students if more than one is followed. The rubric presented in Table 12.7 can be used as a reference point for interpreting the student's understanding of literacy environment.

Just as the student interview yields valuable insight into the ways that a student thinks about literacy, so does the teacher interview. In the full TEX-IN3, the teacher interview involves two related tasks: rating the various text types and then ranking them. Both tasks are designed to get at the deep understandings, intentions, purposes, and beliefs of the teacher with regard to the literacy practices in which she or he engages the children. The teacher interview begins by the teacher rating each of the 17 text types in terms of their importance in the classroom. It is best to think of something like a five-point scale (5 = very important, 3 = important, and 1 = not very important). With the rating of the text types, the teacher talks about "why" and "in what ways" and "with what purposes" these texts function in the classroom. This task allows the teacher

TABLE 12.7
TEX-IN3 (M): Holistic Rating Student Interview

---

5. Elaborated/Enriched
Has a rich understanding, valuing, and use of texts;
Is able to express critical insight into quality of texts;
Has a sense of pride and ownership in the texts;
Has an awareness of what is there as well as what might be added to enrich the literate environment.

4. Good Understanding
Has a good understanding, valuing, and use of almost all texts;
Understands and describes purposes of texts;
Describes text use as primarily dictated by teacher with some personal choice in use.

3. Basic Understanding
Has a basic understanding and use of most texts;
Describes texts in terms of fulfilling specific purposes;
Text is assigned by teacher (no initiation by student);
Student values text but is not articulate about text in relation to learning goals.

2. Vague Awareness
Vague or general understanding of basic texts;
Limited sense of how texts work and function;
No knowledge of some of the texts.

1. No Knowledge
Describes many of the texts as "there" and not used by any person on any particular frequency;
Limited valuing of the texts in the classroom.

---

more space to talk about the value of all of the text types without setting one in favor over the other, which he or she will be asked to do on the next task.

Next, the teacher is directed to think about the role of the texts in the classroom through a "ranking" task. The teacher is asked to rank (from highest to lowest) the text types in terms of the order of importance they play in the reading/literacy program. Ranking can be a challenge, but it does force us to look at the relative value and importance these texts play as they influence daily decision making. It is through these discussions that the deep sense of practice is uncovered. Many teachers have commented that these exercises give them the opportunity to reflect critically on the types of text with which they surround and engage their children.

A similar procedure can be followed for the modified TEX-IN3(M). As an alternative procedure, we offer a more conversational, dialogic model. We suggest that the teachers, in pairs or in small groups, come together to talk about the text environment. Colleagues can assist one other with questions such as the following:

- Does my text environment reflect the breadth of text types that could be located in my classroom?
- Does my text environment create a rich set of possibilities for the literacy development of my children?
- Do the texts located in my classroom reveal my purposes and goals for the literacy development of the children in my classroom?
- Are the texts in my classroom a rich resource for the literacy practices that I hope to engage my students with?
- Are there alternative ways I might structure my text environment (e.g., by creating spaces; organizing materials differently) to encourage additional understandings and valuing of literacy by my students?
- Is my literate environment a dynamic one, ever-changing as the needs of the language learners in my classroom change?

These questions are intended to serve as a guide for thinking about the texts that are in place and the ways in which the children in the classroom talk about those texts, as well as the teacher's understanding of them.

INTERPRETATION AND USE

We can encircle what we know about learning, embody what we value about wisdom, comprise an ecology of learning. We can become better at creating what we intend for ourselves and our students. (Ayers, 2001, p. 51)

Schon (1983) described reflective practitioners as those who are able to take what is known tacitly and make it explicit as a way of examining that knowledge, questioning it, and reconstructing it. This is one way of improving on the teaching and learning that takes place in classrooms. As the person who structures the literacy practices of the classroom, often it is helpful for a teacher to be able to step out of the daily life of the classroom and take a reflective look at the literacy practices that have been established there. One way to do this is to look at the literacy environment, literacy events, and the understandings of that environment and those events that children encounter on a daily basis. A teacher reflecting on the literacy environment of the classroom might ask how her vision of literacy is represented in the texts in the classroom. In addition, a teacher might also reflect on the connection between her understandings, intents, and practices of literacy and her students' understandings, intents, and practices of literacy.

The data from the TEX-IN3(M) should be used as a basis for reflecting on the literate environment and the literacy practices of the classroom community. If elements of the data seem suspect, then phases of the data collection can be repeated in the same or in adapted formats. There is a real danger in using an instrument and a process like this to fall into a deficit mode of analysis: What's wrong with this classroom? What don't I have? This is not a productive frame for reflection. The goal is to establish a point of reference to begin to think about strengthening the way that literacy is presented and practiced with and among the members of the classroom. There is no magic formula for improvement (i.e, if you score X, do this). The interpretations are made by the teacher for his or her own classroom and are intended to be a guide, and not a "fix-all," for those who are involved in the immediate decision making of the everyday experiences in the classroom. As teachers, we must be willing to step back from these practices so as to see them more clearly, and then be willing to step back in to use what has been learned to grow. Those who have helped you with the assessment are a sounding board but not the final interpreters of what is there and what is needed. The tool can continue to be used over time as a means by which a teacher can track the impact of changes that have been made on the literacy practices of the classroom. This is the essence of reflective practice as a tool for professional growth.

REFERENCES

Ayers, W. (2001). *To teach: The journey of a teacher.* New York: Teachers College Press.

Barton, D. (1994). *Literacy: An introduction to the ecology of written language.* Oxford: Blackwell.

Barton, D., & Hamilton, M. (1998). *Local literacies: Reading and writing in one community.* London: Routledge.

Barton, D., & Hamilton, M. (2000). Literacy practices. In D. Barton, M. Hamilton, & R. Ivanic (Eds.), *Situated literacies: Reading and writing in context* (pp. 7–14). London: Routledge.

Barton, D., Hamilton, M., & Ivanic, R. (2000). *Situated literacies: Reading and writing in context.* London: Routledge.

Bruner, J. (1990). *Acts of meaning.* Cambridge, MA: Harvard University.

Cazden, C. B. (1988). *Classroom discourse: The languages of teaching and learning.* Portsmouth, NH: Heinemann.

Duffy, G. G., & Sailors, M. (2001). The development, training, and reliability of the Text Inventory, Text Interview and Texts In-Use Observation System. Unpublished document, The University of Texas at Austin, Austin, TX.

Duke, N. K. (1999). *Print environments and experiences offered to first-grade students in very low- and very high-SES school districts.* Unpublished doctoral dissertation, Harvard University, Boston, Massachusetts.

Duke, N. K. (2000). 3.6 minutes per day: The scarcity of informational texts in first grade. *Reading Research Quarterly, 35,* 202–224.

Edelsky, C. (1994). Education for democracy. *Language Arts, 71,* 252–257.

Gee, J. (1996). *Social linguistics and literacies: Ideology in discourses* (2nd ed.). London: Falmer Press.

Henk, W. A., Moore, J. C., Marinak, B. A., & Tomaseiit, B. W. (2000). Lesson observation framework for elementary teachers, principals, and literacy supervisors. *The Reading Teacher, 53,* 358–369.

Hoffman, J. V. (2001). *Assessing the literacy environment of the elementary classroom: The TEX-IN3.* Unpublished document, The University of Texas at Austin, Austin, TX.

Langer, J. A. (1987). Literacy and schooling: A sociocognitive perspective. In J. Langer (Ed.), *Language, literacy, and culture: Issues in society and school* (pp. 1–20). Norwood, NJ: Ablex.

Loughlin, C. E., & Martin, M. D. (1987). *Supporting literacy: Developing effective learning environments.* New York: Teachers College Press.

McGill-Franzen, A., & Allington, R. L. (1999). Putting books in the classroom seems necessary but not sufficient. *Journal of Educational Research, 93,* 67–74.

Sailors, M. (2001). TEX-IN3 Training Manual. Unpublished document, The University of Texas at Austin, Austin, TX.

Schon, D. A. (1983). *The reflective practitioner.* New York: Basic Books

Shulman, L. S. (1986). Paradigms and research programs in the study of teaching: A contemporary perspective. In M. Wittrock (Ed.), *Handbook of research in teaching* (3rd ed., pp. 3–36). New York: Macmillan.

Street, B. (1995). *Social literacies.* London: Longman.

Author Index

Subject Index

A

Abbott, J., 70
ABC Discovery! (Cohen), 102
ABC Kids (Williams), 102
Accessibility principle, 117–119
Action Alphabet (Rotner), 102
Adams, M. J., 40–41, 44, 50, 51
Alao, S., 76
Alphabetic principle, of reading, 43
Alvermann, D. E., 76, 148
Amber Brown books, 99
Amber Brown Is Not a Crayon (Danziger), 99
American Library Association, 199
Amos and Boris (Steig), 90
A My Name Is Alice (Bayer), 102
Anchor words, 48
Anderson, E., 76
Anderson, V., 186–187
Angelou, Maya, 199
Animorphs (Applegate), 196
Aoki, P., 161
Ardley, N., 138
Arthur series, 106
Ashton-Warner, Sylvia, 7, 148
Assisted Reading, 53
Automatic word recognition
   development of, 42–44
      reading words in context, 44
   development of automaticity model
      orthographic, 40–42

B

Baker, L., 71, 119
Barnhart, C., 120–121
Barton, D., 146, 214, 215

Basal reader, 121–122
Battle, J., 87, 185, 191
Bauer, E. B., 180, 183, 185, 188, 190
Baumann, J. F., 85, 87
Bean, K., 95
A Bear Called Paddington (Bond), 57
Beck, I. L., 52, 119
Becoming a Nation of Readers, 87
Beginning reading instruction, method of
   stage of
      semiotic nature of print, 17
      short vowels, 17–18
      story/information text difference, 18
      word concept, 17
   type of, 16
Betts, E. A., 55
Biography, 135–137
Black, White, Just Right (Davol), 188
Blanchard, J. S., 53
Bloomfield, L., 120–121
Blue-Back Speller, 114
Blume, Judy, 198, 199, 208
Blunden, D., 52–53
Bomer, K., 148–149
Bomer, R., 148–149
Bond, G., 50
Book selection issue
   outside pressure on trade book, 199–201
   recommendation for trade book, 205–207
   stealth censorship, 204–205
   teacher self-censorship, 201–204
      example of censorship *vs.* selection, 202 (tab)
   in textbook adoption, 196–198
   using distance/rate/time to select book, 207–209

247